Herbert McCabe

Herbert McCabe

Recollecting a Fragmented Legacy

By

FRANCO MANNI

Foreword by David B. Burrell, CSC

CASCADE *Books* · Eugene, Oregon

HERBERT MCCABE
Recollecting a Fragmented Legacy

Cascade Books
An Imprint of Wipf and Stock Publishers
199 W. 8th Ave., Suite 3
Eugene, OR 97401

www.wipfandstock.com

PAPERBACK ISBN: 978-1-7252-5330-8
HARDCOVER ISBN: 978-1-7252-5331-5
EBOOK ISBN: 978-1-7252-5332-2

Cataloguing-in-Publication data:

Names: Manni, Franco, author. | Burrell, David B., foreword writer.

Title: Herbert McCabe : recollecting a fragmented legacy / Franco Manni, with a foreword by David B. Burrell.

Description: Eugene, OR: Cascade Books, 2020 | Includes bibliographical references and
index.

Identifiers: ISBN 978-1-7252-5330-8 (paperback) | ISBN 978-1-7252-5331-5 (hardcover)
| ISBN 978-1-7252-5332-2 (ebook)

Subjects: LCSH: McCabe, Herbert, 1926–2001 | Catholic Church and philosophy |
Philosophical theology | Catholic Church—Doctrines | Christianity—Philosophy |
Theology

Classification: BX1746 M36 2020 (paperback) | BX1746 (ebook)

03/24/21

Cover illustration by Adriano Bernasconi

Contents

Conclusions

Acknowledgments

This book is an elaboration of a doctoral dissertation of a (very) mature student. I thank Susannah Ticciati, who chose my research proposal for a PhD at King's College London. Throughout all those years she provided me an environment of optimism, and sharp intellectual dialogue.

I thank also the Italian Ministry of Education, which, according to a very progressive law made in the better years of old (1984), allowed me to stay in London on a paid leave meant for my doctorate. I thank King's College London whose facilities I took full advantage of.

I thank the people who knew well McCabe and his works and who throughout the years allowed me to interview them or ask for information: McCabe's Dominican brethren and former students of Blackfriars-Oxford (Timothy Radcliffe, Robert Ombres, Simon Gaine, Richard Conrad, Fergus Kerr, and Peter Hunter), his literary executor and disciple Brian Davies, another disciple of his, Denys Turner (and Denys Turner's disciple Eric Bugyis), and his former schoolmate at Manchester University, Thomas Markus. I also thank Terry Eagleton, who was my first interviewee in 2014 and who encouraged me to undertake this task.

In particular I thank four old men, genuine kindred spirits and admirers of McCabe: David Burrell, Alasdair McIntyre, Stanley Hauerwas, and Anthony Kenny. I thank them because they read my work, and encouraged me to publish it. Their acknowledgment was morally supporting along my path.

I want to thank my friends in Italy and England without whom I could not have survived alone abroad and committed to a lonely task. Among them I want to mention Massimo Seneci, David Pedder, and Sam Jefferey. Thank you.

EDITORIAL CREDITS

Most of parts 1, 2, 3 and much of part 8 have been published in my article 'An Introduction to Herbert McCabe OP', *Angelicum*, volume 95, 4/2018; most of part 7 has been published in my article 'Herbert McCabe Proving the Existence of God', *Lumen Veritatis*, vol 11, issue 44–45, Oct-Dec 2018, pp. 405–422;

most of part 9 has been published in my articles 'God as a Creator according to McCabe', *Divus Thomas,* vol. 120, Sept /Dec 2017, pp. 72–95, 'An Apophatic view of God and Creation', *Religious Inquiries*, vol. VIII, issue 15, Winter/Spring 2019 pp. 82–105 and 'Atheistic Scientists and Christian Theologians as Travel Companions', *Theology and Science* vol 18, issue 1, January 2020, pp. 46–58;

much of part 11 has been published in my article 'Herbert McCabe's Philosophical Anthropology', *Politeia*, vol. II, issue 4, November 2019, pp. 244–266;

much of part 14 has been published in my article 'Herbert McCabe's Christology', *Acta Theologica* vol. 39, issue 1, June 2019, pp. 181–199.

Foreword

A group of us invited by Enda McDonagh were gathered in his "rooms" for the second bi-centenary of Maynooth, as Irish love to celebrate, when a Texas voice blared out: "Herbert, when is the big book on Aquinas coming out?" "Stanley," was the answer, "you don't do that; your students do."

Although Franco Manni came too late to be his actual student, this systematic study of Herbert McCabe qualifies him as a virtual student and mentee. He aims to present to a subsequent generation something of the exceptional quality of McCabe's work, fleshing out where Herbert was inclined to be more topical. So Franco Manni helps us to imbibe Thomas from Herbert, as a master among us did for his master, Thomas Aquinas. And in doing so, the author succeeds in finding an incisive rigor in McCabe's disparate deliverances, often deftly elided.

That is what gives this study its comprehensive scope. The section on "the problem of evil," for example, watches him cut a swath between contemporary debates by acutely employing Aquinas, as was his wont. So it is illuminating to trace how clearly Manni expounds McCabe's deft moves—not an easy task. It would be difficult to find another exposition of McCabe's philosophical wit as competent as Manni—a herculean task.

My only fear with such a rendition of Herbert's work is that readers would miss the very verve of his own idiom. Yet Manni has incorporated enough of that to taste it, and succeeds in contextualizing the often topical in McCabe. So it is with great joy that I present a study that clearly shows why thinkers like Stanley Hauerwas and Denys Turner continue to attribute so much to him.

David Burrell, C.S.C.
Hesburgh Professor emeritus, University of Notre Dame (IN, USA)

Herbert McCabe

1

An Elusive Presence
and a Problematic Absence

Herbert McCabe's presence in the fields of theology and philosophy is elusive. It is true that there are still a few distinguished scholars who appreciate McCabe. However, when in September 2016 the first anthology of his writings was published, no reviews appeared in magazines or newspapers. On the one hand, if we search the occurrences of his name on Google,[1] we get 47,600 entries, most of which are sites about religion. On the other hand, articles about his works in journals are few and mostly on limited aspects of his thought. Apart from three exceptions (many years ago and never reprinted),[2] his works are not translated into other languages. Furthermore, there has never been any published book-length study on McCabe. Granted, he did influence other scholars and schools of thought, but only sometimes is it easy to detect such influences; other times we just speculate.

Overall his work is little known. Studies on it have been diminishing throughout the years. Most of his books are only collections of short writings: texts for homilies, texts for classes at the Dominican school, texts for

---

1. On 11 February 2019.

2. *The New Creation* has been translated into Dutch (1966) and Portuguese (1968), *The Good Life* into Slovenian (2008), and *The Teaching of the Catholic Church* into French (1986).

3

public lectures, articles for journals. Given this fragmentation, it is difficult for the reader to become aware of both the complexity and the consistency of McCabe's thought. Moreover, most of his books have been published posthumously, when McCabe was no longer able to debate with other philosophers and theologians. The lack of translations narrowed the scope of the readers and scholars who could be aware of his very existence. This was compounded by the fact that he was not accustomed to travelling in Europe. Furthermore, his literary genre is somehow peculiar: Timothy Radcliffe advocated French translations to Les Editions du Cerf, who refused because the writings are difficult to categorize: they require of the reader a deep knowledge of philosophical concepts and a committed attention in following the logic of the arguments. They are not "books of spirituality" for bedside reading. However, most of them are not, either, academic books involved in dialogues with other scholars and schools of thought; even when they allude to contemporary debates, they provide very few, if any, references to other books.

This book therefore aims at making a readership aware of the comprehensiveness of McCabe's work. In fact, it is not well known, even among scholars, that he actually treated all the principal classical topics of philosophical and theological tradition: ontology and natural theology, anthropology (including epistemology), ethics, and an articulate revealed theology.

Another purpose is to show the systematicity of McCabe thought, that is, the connections among the parts. For example, within the dedicated chapter I showed the connections of the doctrine of creation with the knowability of God, ontology (i.e. existence as such), the relationship between faith and reason, the relationship between philosophical theology and science, the history of philosophy, ethics, and a theology of grace.

In order to achieve this, given the scattered nature of his writings, I have examined all the passages that relate to each of the philosophical and theological topics he dealt with. For example, for the chapter on creation I consider his 1957 dissertation on the problem of evil, the appendix "Causes" in his 1964 commentary of *Summa Theologiae*, the 1964 book *The New Creation*, the 1980 Cambridge lecture "Creation," the 1985 Leeds lecture "The Involvement of God," the 1987 book-chapter "Freedom," his posthumous writings "God" (2002), "Causes and God" and "On Evil and Omnipotence" (2007), and "God and Creation" (2013).

Another goal of this volume is to put McCabe's ideas into a historical context. For example, while presenting his ideas about the knowability of God, I show that they are inserted within a line of Thomism which from Sertillanges through Gilson and White arrives to him, in contrast with another Thomistic stream shared by Cardinal Mercier, Garrigou-Lagrange, and Richard Phillips. Similarly, I provide historical connections between McCabe and other writers on the problem of evil, creation, anthropology, and ethics.

Another purpose is to make manifest the profundity, sophistication, and brilliance of McCabe's thought. Brian Davies and Denys Turner said that McCabe was the most intelligent person they had met. I acknowledge that the word "intelligent" is not fashionable in our times. To be more precise, I would say that McCabe, like Stephen J. Gould and the post-war Popper, was one of the few intellectuals able to introduce the great thinkers of the past to people who have never read their works and to explain their difficult ideas to those who read their books but did not fully understand them. He heads straight towards what is essential, that is, the analysis of the ideas themselves, showing both their depth and their applicability to human problems. As a consequence, McCabe's readers understand and appreciate his work, because of the relevance of the topics and the clarity of the writer.

If we turn now to the contents themselves, why is his work worth knowing? What validity can it still have for today's reader? First of all, he tells us that "God matters": whatever topic he deals with—from the Vietnam war to animals' sensitive life, from Jane Austen's novels to the theories of Marx and Freud—the reader is always made aware that a particular point is framed within a worldview where God and his continuous loving initiative are a reality. This awareness of God's "omnipresence" within every piece of our lives does not place a uniform blurry "religious" film over the particular experiences but, on the contrary, makes them more realistic and detailed according to their own uniqueness.

A second message of McCabe with perennial value is a strong and pioneering apophaticism: we do not know what/who God is, neither by reason nor by faith. However, philosophically, God allows us to make sense of both the world and our thought, and, as believers, while considering Jesus' life and promises, he gives us hope. What is the function of such apophaticism? First of all, it stops us confusing God with cosmic and historical powers and with the features of human nature. If such a confusion is avoided, or at least reduced, our reason will be less and less hindered, and so will our faith too: we are not meant to blindly follow mere human traditions, because they hinder faith itself, which is something unique for each of us; faith certainly needs a community, but an "apophatic" community that is respectful of the mysterious path by which God reveals himself throughout each individual life, in a non-repeatable way. Peter, the Samaritan woman, the good thief, the apostle Paul, Jesus' mother Mary, and many others show us a faith that is not standardized at all. By contrast, a non-apophatic community is at risk of hindering our faith, while intrusively proposing and even imposing—in

God's name—mere human traditions bound to fashions, ideologies, and transient social conventions.[3]

A further relevant message is the strong emphasis given by McCabe to the tragedy of human life. He indeed appreciates and promotes Aristotelian ethics, but only as clothing—albeit the best clothing available—worn by the wandering nomad throughout his journey, which is tiring, dangerous, toilsome, painful, and eventually lethal.

Finally, here I want to hint at a fourth message that I will develop below when speaking of his intellectual life: McCabe was a master in approaching openly the problems of today's society, and in relying on our contemporary language and mind-set; however, he did this without getting rid of tradition. He is a model for us of how the treasures of the past can be revived and made available for the needs of the present, for those of us who live today.

3. If I am a bishop or a theologian and I claim to speak on behalf of God, while in reality I am just expressing the ideologies of my times, I am behaving like the old Pharisees who—in Jesus' words in Mark 7—were just observing their own traditions. If I say too much about the will of God (there about washing hands and kettles) I can hinder the faith of others. In fact, there could be someone who could lose his faith if he thought that the God he is asked to believe in is a God who cares for material cleanliness, or circumcision, or for ruling out Darwin's evolutionary theory. One of the first steps undertaken by Aquinas to go through the apophatic "via negativa" is to say that God is not material. We remember how much Augustine's faith was hindered by the idea that God was material.

2

Intellectual Life

AFFILIATIONS

Herbert McCabe was born in 1926 in Middlesbrough, Yorkshire, and from the age of eighteen lived in various English cities, before moving to Oxford in 1968, where he remained until his death in 2001.[1] "At Saint Mary's College in Middlesbrough he had received that solid

1. 1926 John Ignatius McCabe was born in Middlesbrough.
1944 he started studying chemistry at Manchester University, but then swapped to philosophy with Dorothy Emmet (she said she could never forget this student).
1949 he entered the Dominicans in Woodchester and given the name Herbert: then he studied philosophy and theology in Hawkesyard (Columba Ryan) and Oxford (Victor White).
1953 he made his solemn profession and in 1955 become a Catholic priest.
In 1958 until 1960 he was priest in Saint Dominic's parish in Newcastle-upon-Tyne.
In 1960 until 1965 he was assigned to St Sebastian's parish in Manchester living together with other Dominicans. From there he travelled to give lectures on philosophy and theology to student societies at various British universities.
In 1964 he became editor of *New Blackfriars*.
In 1966 he was transferred to the Dominican Priory of Cambridge where he came to know many students, notably Terry Eagleton, and was one of the main inspiring minds of the leftish student magazine *The Slant*.
In 1967 there was the "Davis affair" also known as "The McCabe's affair" and he was relieved from *New Blackfriars*' editorship.
In 1968 he moved to the Dominican convent in Oxford and lived there until his death. During the Oxford years he taught Dominicans in formation at Blackfriars.
In 1970 he was reappointed as editor of *New Blackfriars* until he resigned in 1979.

grounding of a conventional kind that is indispensable for those who are
going to be able to break out into genuine originality."[2] His experience as a
student at Manchester University was, on the one hand, that of a "conventional" study in the British analytical philosophy syllabus of those times;[3] on
the other hand, it was better than the average because his teacher Dorothy
Emmet debunked the monopoly of this approach to philosophy and taught
the classical themes of Truth and Good in a historical way.[4] When he decided to enter the Dominican order, during his first studies at Hawkesyard
and then in Oxford, his teachers belonged to the "old guard of scholastic
Thomists," actually without notable excellences, but treating the whole
range of philosophical disciplines, as we can deduce from what one of them,
Columba Ryan, recalls.[5] In fact, a classmate of his remembers that:

> The men who taught McCabe theology at the Dominican House
> of Studies at Oxford were—with the exception of Jung's friend
> Father Victor White, who only taught McCabe for a year—not a
> particularly imaginative group, likely to respond to a mind like
> his. They were uneasy about him.[6]

I conjecture that McCabe, throughout his education, had received a
good input of "common sense" from his teachers, so that he was not much
attracted by intellectual fashions of those times. Moreover, since he was
not going to become an academic, he was safely far away from the anxious
"duty" of keeping himself "updated" about what was popular among the
professional thinkers.

When he was still young, he "settled down" forever within the Dominican family. They returned his affection:

From 1981 till 1988 he was Novice Master for England.

In 1989 he was given the STM (master of sacred theology), the highest academic
degree in the Dominican order.

In 2001 he died in Oxford. Four books of his work were published during his life, six
others posthumously. He is almost unknown outside the Anglophone world.

2. MacIntyre, "Foreword," in McCabe, *God Still Matters*, vii.

3. MacIntyre, "Foreword," in McCabe, *God Still Matters*, vii.

4. "At a time when philosophy was becoming obsessed with understanding the mi-
nutiae of supposedly ordinary language, she was unpersuaded by colleagues who tried
to avoid basic questions of truth by holding that all claims were internal to a 'language
game.' Her question was: 'But, then, why play the game?'": "Obituary: Dorothy Emmet,"
The Guardian, 25 September 2000.

5. Ryan, "Homily at Herbert McCabe's Funeral," 309: "I, under a kind of religious
compliance, was required to teach him a strange scholastic psychology in dog Latin. I
hang my head in shame at the remembrance."

6. Orme Mills, "Fr Herbert McCabe," in *The Independent*, 25 July 2001.

Not to say that all of his brethren found him personally conge-
nial. Some did not, largely because he could sometimes be ex-
tremely acerbic, not to say bellicose, especially when under the
influence of alcohol. But his Catholic orthodoxy and loyalty to
Dominican ideals were recognized by everyone in his province.
Even those Dominicans who found McCabe difficult to tolerate
in certain ways would never have denied that he was an excep-
tionally talented preacher.[7]

In one way or another, he brought every reading and every friendship
back to his Christian identity. He was indeed a reader of Aquinas and Chesterton; however, while reading Jane Austen or Marx, he was always bringing
them back to the church's theology and life as well.

Being Catholic in Great Britain, he conversed with Protestants of
various denominations. While he speaks of the "church" as forerunner of
the future unity of humankind, he does not say "Catholic church," but just
"church." As a Catholic, he was not keen on identitarian boastings. The only
time he became "famous," in fact, was because of the so called "McCabe's
affair":[8] in 1967 Charles Davis, a Catholic priest who was the best-known
Roman Catholic theologian in Britain, announced his departure from the
church. McCabe tried to persuade Davis to remain in the church but, as
editor of *New Blackfriars*, McCabe wrote that the Catholic church was "corrupt." As a consequence he was removed from his editorial position. However, his editorial was, in the words of Brian Davies, "full of pastoral concern
and aims to explain why Charles Davis should not have left the Church. It
can be best described as an essay in bridge-building."[9]

He was a progressive person within a then mostly conservative Catholic church and conversed with both Catholic conservatives and Catholic
progressives. He was a friar, a priest, and a theologian, and also a mentor to
youths who were already Christians or became such thanks to him. However, he did not idealize the church: "his view of the Catholic church was
thoroughly unsentimental"[10]; he looked at it critically and self-critically.
For instance, even before the council, he had backed the "liturgical movement." However, in his last column as editor of *New Blackfriars* in 1979 he
acknowledged that the liturgical reform had not fulfilled what was hoped

---

7. Davies (ed.), *The McCabe Reader*, Kindle edition, loc. 174–76.

8. Clements, Simon. *The McCabe Affair. Evidence and comment.*

9. Davies (ed.), *The McCabe Reader*, 133.

10. Davies, "Introduction" to McCabe, *God Still Matters*, xi.

for, and so, perhaps, the progressive Catholics of Vatican II had put their hopes into the wrong place.[11]

This affiliation to the church was more important than others; for example, more important than his affiliation to the world of professional scholars, or than his affiliation to the Irish cause. Although he presented himself as a republican Irishman, this was an occasional and semi-private behavior, never a public identity, as his readers know well.

Apart from being a "child of the church," he was also a "child of his times." When he wrote his short catechism, he hoped it could represent the spirit of Vatican II's years, as the Trent catechism had done for its.[12]

His hero was Aquinas, but he disliked being called a "Thomist" because he approached Thomas just as a help for "contemporary discussions."[13] On the one hand, he kept himself updated about strictly conventional Thomist scholarship, as we can see when he reviews—in *The Thomist* journal—an article about scholastic logics, where he shows himself to be fully acquainted with its technicalities about concepts, judgements, and enunciations.[14] On the other hand, however, McCabe acknowledges his debts to Victor White—being aware that White's "apophatic" Thomism (which was quite a new strand in Thomist scholarship) and commitment to Jung's psychoanalysis were something new and suitable to modern thought—and thanks him on the same page as he does Wittgenstein for his anti-dualism and Terry Eagleton for his Marxism.[15]

He followed also—at least for a few years, when he was young—the mainstream so-called analytical philosophy so popular in the Anglophone universities of his times. Reading his review of a book by Anthony Flew, we get evidence of his expertise and clarity while discussing "explanation," "referring," "facts," "meaning," "paradigm cases," "probability," and "parenthetical verbs."[16] In his thorough analysis of a similar book written by Gilbert Ryle, he says that it is neither profound nor new, but "the most important thing we do get is a valuable lesson on how to write philosophy in English," therefore he hopes that this book "will have a large sale amongst Thomists and neo-scholastics."[17]

11. McCabe, "Comment" (1979) 402–3.

12. McCabe, "Introduction," in *The Teaching of the Catholic Church*, x.

13. Davies, "Introduction," in McCabe, *God Still Matters*, xii.

14. McCabe, "The Structure of the Judgement," 232.

15. McCabe, "Preface," in *God Matters*.

16. McCabe, "Essays in Conceptual Analysis by Antony Flew," 539–40.

17. McCabe, "Dilemmas by Gilbert Ryle," 548–55.

It is true that, especially in his writings of the 1990s, he seldom mentions contemporary theologians, nor did he while teaching at school.[18] However, surely, he used to read them and also—from the 1960s till the 1980s—to debate with them. Good examples of this are: his review of a book by Eric Mascall, where he discusses Bonhoeffer, van Buren, Schubert Ogden, and Bultmann;[19] a review of Bishop John A. T. Robinson's controversial theological best-seller *Honest to God*, where we realize McCabe knew well both Robinson and Tillich;[20] a review of an anthology edited by Hick, *The Myth of God Incarnate*;[21] his critique of "process theology";[22] and his critical dialogue with J. Fitzpatrick about Eucharist.[23]

From his contemporary context he took also some traits of behavior, like being much more informal than was typical of Dominicans. Timothy Radcliffe, who was a student of his, contrasted this informality with the more conventional behavior of Fergus Kerr and Cornelius Ernst towards their students. He was fond of attending pubs and used to knock at Radcliffe's door at the monastery and propose to have a "smallest half pint" of beer, whereas he used to have two pints for his part. He loved conversation and conviviality.[24] Eamon Duffy recalls that McCabe was not "conventionally pious"; in his cell he did not keep devotional books, and the real purpose of his prie-dieu (prayer desk) was to support the dictionary for his crosswords.[25] And from his context he took also a new appreciation of sexuality: he defined chastity as "being warm and affectionate with others,"[26] and when asked what the worst offence against chastity was, he replied: disliking sex.[27]

How are we to relate these two affiliations of his—being a child of the church and a child of his times—to each other? I would say that his affiliation to the church, which already began within his own family in Middlesbrough, gave him the long-lasting motivations for his life. Whereas his will to be a person of his times, one who speaks to his contemporaries, fed him with live ideas and experiences, which, in turn, were essential to him in

---

18. As his former students Fr S. Gaine and Fr Hunter told me when I interviewed them on 24 November 2015.

19. McCabe, "The Secularisation of Christianity," 696–98.

20. McCabe, "Dr Robinson's Book."

21. McCabe, *God Matters*, 54–73.

22. McCabe, *God Matters*, 39–51.

23. McCabe, *God Matters*, 116–162.

24. Radcliffe, my interview.

25. Duffy, "Herbert McCabe."

26. Radcliffe, interview.

27. Cunningham, "Herbert McCabe," in *The Guardian*, 16 July 2001.

order to remain within the church till the end. A fictitious McCabe who—deprived of the food for thought coming from sciences and without a lively commitment into the political struggles of his times—had been unable to think of himself as a man of his times, could not have continued thinking of himself as a child of the church either. In fact, he was not much a conservative creature of habit set in his ways, but, rather, a progressive person without nostalgia, and an enthusiast for the new things that were coming up in the church (because of Vatican II) and in the secular world as well.

PSYCHOLOGICAL TRAITS

I have said above that McCabe was not a creature of habit. Here I suggest that, rather, he was a restless person. Two people who knew him well speak of his "restlessness" due to his insecurity, like that of the eternal adolescent who likes to shock,[28] or even a "dark" insecurity "that went deeper than passionate inquiry and penetrating interest in people."[29] One effect of his restlessness might has been the variety of his relationships. He himself said that "being one of the brethren is the whole of our human identity,"[30] but one of his brethren noticed that almost all his closest friends were not Dominicans.[31] He himself said that several times he wanted to sleep with someone,[32] but he remained always single and his affection "matured into a rare capacity for love of all kinds and conditions of men and women."[33]

He did not like to exercise the art of compromise. In Cambridge, while addressing another theologian, he said that he did not want to argue that the truth lies somewhere in the middle between him and his interlocutor, but he wanted to argue in order to demonstrate that he was right and his interlocutor wrong.[34] He could be arrogant in his convictions, but not because he could not tolerate disagreement: it was because he did not brook people who were "playing games" rather than sincerely holding a well thought out argument. Most of all he was "outrageous at the expense of pompous authority";[35] while meeting pretentious people he liked to take them down

28. Ryan, "Homily," 308.

29. Cunningham, "Herbert McCabe."

30. Cunningham, "Herbert McCabe."

31. Orme Mills, "Fr Herbert."

32. In an editorial about celibacy reported in "Father Herbert McCabe," *Irish Times,* 3 September 2001.

33. Ryan, "Homily," 308.

34. Eagleton, my interview.

35. Ryan, "Homily," 308.

a notch.[36] However, most people where not offended by his way of arguing, since it was visible to many that he was more concerned with defending the truth than with affirming his own personality as a winner. One fellow friar said that McCabe was so absorbed in philosophizing that at table he did not use to speak of weather or health, but instead he used to ask questions like: "Bob, why are you not able to bilocate?"[37]

Overall his personality and his religious family matched each other: the Dominicans appointed him editor of *New Blackfriars* for fifteen years, Novice Master for England for seven years, and in 1989 awarded him the STM, the highest Dominican academic degree. Even with brethren very different from him in temperament, such as Fergus Kerr and Cornelius Ernst, there were not explicit ideological differences, and there was an external reciprocal respect.[38] McCabe himself in his last editorial on *New Blackfriars* wrote that if a human being "does his job well," he will be persecuted. But immediately afterwards speaking of his fifteen-year-long editorship he does not mention any persecutions, and merely describes himself and the journal (that is, the English Dominicans) supporting socialism while the majority of Catholics were against it.[39]

What should we think? I mean "we" as readers of McCabe, who have so many times read his maxim "you cannot live without love, but, if you love enough, you will be killed."[40] Could we argue that both McCabe and his supportive Dominicans did not "love enough" and, therefore, have never been requested to shed their blood? As for McCabe himself, we can certainly say that he dedicated most of his life to intellectual activities, prioritizing listening to, studying, and absorbing the teaching of his mentors and the authors who had lasting influence on him.

VOCATION

McCabe read many books by many writers and was influenced by some of them. Did he become a committed writer as well? Did his existential vocation call him to become a typical scholar? The very nature of most of his writings is peculiar: most of them are texts he used to prepare for preaching at church, teaching at school, and giving open lectures. Terry Eagleton says that McCabe was not interested in long theological research. The only reason

36. Radcliffe, my interview.
37. Ombres, my interview.
38. Radcliffe, my interview.
39. McCabe, "Comment" (1979), 402–3.
40. E.g., McCabe, *God Matters*, 23, 95, 124, 218.

he wrote *The New Creation* is because he had an accident and had his legs broken; and he wrote *Law, Love and Language* because he was asked to give a series of lectures.[41] Denys Turner observes that McCabe's very closeness to Aquinas prevented him from being patient enough to expound Thomas' works in detail.[42] Brian Davies says that McCabe always prepared a text before preaching,[43] and Conrad says the same about teaching.[44] Davies tells us that all the posthumous books are compilations of typescripts from around 1970 onward, which McCabe wrote for the aforementioned purposes.[45]

Not surprisingly the literary quality of these writings reflects this origin. He did not write long texts because he preferred oral communication; in fact, they are written as a teacher speaks, with "abrupt shifts from extreme conceptual exactness to an equally exact but tellingly home example."[46]

Moreover, he does not fill his writings with footnotes, nor does he put a topic into the broader context of studies (the "secondary literature" of an academic discipline), but, quite differently, he focuses on an idea and goes on to dig into it more in depth. Perhaps it is because of this that today he is not remembered, valorized, nor much appreciated within academia, and is not considered as a true scholar by some, as Robert Ombres recalls.[47] As does Denys Turner:

> Herbert was a fresh thinker, drawing on sources in Wittgenstein, Thomas, Marx, Chesterton, Dominican traditions, intellectual, moral, literary and spiritual. And it is often noted that Herbert rarely footnotes his sources. This is because he doesn't have sources, he is in constant dialogue with all the above and many others (Seamus Heaney was another) and I don't think he had any interest in breaking those vibrant intellectual exchanges (often in pubs) down into the identities of who said what and when, considering that to do so would misrepresent the interactive character of thinking itself.[48]

McCabe's attitude towards writing is related to his not being an academic himself,[49] since the vast majority of academics are much keener on

41. My interview.
42. Turner, "Foreword," in McCabe, *Faith within Reason*, x.
43. Davies, "Introduction," in McCabe, *God, Christ and Us*, x.
44. Conrad, my interview.
45. Davies, "Introduction," in McCabe, *God and Evil*, xiv.
46. Turner, "Foreword," in McCabe, *Faith within Reason*, viii.
47. Ombres, my interview.
48. Turner's email to me (22 May 2018).
49. For a few years he lectured regularly at Bristol and occasionally in Oxford,

writing than on teaching. A typical academic such as Anthony Kenny thinks that, had he chosen to, McCabe would have arrived at the top of the profession. However, did not want to be an academic, because he preferred to live the life of a Dominican friar.[50] Another academic, Eamon Duffy, thinks that, more than an existential choice, this was an intellectual attitude: "McCabe was a reasoner, not a scholar: he was not deeply read in the fathers or scholasticism beyond St Thomas. He thought most modern theology intellectually vacuous."[51]

John Orme Mills, a fellow Dominican, argues that McCabe's intellectual orientation was a consequence the will of his teachers and seniors, who were "uneasy about him":

> So he was not sent abroad for higher studies, to equip him to teach in Oxford. Instead, he was sent to work in the Order's parish house in Newcastle and then in Manchester. This, however, was providential. He became an enormously successful teacher.[52]

And Denys Turner observes:

> He didn't fit the fashions of the academic world, either in style or theological method. So much the worse for that world, of course: he was simply a whole lot better than his theological peers, sharper, clearer, remorselessly more precise, and impossible to pin down to any fashion; and to this day the professional theologians find it difficult to know what to do with him just because his conception of theology, and his practice of it, is so distinctively Dominican, engaged by and rooted in the practices of preaching.[53]

McCabe himself, while introducing himself as newly appointed editor of *New Blackfriars,* underlines that the journal "has no other purposes than to use the resources of theology, not as a private language for specialists, but as a contribution to a living debate that concerns us all."[54] Using the words of Turner, we could say that McCabe embodied "the genius of the Dominican vocation [which lies] in the essential connection between poverty of spirit

---

Cambridge, USA, South Africa, and elsewhere, but always without any formal affiliation to any university.

50. Kenny, "Foreword," in McCabe, *On Aquinas*, vii.
51. Duffy, "Herbert McCabe."
52. Orme Mills, "Fr Herbert McCabe."
53. Turner's email to me.
54. McCabe, "Comment" (1964), 2–5.

and the effectiveness of the preached word, the first being the condition of the second."[55]

On his part, Brian Davies, one of McCabe's students, builds a complex definition: McCabe was a philosopher and a theologian, but, as a Dominican, he was first of all, a preacher. However, his preaching benefited a lot from his theological and philosophical culture, and, so, "he was an extraordinary preacher."[56] Anthony Kenny remembers:

> If you went to a sermon by Herbert, you knew you were in no danger of falling asleep: his style as a preacher was at the furthest possible remove from the bland truisms one hears so often from the pulpit. One of his favourite devices was to take some ecclesiastical commonplace—such as "the church welcomes sinners"—and spell out what it meant, freed of cant. "People who are really welcome to the Catholic Church are the murderers, rapists, torturers, sadistic child molesters, and even those who evict old people from their homes." It was for such people, he said from the pulpit, that the Church existed: but he went on to admit, with a certain show of reluctance, that many of his congregation, perhaps even a majority, did not come into any of these categories.[57]

Turner prefers to call McCabe "essentially a teacher."[58] Cunningham sums everything up saying that "in his view, preaching was a form of talking, and the compelling conversational style of his writing—no footnotes, no bibliographies—follows from this."[59]

I would say that McCabe was an educator, a counsellor, a mentor, an eye-opener while teaching, preaching, writing, taking part in groups, such as the December Group (which he cofounded in 1958 to discuss social and political issues from a Catholic point of view) or the Slant Group in Cambridge (in 1966, around a Marxist student-led magazine), and, also, meeting individuals as a friend. Historian Jay Corrin writes that McCabe converted several students at Manchester University[60] and reports Terry Eagleton's gratitude: "without my friendship with Herbert McCabe I wouldn't be at all

55. Turner, *Thomas Aquinas*, 18.

56. Davies, "Introduction," in McCabe, *God, Christ and Us*, ix.

57. Kenny, *Brief Encounters*.

58. Turner, "Foreword," in McCabe, *Faith within Reason*, vii.

59. Cunningham, "Herbert McCabe."

60. Corrin, *Catholic Progressives in England after Vatican II*, 187.

what I am."[61] Brian Davies reports that Alasdair MacIntyre said: "McCabe played a key part in my own acceptance of the Catholic faith."[62]

However, his particular way or method of being a mentor was not in leading groups of spirituality and prayer. Rather, most of all, he wanted to share the "treasures" he found in Aquinas, Wittgenstein, and the Gospels: "it was his life, for as he used to say, 'Dominicans do not pray. They teach.'"[63] According to Duffy, McCabe was seen as a radical, not because he was liberal, but because of "his ability to present the affirmations of classical Christianity as fresh, exciting, and new."[64] Eagleton says that McCabe's motto was "to bring the light of contemporary thought to bear on the gospel."[65] To do this, he was keen on clarity and essentiality. One of his former students, Richard Conrad, gave me the handouts McCabe wrote for a class about the act of will, and there he simplifies Cajetan's twelve phases of deliberation into only four. Another good example of essentiality and clarity is when McCabe summarized the long-lasting impervious debate about Aristotelian theory of intellect, saying that the passive intellect is the capability of humans for learning a language, while the active intellect is the actual knowledge of a language.[66]

In conclusion, the intellectual piece was an essential element of his formula for mentoring. The other one was friendship, that is, he did not want to be an inspirational guru or wise "spiritual father," but a real friend to his interlocutors: "Herbert genuinely believed that good theology was possible only as the outcome of good company—and friendship was his model for 'good company.'"[67]

If we wanted to summarize the purposes of his activity as educator, we could say, in accord with his Dominican friend J. O. Mills, that he wanted "to make people aware that the fundamental teachings of their religion spoke to their needs and the needs of their time";[68] and, in accord with Denys Turner, that McCabe "thought with Thomas and Thomas comes alive in Herbert's theology" and the paradox is that Herbert also comes alive through Thomas; this is what characterizes his vocation, to show how intellect "is a way of being alive."[69]

61. Corrin, *Catholic Progressives in England after Vatican II*, 223.

62. Davies, *The McCabe Reader*, Kindle loc. 103–10.

63. Turner, "Foreword," in McCabe, *Faith within Reason*, viii.

64. Duffy, "Herbert H. McCabe," ad locum.

65. My interview.

66. McCabe, *On Aquinas*, 140.

67. Turner, "Foreword," in McCabe, *Faith within Reason*, vii.

68. Orme Mills, "Fr Herbert McCabe."

69. Turner, "Foreword," in McCabe, *Faith within Reason*, x.

ATTITUDE

Relying on what we have just seen in the previous section, if we are reason-ably allowed to define McCabe's personal vocation as that one of an educator who inspires and vivifies other persons by friendship and by a sincere ap-preciation of human intellect, then now we should ask ourselves what were his attitude and endeavor towards culture and intellectual activity itself.

His was a conservative theology whose hero was Aquinas, but he meant it be revived in such a way as to meet our contemporary life needs.[70] He thereby "transcends the distinction between conservative and progres-sive"; he was rooted in the tradition but "longed for the transformation of the world, the revolution as he called it."[71]

Because of this, McCabe was able to influence other people in a com-plex way. Consider, for instance, Eugene McCarraher. He came across Mc-Cabe while reading some of the early works in Radical Orthodoxy (RO) published on *New Blackfriars*. Of RO he appreciated "the idea that theology can be a distinct and compelling form of social and cultural criticism," a feature he found in McCabe as well. However, later on he was disappointed by some "bad mental and political habits" stemming from RO, for instance their contempt for liberalism, modernity, and Enlightenment, treated as though they were "the spawn of Satan" and blamed for being the alleged cause of genocides, nuclear war, and harsh capitalism. Whereas, McCabe, who was so keen on medieval tradition but also always remained bal-anced and grateful for the many achievements of modernity, "kept him a Christian."[72]

We can see McCabe's attitude towards tradition as a living thing (which is enriched by the further developments of our civilization and organically flows into the new things of the present) in his appreciation of Vatican II's liturgical and biblical movements, which caused significant innovations in the Catholic church precisely by means of looking back to ancient sources.[73] Even more so, as a disciple of Aquinas, he was well aware of how a new avail-able source—the works of Aristotle—could be so effective in innovating the philosophical landscape of Aquinas' contemporaries without warping the previous theological tradition, and, so, he thinks that the same could hap-pen by introducing Marx's ideas into Christian thought.[74]

---

70. Orme Mills, "Fr Herbert McCabe."

71. Radcliffe, my interview.

72. Keller and McCarraher, "Meet the New Boss, Same as the Old Boss—Interview."

73. McCabe, "The Word in Liturgy," 57–65.

74. McCabe, "Catholic Marxists," letter to *The Spectator* (1 July 1966), 13.

To stick to tradition does necessitate that one be conservative or tra-ditionalist. On the contrary, a tradition is something that always changes, and requires an active engagement from the individual, who is asked to give his or her own contribution to these changes: "To be within a tradition is to be able to alter it in significant ways. To refuse to be traditional is usually to want to stick unchangeably to present ways."[75] Therefore, it is worth criticiz-ing both the "traditionalists" and the "iconoclasts," since both of them fail in understanding the true nature of tradition. To the traditionalists it has to be said that "In theology, as in liturgy, to be truly traditional is not to repeat past formulae."[76]

And he put this idea into practice many times with regard to para-mount theological topics, and innovated within Catholic doctrine, albeit in strong continuity with the best tradition and being cautious of any pos-sible iconoclasm. For example, there is not any God before the Universe; transignification in Eucharist; never use the word "soul" while speaking of human beings; the "pre-existing Christ" did not pre-exist; the "persons" of the Trinity are not persons but substantial relationships; in ethics natural law is universal just in potency, but, in act, is both objective (not a matter of individual subjective desire, but of rules in a community) and "relative" because it is related to a particular community or tradition.

McCabe considers iconoclasts, who sit loose to tradition, to be poten-tially counterproductive despite their best intentions. Thus, in his review of Bishop John A. T. Robinson's book *Honest to God* (1963), a book considered by many as a progressive turning point in theology, McCabe observes that "the air of iconoclasm which the author evokes has merely led to his being interpreted in a non-Christian sense."[77] McCabe seeks to pursue a different path, one that draws on the wealth of tradition while seeking to avoiding the fossilization of traditionalism.

75. McCabe, *God Matters*, 148.
76. McCabe, "Received Wisdom?" 580.
77. McCabe, "Dr Robinson's Book," 30–31.

3

Influences

VICTOR WHITE

Victor White was the most important teacher of Herbert McCabe, because he made him love Aquinas. McCabe met White while studying theology as a Dominican in Oxford. White was thoroughly learned in scholastic thought:

> For him, not only Albert and Thomas but also Bonaventure, the Victorines, William of St Thierry, Rupert of Deutz and even St Bernard were at one and the same time mystics and scholastics. . . . His account of Aquinas was especially indebted to Père Antonin-Dalmace Sertillanges.[1]

In particular, in presenting his "treatise on God," White maintains a radical apophaticism underlining how much God's infinity goes beyond any human concept: "the most perfect union with God is union with the utterly Unknown."[2] This stand does not entail that we should be agnostic about the existence of God: the mystery is not *that* he is but *what* he is.

Moreover, it is worth noticing, both White and McCabe maintained a "philosophical" or "natural" theology, that is, a discourse about God by means of rational arguments. In fact, although White sympathized with the

---

1. Nichols, *Dominican Gallery*, 63.
2. Nichols, *Dominican Gallery*, 72.

"ground" of Barth's criticism of natural theology—that is, a concern for preserving the radical transcendence of revelation—he disagreed with Barth about ruling out natural theology itself.[3]

McCabe shared with White this moderate and balanced appreciation of human reason in the service of religious belief.

Through White and the other Dominican teachers, McCabe became aware of the work of Thomas Aquinas, which was rare in the European culture of that period. In fact, outside the Catholic seminaries European culture of those years did not provide any account or appreciation of scholastic philosophy, and most times even in the Catholic syllabuses the thought of Aquinas was watered down by the insertion of many other schoolmen and commentators, and filtered by the systematizations of modern Neo-scholastic authors of handbooks.

THOMAS AQUINAS

Aquinas is by far the most formative author for McCabe, and Aquinas' ideas ubiquitously fill McCabe's philosophical and theological thoughts. Sometimes he presents Aquinas' doctrine just in a plain didactic way, for example when he describes the Aristotelian doctrine of the four ethical states.[4] He could be called a good explainer of Aquinas.

But, he was not just that. At other times, he interprets freely and cleverly the spirit of Aquinas' passages and provides fresh, original insights that could hardly have been grasped by the reader of those texts who was trying to understand them by him- or herself. We can see this, for example, when McCabe effectively draws a crucial idea from Aquinas' treatise on creation and is able to explain it quite clearly: since God creates everything from nothing, he is not part of that everything and thus he does not make changes in this universe. Another example is when McCabe is able to make clear for us—people who live after five centuries of the development of the natural sciences—that what Aquinas meant by the "spirituality" of the human intellect is actually its interpersonality, its non-individual and non-private nature, which brings us to see that the biological brain is not the "organ" of thought but, instead, *language* is.

Anthony Kenny recalls: "He only rarely provided textual documentation for the ideas that he credited to Aquinas, yet his exposition has a ring of authenticity often lacking in commentators of a more scholarly bent."[5]

3. Nichols, *Dominican Gallery*, 73–74, 82.

4. McCabe, *On Aquinas*, 91–102.

5. Kenny, *Brief Encounters*, Kindle loc. 375.

Therefore, since Aquinas' pervasive influence is evident in most of Mc-Cabe's works, it is not worth insisting here on providing evidence of this. We will see the evidence as we explore his thought later. Here I just report two testimonies from his former students and fellow Dominican friars. Fr Peter Hunter says that, for McCabe, Aquinas was not just an author, however important, who adds to scholarship, but rather was "a living system of ideas."[6] Roberto Ombres recalls that when at dinner in the monastery he once asked McCabe what was his thought about a topic, he replied: "Bob, you mean what Thomas thinks. I have no thoughts."[7]

As for me, I notice that, in contrast to the majority of the Thomists I have read, McCabe has the capacity to provide expositions of Aquinas' thought that are readable, interesting, illuminating, relevant for our lives and also, sometimes, resulting in beautiful sentences that are paradoxical, moving, witty, and memorable.

However, as for McCabe himself, the older he grew, the less he claimed for originality: "If readers discover any new truths in the course of reading this book, they should not attribute it to any originality of mine."[8] Brian Davies comments on this passage saying: "McCabe did not like to be called a Thomist, but that was because he thought that, given what most people who use the word 'Thomist' seem to have in mind, Aquinas himself was not a Thomist."[9]

Who are these "most people"? McCabe and Brian Davies do not provide names; both Dominicans could only think of a very limited group of scholars, mostly belonging to the Anglophone world and certainly related to a particular time. It is better, therefore, to listen to McCabe himself while he tries to narrow down this category, timing it from the Leo XIII encyclical *Aeterni Patris*, and consequently casting aside six centuries of commentators on Aquinas. That pope—says McCabe—wanted to criticize the mindset of liberal capitalism and "the worship of the ruthless free market and the elimination of friendship as a basic social value" and "coopted" Aquinas in this campaign, so that "Thomism" had to become "legalistic and voluntaristic." McCabe agrees with that pope's critique of ruthless capitalism, but he deplores the legalistic and voluntaristic approach adopted in doing so, which distorted Aquinas' authentic virtue-based and intellectualistic thought. Whereas, McCabe praises some French and English Dominicans who rediscovered the authentic thought of Aquinas: Gerald Vann, Thomas

---

6. Hunter, in my interview.
7. Ombres, in my interview.
8. McCabe, "Preface" to *The Good Life*, 1–2.
9. Davies, "Introduction" to *The McCabe Reader*, Kindle loc. 481.

Gilby and above all Victor White.[10] They were not alone, because McCabe praises also Peter Geach, Daniel Westberg, Michael Nolan, and Elizabeth Anscombe.[11]

On his part, the longtime British academic philosopher Anthony Kenny is aware of the differences within this allegedly monolithic "Thomism" and distinguishes four groups: the followers of Maritain and Gilson, who are more traditionalist; the "transcendentalists," such as Marechal, Hoenen, and Lonergan; the "Radical Orthodox," such as Milbank and Pickstock; and finally, the analytic, keen on the philosophy of language, such as Geach, Finnis, MacIntyre, Kretzmann, and Herbert McCabe.[12]

WITTGENSTEIN

McCabe read other philosophers, though. He mentioned Karl Marx and his ideas many times throughout the 1960 and 1970s, and both Radcliffe and Eagleton, who stayed in touch with McCabe for decades, think that he read Marx's works directly, at least to some extent.[13] The contribution from Marx to McCabe was a strong criticism of liberal Western capitalism and an appeal for a "revolution" by and for the poor to change the current system radically.

Friedrich Nietzsche is also mentioned many times in McCabe's writings as an effective example of demystification of idolatrous ideas about God. In particular, several times McCabe agrees with Nietzsche that a benevolent paternalistic protector cannot be a true God but just a vast omnipotent baby unable to grow up and to abandon himself in that true love that requires equality.[14]

Apart from Aquinas, however, the most influential philosopher for McCabe was without doubt Ludwig Wittgenstein. Any reader of McCabe's writings is aware of this, both because of the quantity of references and the positive role played by Wittgenstein's ideas within them. McCabe many times openly recognizes this, for example when he writes of being in debt not only to Aquinas but also to Wittgenstein and to those who were influenced by Wittgenstein: Anthony Kenny, Peter Geach, Philippa Foot, Elizabeth Anscombe, Gilbert Ryle, and Alasdair MacIntyre.[15]

---

10. McCabe, *On Aquinas*, 102–3.

11. McCabe, *On Aquinas*, 141, 145, 162.

12. Kenny, "Foreword," in McCabe, *On Aquinas*, vii–viii.

13. My interviews.

14. McCabe, *God Matters*, 21; McCabe, *God Still Matters*, 6.

15 McCabe, "Preface," in *The Good Life*, 2.

His former teacher Columba Ryan says: "It was from Victor and the companionship of Cornelius Ernst, who had studied under Wittgenstein, that he derived his abiding concern with the theory of meaning."[16]

Anthony Kenny observes:

> [McCabe] sought to graft the insights of the twentieth-century thinker on to those of the thirteenth-century thinker not out of a desire to appear up-to-date—he showed no inclination to endorse any of the trendy intellectual fashions of the age—but because he recognized a genuine affinity between the two masters. Both shared a conviction that it is through an unconstrained attention to the operation of language that we achieve philosophical understanding of human nature. The two philosophers present a vision of human beings as intelligent bodily agents that is far removed from the dualisms or physicalisms characteristic of the ages that separate them in time.[17]

Quoting McCabe's former university colleague Alasdair MacIntyre, McCabe's former student Brian Davies says that McCabe

> owed much to the thinking of Ludwig Wittgenstein (1889–1951). As Alasdair MacIntyre observes, by the time McCabe began writing "it had become impossible to avoid reckoning with Wittgenstein. . . . So good work in philosophy required Herbert to learn how to address both Thomas's questions and Wittgenstein's within a single enquiry."[18]

Where can we see this "reckoning"? Certainly, in McCabe's anthropology, a very original constituent of his philosophy, which deserves a dedicated study on its own. Wittgenstein's philosophy of language could improve Aquinas' statement that thoughts have to be related to images because now analytical Thomists "in explaining the essential connection of thought and language, start from the language end instead of, as Aquinas does, starting from the thought end"; now we analyze understanding in terms of human communication whereas Aquinas analyses communication in terms of understanding.[19]

Another aspect of Wittgenstein's influence on McCabe is a sort of "encouragement," coming from a renowned non-religious contemporary philosopher, in respecting the philosophical rights of metaphysics, a backing

16. Ryan, "Homily," 309.

17. Kenny, *Brief Encounters*, Kindle loc. 384.

18. Davies, "Introduction," in *The McCabe Reader*, Kindle loc. 485.

19. McCabe, *On Aquinas*, 132–33.

that did not come, instead, from Bertrand Russell, who, according to Mc-Cabe, arbitrarily stated that the universe "is just there" and we do not have to seek God, whereas Wittgenstein held a better position, saying: "not *how* the world is, but *that* it is, is the mystery."[20]

More generally, Wittgenstein, because of his "philosophical respect-ability," acted like a "bridging-character" between a medieval thinker, Aqui-nas, who was not popular at all among the vast majority of eighteenth- to twentieth-century philosophers, and contemporary thought. For example, when McCabe is arguing in defence of the logical principle *saltem ut in pluribus* (at least for the most part), held by Aquinas, he seeks support adding that: "Wittgenstein rediscovered this point."[21]

Apart from White and Ernst, McCabe appreciated Wittgenstein also thanks to the work of Anthony Kenny, one of the few contemporary philosophers he used to read,[22] whose writings he quotes often and of whom he provides a short "biographical note":

> Dr Kenny is a very definitely ex-Christian, a genuine agnostic who is profoundly sceptical (to say the least) about such notions as the immortality of the human soul. Nevertheless holding, as he does, very similar views to those of Aquinas about what is to be a rational animal (it means to be a linguistic animal) he shares Aquinas's puzzlement.[23]

I would say that McCabe follows the example of Kenny: when he has to deal with complex scholastic topics like, for instance, the relationships between intellect and will, Kenny provides a solution that is, on the one hand, consistent with the tradition, but, on the other, is simpler and takes advantage from what modern philosophy has developed.[24]

THEOLOGY, SCIENCES, AND LITERATURE

Apart from philosophers, we should pay attention to theologians as well. His former student Richard Conrad says that McCabe was particularly keen on St John the Evangelist, used to mention Cyril of Alexandria and Leo the Great (preferring the former to the latter), strangely enough did not

20. McCabe, *God Matters*, 5.

21. McCabe, *God and Evil*, 36.

22. As Robert Ombres recalls (my interview) and as we see from the number of quotations.

23. McCabe, *On Aquinas*, 118.

24. McCabe, *On Aquinas*, 89.

mention Augustine while speaking of Christ's predestination (when this is a fundamental source for the topic), gave a series of lectures on Aquinas' Christology, and was very interested in sacramental theology.[25]

Since he discusses and criticizes their writings, he also certainly read many contemporary theologians—I have listed them above—even though here the "influence" is to be understood in a Popperian sense, i.e., to serve for contrast.

Two people who knew McCabe well for many years, Terry Eagleton and Timothy Radcliffe, sharply state that he never mentioned Karl Barth in his conversations and classes.[26] However, I would say that, in another sense of "influence" (i.e., that which comes from the broad cultural environment), a theologian like Barth could not help but influence McCabe; in particular, the sharp Barthian distinction between God and the gods comes to McCabe as well. And so does the idea of God-not-filling-the-gaps from another great twentieth-century theologian, Dietrich Bonhoeffer. In any case, these, like other particular theological influences (for example, that one of Edward Schillebeeckx, reported by Timothy Radcliffe),[27] should be checked more closely while studying McCabe's revealed theology.

McCabe used to read works in the sciences also. He read Charles Darwin's evolutionary theory, Karl Lorentz's ethology, and physicists' writing on Big Bang cosmology. He mentions also the Gestalt psychologists (Köhler, Koffka, and Wertheimer) and the authors of *Naked Ape or Homo Sapiens?* John Lewis and Bertrand Towers.[28] Most of these readings focused on the animality of human beings, who are linguistic animals and not the "souls in the machines" of Cartesian tradition.

McCabe was also keen on fiction: the writer he mentions most frequently is Jane Austen. Both from his writings and the people who knew him, we know that he read G. K. Chesterton, William Shakespeare, P. G. Wodehouse, Brian O'Nolan, James Joyce, and Seamus Heaney.[29] We might notice that in this list, apart from Joyce, the most typical representatives of mainstream modernism are missing (say Virginia Woolf or T. S. Eliot).

25. My interview.

26. My interviews.

27. My interview.

28. McCabe, *On Aquinas*, 124–25.

29. Davies, "Introduction," in McCabe, *The Good Life*, vii. Eagleton, Radcliffe, and Ombres, my interviews.

4

Recollecting a Fragmented Legacy

TWO RECOLLECTIONS

My "recollection of McCabe's fragmented legacy" (which gives my work its subtitle) is not primarily meant to provide a synthesis of the scholarship affected by McCabe that was or is present in the cultural world, but to put together the scattered ideas that McCabe expressed in his short, focused writings (as I said in my first chapter) and to show their systematic connections. This work, at length and directly, addresses this task throughout all its parts. In a secondary and subsidiary sense, however, the "recollection of the legacy" is a recognition of the scholarship influenced by McCabe and this task is addressed in brief here in this chapter.

From several sources I examined, I drew a list of scholars that were influenced by McCabe in different ways and to different extents. Although here I must be brief, the list is not short. It includes some who explicitly acknowledge their debt to him (and some who do not), others who admire his work and follow or share some of his ideas in their own works, and still others who, although they admire him, have trodden different paths in their research. I use the word "disciples" to refer to those scholars who both implicitly and explicitly relied on some of McCabe's ideas for years and to a large extent; scholars who are admirers and supporters of McCabe's intellectual role but are also proactive users of his ideas, applying them both to the same matters he had already dealt with and also to new and different ones. These disciples are Terry Eagleton, Denys Turner, and Brian Davies.

THE DISCIPLES

The Disciples: Terry Eagleton

Terry Eagleton met McCabe when he was young and both were living in Cambridge, and they remained friends until the end. Since Eagleton's major was in literature at the university, and outside it he agitated as a polemist and militant on the battlefield, becoming learned in Marxism, he was completely ignorant both of Thomistic philosophy and of theology. He himself and the scholars who wrote about his intellectual life said repeatedly that "without Herbert" he would not have had any knowledge of these matters. In his celebratory biographical sketch of McCabe—after having found in him a kindred spirit of Chesterton, Shaw, Joyce, and Wilde, Eagleton describes McCabe's style this way:

> Stylistically speaking, he trades in paradox, epigram, estranging inversions, sudden semantic subversions, all of which disruptive activity lurks beneath the cover of a breezily colloquial tone. The style strikes up a pact with the reader in its very button-holing lucidity, only to leave her routinised assumptions as upended as with the reader of Swift. As such, it is a form of writing which mimes the contradictions of Christian faith, its simultaneous reinforcement and disruption of common perceptions, its pivoting of unthinkable paradoxes around the aporia of the cross.

Then he makes a passionate statement:

> Dismally few people, when you come to weigh it up, really change your life, even those who are traditionally supposed to. My supervisor at Cambridge changed my life about as much as Vera Lynn did. But without my long friendship with Herbert McCabe I wouldn't be at all what I am. So, you can blame it all on him.[1]

Terry Eagleton is the faithful quintessential disciple, the only person who for decades has continued both mentioning explicitly McCabe as his most important mentor and, more importantly, using his ideas (and style)

---

1 Eagleton, "Priesthood and Paradox," 316–19.

in the many books he has written. Into his *The Body as Language* (1970) he draws the main ideas from *Love and Language* and thanks McCabe "whose seminal work stands behind most chapters of this book and from whom I have learned continually."[2] In *After Theory* (2003) he says that McCabe's influence is so pervasive that it is impossible to localise. *Sweet Violence: The Idea of the Tragic* (2003) is dedicated to "the memory of Herbert McCabe."

In his presentation of Eagleton's works, James Smith writes that McCabe's influence has come to the forefront in recent years.[3] In fact, in the last fifteen years Eagleton published more books on philosophy than on literature and there he relies on McCabe's bequest of Aquinas about God and human nature. As for God, typical is Eagleton's book, *Reason, Faith and Revolution: Reflections on the God Debate* (2009), where he uses the Thomistic view of creation to bewilder the new atheists or, as for human nature, typical is his *Materialism* (2017), where the reader is put before an unexpected Aquinas, as much materialistic as Marx.

I must notice, however, the differences, the most important of which concerns erudition: while his career was developing, Eagleton devoted himself more and more to a sort of complex analysis of Western culture, throwing into it a huge quantity and variety of knowledge, mostly literary and philosophical, but also from history, religion, psychoanalysis, arts, and current affairs. Since he takes the floor about many topics and is able to disseminate high culture to educated laypeople, he has become one of the few "public" intellectuals in the UK. McCabe, for his part, was different, because his erudition was nowhere near as wide as Eagleton's and he was not particularly interested in the idea of "culture."

Going back to the similarities, James Smith strongly maintains that a long-lasting feature that Eagleton received from McCabe is the style, logic, and rhetoric of his prose. His way of writing is

> a flexible polemical device which takes the form of a rhetorical flourish designed to debunk an image of high culture, through a gesture in the direction of some banal, bizarre or brute reality . . . against the exorbitant claims of metropolitan high culture, . . . yet it appears that the Eagletonism is less a distinct invention, and more an interesting mutation of an older "McCabeism."[4]

I agree with Smith because both authors, although being very high-cultured themselves, share the same critique towards some widespread habits present in high-culture, like unnecessary technical words and a

2. Quoted in James Smith, *Terry Eagleton*, 25.

3. James Smith, *Terry Eagleton*, 10.

4. James Smith, *Terry Eagleton*, 30.

concealed detachment from everyday life issues. Eagleton says that McCabe had a talent for showing how much some ideas are relevant, even though, according to commonplaces, they are not.[5] I think that to some extent the same applies to him.

Coming to the ideas themselves, both authors underline the drama or tragedy of human life: despite contrary appearances, every individual and every group or institution is spoiled in some way or another, decline and perish. Both authors oppose the overoptimistic view of liberal thinkers about the future and hold that whatever the future will be, it will never rule out suffering, conflicts, hatred, and wickedness. In *Hope without Optimism* Eagleton quotes McCabe (human hope goes through defeat and crucifixion to resurrection)[6] and, as we have seen already, dedicates to McCabe his book about tragedy. In a recent book, *Radical Sacrifice* (2018), he quotes McCabe again, saying "Jesus, for the sake of his fellow men and women, accepted total failure, death and crucifixion and left it all to the will of the Father," and comments: "the theologian Herbert McCabe speaks bluntly of death as 'an outrage.'"[7] Eagleton's favorite quotation from McCabe says that without love it is impossible to live a human life, but, if you love enough, you will be killed. For example, in the beginning of his autobiography:

> Marx called history a nightmare . . . . But if history was to be undone, it could only be from the inside. The Christian gospel invites us to contemplate the reality of human history in the broken body of an executed political criminal. The message this body proclaims, as the theologian Herbert McCabe puts it, is uncompromising: if you don't love you're dead, and if you do love you'll be killed. Here, then, is the pie in the sky, the opium of the people, the sentimental twaddle of salvation.[8]

This appreciation of the tragic side of our life is strongly connected with his long-lasting respect and interest for Christianity. Personally, Eagleton does not consistently define himself as a believer, at least in public statements, even though he does not claim to be an atheist either. However, in 2014 he said that without McCabe he would not have remained a Christian.[9] Apart from his personal belief, for fifteen years he has written books that eventually made a reviewer in *The Guardian* declare *Reason, Faith and Revolution* to be "one of the most important works of Christian apologetics

---

5. My interview.

6. Eagleton, *Hope without Optimism*, 133.

7. Eagleton, *Radical Sacrifice*, 45, 82. He quotes McCabe, *Hope*, 4.

8. Eagleton, *The Gatekeeper*, 16.

9. My interview.

to have emerged in recent years,"[10] and, on the negative side, a reviewer of his *Trouble with Strangers* (2008) blames him for being a "part time theologian of the Roman Catholic left" who repeats always the same worn arguments "with occasional references to Thomas Aquinas and his old mentor, Herbert McCabe."[11]

However, despite these generic allegations of banality and staleness, when Eagleton uses the theology that McCabe provided him with, he shows himself as powerful a critic of his opponents as the best apologists ever were. For example, when he starts his highly successful review of Richard Dawkins' most notorious book, *The God Delusion*, he writes, "Dawkins might also have avoided being the second most frequently mentioned individual in his book—if you count God as an individual."[12] That view of God is a typical McCabe idea, deployed in a humorous yet biting way.

Another idea that pervades Eagleton's works is materialism, but not in its positivistic version, where "matter"—be it the atoms of Epicurus or the economic "structure" of orthodox Marxists—is opposed to ideas, theories, politics, and religion. When Eagleton uses this word, he means the Aristotelian view of substances as, first of all, living bodies where the "soul" is just the structure of their bodies. In this sense, he maintains that Aquinas was a "materialist" and a companion of Marx, as read by Gramsci and not by Bucharin: "History, culture and society are specific modes of creatureliness, not ways of transcending it."[13] This kind of materialism comes to Eagleton directly from McCabe and his long-lasting concern for presenting Aquinas' anthropology through Aristotle and Wittgenstein in order to make it compatible with Marx.[14]

To sum up Eagleton's reception of McCabe's legacy, on the one hand we notice that he did not develop a theology of his own since he was never interested in committing himself in this field of professional research, but on the other hand he received the indelible conviction that religion is a living and powerful system of symbols without which we would be not able to understand the history of our culture, and which no one can dismiss as an obsolete delusion.[15]

10. Hobson, "Eagleton the Apologist," *The Guardian*, 9 January 2010.

11. Boer, "The Ethical failure of Terry Eagleton," *Monthly Review*, 22 September 2010.

12. Eagleton, "Lunging, Flailing, Mispunching," *The London Review of Books*, 19 October 2006.

13. Eagleton, *Materialism*, Kindle loc. 538.

14. Eagleton, "Portrait of Thomas Aquinas."

15. In recent years Eagleton has been delivering lectures in different countries and universities about the presence of religion in Western culture as the principal "symbolic

Asked for the reasons why McCabe did not establish any "school," Eagleton answered: because he did not publish much, was not an academic (and, also, was anti-academic), and was a friar in a society where there is a separation between ecclesiastical culture (seen as something specialized) and secular culture (seen as mainstream).[16] We can easily see how much Eagleton himself was not at all a disciple of his mentor in these three regards.

The Disciples: Denys Turner

Unlike Eagleton, Denys Turner is not a public intellectual and we could define him as a specialist in medieval philosophy and theology. Like Eagleton, he used to be Marxist in his youth, even though, unlike him, he is not any longer. Marxism was one reason why he met McCabe and afterwards, again like Eagleton, McCabe encouraged him to study medieval philosophy and theology.

Turner met Herbert in Dublin in 1965, while Tuner was a graduate student in philosophy there. In fact, McCabe used to come over to Dublin quite regularly to speak to groups and societies engaged in thinking through the consequences of the Second Vatican Council for the church, and for theology. Since then, until the day McCabe died, Turner was in regular contact with him.[17]

From McCabe he took an example for how to write his prose: in fact, unlike other scholars of Aquinas—like John Wippel, for instance—he is able to disentangle himself from any specialist's paraphernalia. In his book on Aquinas Turner writes:

> What herein I offer is more a point of entry into the man's thought obstructed by as little of the technical jargon of the medieval philosophers and theologians as is consistent with accuracy of exposition.[18]

And the writer keeps his promise, since he provides his audience with an introduction to Aquinas that is both deep and pleasant to read.

Turner openly acknowledged his debts towards McCabe ("the influence of the late McCabe on my reading of Thomas will be too obvious to all

system."

16. My interview.

17. Turner's email to me on 22 May 2018.

18. Turner, *Thomas Aquinas*, 1.

who know"[19]) and praised the person: "Herbert was perhaps the cleverest man I ever met."[20] Also:

> although Herbert's was the cleverest, most philosophically acute theological mind that I have ever encountered in more than fifty years of academic life in Britain and United States (let alone continental Europe) he didn't fit the fashions of the academic.[21]

A few scholars, such as Timothy Radcliffe, Terry Eagleton, and Susannah Ticciati, failed to notice this influence and attribute ideas that originate from McCabe to Turner.[22] This move is so pervasive that even Terry Eagleton, while reviewing Turner's book on Aquinas, attributes to Turner very typical ideas of McCabe, like the one about humans being "wholly animals from top to toe."[23] The same is done by Stephen Mulhall who, while reviewing another of Turner's book, presents what is in fact McCabe's arguments about creation out of nothing saying: "Denys Turner puts the matter this way."[24] One of them—Cyril O'Regan—even highlights "the difficulty of determining the relation between Turner and McCabe. For surely Turner and McCabe are not identical in every respect."[25] It is a pity, however, that O'Regan does not provide us with more information on the differences. However, I will do myself below, after I had highlighted the similarities .

The first and most important similarity is a shared theological apophaticism. Already in his *Darkness of God* (1998), a book about medieval mystics, Turner adopts this concept, which he has learned from McCabe, and so presents mysticism not as an esoteric non-rational private experience but as an exoteric theological teaching about the unknowability of God.[26] It is what "the Latin tradition of Christianity called the *via negativa*."[27]

Years later Turner realized how much this apophaticism was not confined to the "mystics" but was a distinctive feature of Aquinas as well, and so belonging to a mainstream Christian tradition. Gradually he studied that

19. Turner, *Thomas Aquinas*, 271.

20. Turner, "Forward" to McCabe, *Faith within Reason*, viii.

21. Turner's email to me on 22 May 2018.

22. As for Radcliffe and Eagleton, I take this opinion from my interviews (cited above) and as for Ticciati in conversation. I add Oliver Davies and Paul Joyce who expressed the same view.

23. Eagleton, "Disappearing Acts," a review of *Thomas Aquinas: A Portrait* by Denys Turner, *The London Review of Books* 35.23, 5 December 2013.

24. Mulhall, "What Is 'Grammatical' about Grammatical Thomism?"

25. Bugyis and Newheiser (eds.), *Desire, Faith, and the Darkness of God*, 212–13.

26. Turner, *The Darkness of God*, 268.

27. Turner, *The Darkness of God*, 19–20.

huge corpus of writings, more and more holding that Aquinas is the greatest of all Christian philosophers.[28]

So therefore, thanks to McCabe's influence, Turner contributed significantly to the recent revival of Aquinas in Anglophone academia.[29]

Another major idea Turner took from McCabe is the validity of "natural" (philosophical) theology. Especially in his *Faith, Reason and the Existence of God* (2004) he was committed to re-establish its importance after decades of decline, mostly among Protestant but also among Catholic theologians. McCabe took this stand: the "God of philosophers," of Augustine and Aquinas, is the same God as the God of Abraham, Isaac, and Jacob. The philosophical comprehension of God is a necessary precondition for Christology. By analogy, we could not speak of cricket with an American unless we say that it is a sport.[30]

As for Marxism, a sympathy that Turner shares with McCabe, we should not treat it as a direct influence: Turner says they he "fell" into Marxism because of Terry Eagleton in Dublin in 1965, adding that McCabe told him about why Catholics should be Marxists.[31] The three of them, also, may be seen as a "group" of English progressive Catholics, as Eric Bugyis, an American scholar, does while looking for an inspiration for those "secular leftists and Christian theologians" of today, who want "to confront the corruption in our late capitalist societies."[32] The same grouping is made by Eugene McCarraher:

> Immune to political trendiness, McCabe remained in the church when many of his left-leaning comrades walked out. By the mid-'60s, the "Marxist-Christian dialogue" was on, and the English Catholic Left took part in this conversation through *New Blackfriars* and *Slant*. . . . Audacious and energetic, . . . the new Catholic Left served as incubator for a motley array of intellectuals, from Eagleton and philosopher Charles Taylor to theologians Brian Wicker and Denys Turner.[33]

From McCabe Turner takes also the attitude of applying metaphysical distinctions onto important current debates, like, for example, speaking

---

28. Eagleton, "Disappearing Acts."

29. Timothy Radcliffe (my interview).

30. Turner, *Saint Thomas Aquinas*, 105, 100.

31. Turner, "If You Do Love, You'll Certainly Be Killed," in Bugyis and Newheiser (eds.), *Desire, Faith*, 312.

32. Bugyis, "As We Were Saying," in Bugyis and Newheiser (eds.), *Desire, Faith*, 352.

33. McCarraher, "Radical, OP: Herbert McCabe's Revolutionary Faith."

of the relations between religion and politics within the different circumstances of different states such as Saudi Arabia and the USA.[34]

Any reader who knows McCabe's works can see how extensively most of his views on various doctrines are present in Turner's books: the existence and knowability of God, creation, the problem of evil, the relations between soul and body, the role of language, sacraments and the Eucharist in particular, Christology, and others.

There are two main differences between them, however. First of all, Turner is a scholar who studies medieval philosophy and even when he presents Aquinas, he does it in a detailed historical way, which was not in the style of McCabe:

> The topics I do not rely on Herbert for—it's a field—are all within the worlds of medieval thought, philosophical, theological and literary. It is true that sometimes I read and try to interpret Thomas. But Herbert used to say that he was no "Thomist." Neither am I. So, I am a medievalist of sorts, and Herbert was never that.[35]

Secondly, Turner's commitment in criticizing the "New Atheism" is something that we do not find in McCabe. The times were different, of course, and McCabe used to mention atheism with sympathy, presenting it as something nobler than the lukewarm attitude of "sociological" Christians.

The Disciples: Brian Davies

Brian Davies started his philosophical training defending Alvin Plantinga against J. L. Mackie when they debated the problem of evil and he was working on his PhD dissertation at King's College in London in 1976; he says that when he bumped into D. Z. Phillips' philosophical works he thought that Phillips was an atheist; however, later on he changed his mind and accepted the core theses of Phillips' "grammar of God," i.e. as a critique of the anthropomorphic understatement of God.

At the end of the 1970s he joined the Dominicans at Blackfriars in Oxford and recalls that the first person who opened the door of that monastery was nobody but Herbert McCabe, who from then onward was his mentor and, also, sponsor: Davies in 1982 started lecturing in philosophy and theology at Blackfriars and in 1988 became the regent of studies of the English

---

34. Turner, "The Price of Truth," 8–9.
35. Turner's email to me on 22 May 2018.

Dominican province. From 1995 till the present day he has been teaching at Fordham University in New York.[36]

His main publication, translated in several languages, is a textbook of philosophy of religion. As a sort of important "side activity," since 2001, he has been working as McCabe's literary executor and has edited six posthumous books which collect the unpublished writings his mentor left, adding to all of them an introduction meant to present the figure of McCabe. In those Davies continually mentions McCabe's "intelligence" and "cleverness," and notices that, although he was a faithful Catholic priest, his view about the Catholic church was "thoroughly unsentimental."[37]

Also, he notices that McCabe's achievements were both in philosophy and in theology:

> for many years now there has been a notable rift between philosophers and theologians. Typically, philosophers have not engaged with theologians . . . and theologians have displayed little interest in (and often little competence in) detailed philosophical analysis.

Unlike them, McCabe mastered both disciplines.[38]

Moreover, according to Davies, McCabe was not a Thomist in the sense that many scholars of Aquinas are, who just report his works in a rather dull way, and thus "do not give us a sense of why Aquinas might be exciting to read for oneself." Rather, McCabe was able to present Aquinas' thought freshly, "as important as coming from an intelligent contemporary."[39]

Davies shares all the main points of McCabe's philosophical theology: central is the idea that God is not an inhabitant of this universe.[40] From this all the rest flows: the why-proof of the existence of God, God's unknowability, the unique causation of creation, and also that God cannot be good in a moral sense and, so, we cannot defend him using the "freewill defence" when we deal with the problem of evil.

In his main text, *An Introduction to the Philosophy of Religion,* Davies maintains a distinction between the "classical theism" exemplified in Aquinas and the "theistic personalism" exemplified among philosophers such as, for instance, Richard Swinburne. This distinction, which he drew

36. I draw this information from the video recording of his lecture "Thomas Aquinas on God and Evil" given at The Lumen Christi Institute on 11 April 2012 and his CV on the website of Fordham University.

37. Davies, "Introduction" to McCabe, *God Still Matters,* xi.

38. Davies, "Introduction" to McCabe, *Faith within Reason,* xi–xii.

39. Davies, *On Aquinas,* Kindle loc. 85.

40. Davies, "Introduction" to McCabe, *God Still Matters,* xiii.

from Phillips, in part, but mostly from McCabe, is a main point of Davies' philosophical theology. Since his book has been an influential text book of religious studies for decades, throughout its three editions,[41] it is interesting to read a review of it that appeared in *The Thomist,* where Davies' and McCabe's rejection of Plantinga's freewill defence is accused of being "deterministic." Here we can see how much the apophaticism handed down by McCabe via Davies is still controversial within Thomism itself.[42]

In concluding this section, we should notice one main difference between McCabe and Davies: Davies is a philosopher, not a theologian, and so in his productions we do not find works on revealed theology dealing with the Christian faith. Consequently, when he edited a selected anthology of McCabe works—*The McCabe Reader*—he was guided by his own interests and did not include examples of the revealed theology that forms a substantial part of McCabe's writings.

THE KINDRED SPIRITS

Kindred Spirits: Alasdair MacIntyre

Within this category I insert authors of around McCabe's own age, who were more colleagues and companions of him. They knew and met him, appreciated his work, and shared some of his ideas, but these scholars studied some similar stream of subjects, being in dialogue with him, proceeding in parallel and quite independently. They did not so much learn new ideas from McCabe as refine their thinking in interaction with him.

Alasdair MacIntyre is just three years younger than McCabe. In his long academic career he was at first a Marxist,[43] then he started a longer phase as an Aristotelian philosopher; in his fifties he converted to Catholicism "as a result of being convinced of Thomism while attempting to disabuse his students of its authenticity."[44] While undertaking this new approach, some role was played by his discussions with McCabe, as MacIntyre recalls:

> I first met John Ignatius—not yet Herbert—McCabe in Manchester in 1949 just before he began his Dominican novitiate and just before I began graduate study in philosophy at Manchester

41. See Roy Jackson's review of this book in *Ars Disputandi* 4 (2004) 125–27.

42. Review by Eleonore Stump, *The Thomist* 49.1 (1985) 128–29.

43. MacIntyre shares his sympathy for Marx with McCabe, Eagleton and Turner.

44. John Cornwell's interview on November 2010 issue of *Prospect Magazine* (#176).

University. I did not see him again until the Fall of 1982, when I gave the Carlyle Lectures at Oxford on "Some Transformations of Justice." He attended every lecture and each of the seminars that followed each lecture. We also had long discussions in various pubs. I took very strong note of his criticisms, as I acknowledge in the Preface to *Whose Justice? Which Rationality?*, the book that resulted from the Carlyle Lectures in 1988. These were the only two occasions on which I met Herbert. He had no further influence on me and I certainly had no influence at all on him.[45]

Actually, it is true that MacIntyre never mentions McCabe in his books and, despite an assertion to the contrary,[46] this is fair: a reader of his books does not perceive McCabe's presence there. But, as for MacIntyre's influences on McCabe, McCabe himself several times in several periods of his life referred to MacIntyre as a landmark for the revived interest in Aristotelian virtue ethics. MacIntyre is the living philosopher he mentions more than any other.

However, I tend to think that MacIntyre is right about his non-debts; as he says:

> It is of course true that we acknowledged many of the same influences and came to be in substantial agreement on a range of central issues. We were both Dorothy Emmett's students, although neither of us held views anything like hers. We were both influenced by Elizabeth Anscombe and Peter Geach. But Herbert's preoccupations were those of a theologian, even if an unusually philosophically skilled theologian, whereas mine are those of an Aristotelian philosopher, even if I take Aquinas to be the most important interpreter of Aristotle. And we each drew on Wittgenstein's insights for our own purposes.[47]

I don't think McCabe quotes and praises MacIntyre because he was grateful to have learned from him new and interesting comments on virtue ethics, an ethical theory opposed to the Kantian ethics of duty. In fact, McCabe had learned such Aristotelian ethics since the 1940s from his Thomist teachers,[48] whereas MacIntyre studied and learned it only in the 1970s,

---

45. My interview.

46. Fr Peter Hunter (private communication to me, December 2015); McCarraher, *Meet the New Boss*: "MacIntyre learned a lot from McCabe, but I don't think he'd quite share McCabe's lifelong commitment to socialism."

47. McCarraher, *Meet the New Boss*.

48. See, for instance, his dissertation on *God and Evil,* completed in 1957.

when he moved away from the Marxism he had followed previously. No. I think that McCabe quotes and praises MacIntyre because the latter was the first famous academic who revalued virtue ethics without coming from the "ghetto" of neo-Thomism in seminaries and Catholic universities, but who belonged to prestigious secular universities (Oxford, Vanderbilt, Boston), and, therefore, gave a new stamp of authority to the ancient doctrine.

Because of his own interests in anthropology, MacIntyre mentions "one aspect of Herbert's theology [that] is particularly worth noting," that is, his Wittgensteinian reading of Aquinas concerning "human beings as embodied minds" and its relation with incarnation.[49] Elsewhere he says, "it is right to emphasise our shared view that human agents are language-using animals, something not taken seriously in the Neo-Thomist tradition."[50]

We see also remarkable differences between the two scholars: MacIntyre is not interested in theology and, as for philosophy, he is much more learned than McCabe on secular (non-Christian) authors. From Hegel and R. G.. Collingwood he has learned that philosophical truth arises only historically and only being a historian is it possible to take account of it. This is a reason why, I think, McCabe liked MacIntyre's virtue ethics much more than that of the Neo-Thomists.

Kindred Spirits: David Burrell

David Burrell is six years younger than McCabe, and he was not his disciple, rather he was one of Bernard Lonergan's. He says that McCabe is a "colleague" from whom he continues to learn. McCabe, he says, led a generation of ethicists (and here Burrell is thinking of Hauerwas rather than himself, I think) and he "taught us all how to read Aquinas through the lens of language; anyone who care about that was instructed by him" (and here he does think of himself).[51]

In his works McCabe almost never mentions David Burrell, whereas Burrell mentions McCabe quite a few times in his writings. For instance, he says that his own book Aquinas: God and Action (1979) is on the same wavelength McCabe's work.[52] In fact, in this book and in Knowing the Unknowable God: Ibn-Sina, Maimonides, Aquinas (1986), David Burrell argues at length and in similar ways about the unknowability of God throughout the best monotheistic traditions, whose culmination is to be found in Aquinas,

49. MacIntyre, "Foreword" to McCabe, God Still Matters, viii, ix.
50. MacIntyre, my interview.
51. Burrell, my interview.
52. Burrell, my interview.

and he explicitly shows his debt to McCabe for this apophatic reading of Aquinas. He also thinks that the current success of Aquinas in the Anglophone academia has McCabe as a significant cause.[53]

Burrell shares also several other major interests of McCabe: for instance, the theme of creation in his books *Freedom and Creation in Three Traditions* and *Original Peace: Restoring God's Creations*, and the theme of friendship in his *Friendship and Ways to Truth*.

This association is recognized by others too. Stephen Mulhall in his *The Great Riddle: Wittgenstein and Nonsense, Philosophy and Theology* (2015) categorizes both McCabe and Burrell as "grammatical Thomists":

> David Burrell and Herbert McCabe are presented by Mulhall as believing that Aquinas—faced with the traditional problem of how to speak about the inexpressible—can somehow be read as resorting to riddles and "projected" language which, if taken literally, seem in every sense nonsensical.[54]

However, this Wittgensteinian interpretation of Aquinas by McCabe and Burrell is criticized by John Milbank, the leading figure of the Radical Orthodoxy movement:

> Milbank's interpretation of Aquinas on analogy is shaped by his dissatisfaction with the grammatical approaches championed by Nicholas Lash, Herbert McCabe, and David Burrell.... Milbank sees in this limiting of our ability to speak adequately of God the consequence of giving linguistics priority over ontology.[55]

In conclusion, here we see two different characters—McCabe, witty and self-contained, and Burrell, serious and passionate—who share a strong interest in the apophatic reading of Thomistic philosophical theology (just as McCabe and MacIntyre share a strong interest in Wittgensteinian readings of Aquinas' philosophical anthropology and the updating of Aristotelian virtue ethics), without sharing others. For instance, McCabe did not share Burrell's interest in Muslim philosophy and Burrell does not share McCabe's concern for Western politics and the class struggle.

---

53. Burrell, my interview.

54. John Rist's review of Mulhall's book *Philosophical Investigations* 40.2 (2017) 188–92.

55. James Keating's review of *Aquinas and Radical Orthodoxy* by Paul DeHart in *The Thomist* 79.1 (2015) 155–56.

Kindred Spirits: Anthony Kenny

Anthony Kenny is five years younger than McCabe. First of all, Kenny has been a sort of ideal academic for his stability (lecturing in Oxford university from the 1970s to the present) and his prolificness: so far, he has published forty books, ten times more than McCabe did in his life. Perhaps thinking of himself, Kenny wrote that had McCabe chosen to embrace an academic career as a philosopher he would have arrived at the top of the profession, but he preferred to live the life of a Dominican friar, "and so his philosophical insights were not widely shared outside the circle of his religious brethren."[56]

He himself, however, was one of the few who took advantage of these insights, as he recalls:

> After studying at the Gregorian, I did graduate work in philosophy at Oxford in the heyday of ordinary language philosophy. I found this much more congenial than Roman scholasticism, but I was fortunate to meet Professor Peter Geach and Fr. Herbert McCabe OP, who showed me that many of the problems exercising philosophers in the analytic tradition at that time were very similar to those studied, often with no less sophistication, by medieval philosophers and logicians. In many ways, indeed, the keen interest in the logical analysis of ordinary language which was characteristic of Oxford in the latter part of the twentieth century brought it closer to medieval methods and concerns than any other era of post-Renaissance philosophy.[57]

This recollection says something that goes beyond Kenny's work itself, because it hints at a new way to tell the story of Anglophone "ordinary language philosophy" as a distinct way of distancing from both nineteenth-century idealism and positivism and twentieth-century neo-idealism and neo-positivism, and reconnecting with what MacIntyre calls the "traditional philosophy," that is, the Aristotelian-Thomistic one, a way that continental philosophy has not undertaken yet, apart from the eccentric neo-Thomistic strand.

ADMIRERS

I categorize as admirers those scholars who are younger than McCabe and did not really influence him, did not have a personal relationship with him, and in their work followed paths mostly different from his, but who, on the

56. Kenny, "Foreword," in McCabe, *On Aquinas*, vii.

57. Kenny, *Medieval Philosophy*, xv.

other hand, appreciate strongly some of his ideas. Here I present only some of them. In addition to those discussed below one could also have considered the impact of McCabe on Paul O'Grady, Karen Kilby, Ian McFarland, Eric Bugyis, and many others.

Admirers: Stanley Hauerwas

Robert Ombres, who lived at Blackfriars together with McCabe for many years, says that Stanley Hauerwas was not a close friend of McCabe, but was an admirer of him.[58] Hauerwas himself recalls:

> I was younger than Herbert, but I had read his book [*Law, Love and Language*] early on when it was published by Orbis Press under the title, I think, "Language and Ethics." I caught how significant the book was as I had schooled myself reading Wittgenstein. So when I went to England in the early 80s we met and I think we hit it off well. Then we had occasional meetings when I came to England and he came to Duke. I read primarily *What Is Ethics All About?* [the American title] under the earlier title early on. Then I tried to read everything I could get my hands on, such as *God Matters.*[59]

Hauerwas wrote a preface for the new edition of this book, which eventually was not included there but published in a journal. In it he wonders

> why McCabe's book did not have the impact it deserves. I believe *What Is Ethics All About?* is one of the most important books to have been written in ethics and theology in the last century. Though it lacks the intellectual mapping of Alasdair MacIntyre's *After Virtue*, I think McCabe's accomplishment in this remarkable book to be as important as MacIntyre's work. But if McCabe's book is so significant, why have the debates in Catholic moral theology and Protestant ethics been carried on as if the book had never been published?[60]

He laments that in America McCabe was too little known, whereas in Britain he was "too well known" for the Davis affair, but perhaps his

> "Notoriety" may have distracted some from recognizing *What Is Ethics All About?* for what it is: that is, an extraordinary

58. Ombres, my interview.
59. Hauerwas, my interview.
60. Hauerwas, "An Unpublished Foreword," 291.

restatement of Aquinas' moral theology made possible by Wittgenstein.[61]

According to Hauerwas, there are other and deeper reasons to explain McCabe's relative lack of impact, which we shall discuss in the conclusion of this chapter.

Here we notice that, as for his own work on ethics, Hauerwas wants to acknowledge in the clearest terms his debt to McCabe: "Anyone reading *What Is Ethics All About?* will quickly discover how 'unoriginal' my work has been. Most of what I have said was said by Herbert in 1968."[62] In particular, he points to McCabe's legacy in his book *Vision and Virtue: Essays in Christian Ethical Reflection* (1974).[63]

McCabe's ethical ideas as appreciated by Hauerwas are several. First of all, he made us aware that

> To be human, to share a common nature, according to McCabe, means we share a biological and linguistic nature. Humans are animals that talk. McCabe thus avoids any account of the human that might tempt us to forget our bodily nature.[64]

Also, he criticized the Humean distinction between "matter of facts" and "values" or "prescriptions," underlining how much this theory is "rooted in the economic structures of capitalism"; today MacIntyre's *After Virtue* allows us to see the importance of McCabe's critique: our lives are made neither of facts nor of values but only of linguistic descriptions, "which means nothing is more important than helping us recover the politics that shape our speech."

Meditating on the *Humane Vitae* he proposed an alternative between the relativism of situationist ethics and the alleged universality of clerical normative ethics, in fact, natural law comes from our life within linguistic communities. In so far as they are several, our apprenticeship in natural law is dramatically incomplete: "Not to be missed, however, is Herbert's equal insistence that every moral problem of the slightest interest is about who is to get hurt." The crucifixion of Christ makes us aware that we cannot avoid "moral tragedy": "The morality we discover through the languages that make us capable of community is, therefore, subject to the new language that is nothing less than God's very word, Jesus Christ."[65]

61. Hauerwas, "An Unpublished Foreword," 291.
62. Hauerwas, "An Unpublished Foreword," 292.
63. Hauerwas, my interview.
64. Hauerwas, "Learning the Language of Peace."
65. Hauerwas, "An Unpublished Foreword," 293–94.

Admirers: Rowan Williams

Rowan Williams, former archbishop of Canterbury, is not Catholic, but, according to Timothy Radcliffe (and Terry Eagleton says the same) was mostly influenced by "the devotional side" of Cornelius Ernst, rather than by McCabe. He also met McCabe and read his books,[66] indeed Williams says *Law, Love and Language* is one of the four books that were most influential on him.[67] He many times mentions McCabe in his books. His biographer writes that McCabe was "a potent prophet of *ressourcement*" to Williams, because the latter shared a common experience of Anglican clergy: in the 1960s the Cambridge theological world knew little of Catholic and Orthodox Christianity and scarcely anything about Christian theology between Chalcedon and the eve of Reformation.[68]

The same biographer in 2016 wrote a book that criticizes the "New Atheists," recalling a similar criticism made by Williams and whose title, *God Is No Thing*, directly echoes the apophatic wording by which McCabe argues that God, since God created everything, cannot be a "thing."[69]

From McCabe Williams draws in particular his philosophical theology about creation: he is ready to revalue natural theology, so neglected and even attacked by the Protestant theologians,[70] and to speak about meaningful questions like "why is there anything instead of nothing?" Williams also says that he drew from McCabe the idea that God is more deeply involved in any creature than we can even imagine.[71] And, in his foreword to *God, Christ and Us*, he writes:

> Christian philosophers do their job so that Christian (and other) people have a better chance of living free from idolatry. . . . There can be few Christian philosophers of the century past who have so fully exemplified this side of their vocation as did Herbert McCabe.[72]

McCabe's ethics also provides some inspiration to Williams:

---

66. Radcliffe, my interview.

67. Rowan Williams interviewed by Terence Handley MacMath, *Church Times*, 18 March 2016, 26.

68. Shortt, *Rowan Williams: An Introduction*.

69 Rupert Shortt, *God Is No Thing: Coherent Christianity*.

70 Williams, "A Future for Natural Theology?"

71. Williams interviewed by Shortt on *Fulcrum Renewing the Evangelical Centre*, 14 December 2010, online.

72. Williams, "Foreword" to McCabe's *God, Christ and Us*, vii.

Herbert McCabe . . . wrote many years ago—not without a touch of mischief—that "ethics is entirely concerned with doing what you want"; he goes on to explain that our problem is that we live in a society—and indeed as part of a fallen humanity—that deceives us constantly about what we most deeply want.[73]

Admirers: L. Roger Owens

L. Roger Owens is an American Methodist priest who in 2005 published an article on McCabe for two purposes:[74] to make him be known by the American public (when he died "there were few ripples in the theological world this side of the Atlantic"), and to show that "McCabe's most important contribution lies in how his theological ethics cannot be separated from his sacramental theology."[75] Before this, he presents the cultural context of the 1930s to the 1980s in England and the Wittgensteinian-Thomistic anthropology of McCabe, and then McCabe debating the *Veritatis Splendor* and criticizing situationists, proportionalists, and traditionalists (nornativists). In fact:

> McCabe's approach to ethics is far from an approach based on principles. Rather, ethics is the study of the meaningfulness of the intrinsically communicative nature of human bodies sharing a common life.[76]

At the end Owens wants "to point to the way McCabe's ethics as language finds its fulfilment, so to speak, in the sacraments of the church."[77] He agrees with McCabe in presenting humankind as something currently fragmented and whose unity is only a reality of the future, and, in the meantime, the church is the "sacrament" (sign which performs what it signifies) of the (eschatological) future united humankind:

> Through the sacraments of the church Jesus is present bodily as the language of the future. . . . McCabe argues that human communication cannot be achieved until all humanity shares bodily

---

73 Williams, "On Making Moral Decisions," 296.

74. Owens, "The Theological Ethics of Herbert McCabe OP."

75. Owens, "The Theological Ethics of Herbert McCabe OP," 572.

76. Owens, "The Theological Ethics of Herbert McCabe OP," 586.

77. Owens, "The Theological Ethics of Herbert McCabe OP," 589.

the life of God. Until then, we share now sacramentally in that life through the eucharistic celebration.[78]

This could seem enigmatic indeed, especially for those people, like Catholics of a certain age, who, differently from the Methodist Owens, have experienced thousands of Eucharists throughout their life and hardly, though, this foresight of the unity among human beings. However, he makes it clear elsewhere when he quotes McCabe:

> I have not, in this book, tried to apply Christian principles to particular moral questions because it seems to me that Christianity does not in the first place propose a set of moral principles. As I suggested in my first chapter [on situation ethics], I do not think that such principles are out of place in Christianity; without them the notion of love may collapse into vagueness or unmeaning, but Christianity is essentially about our communication with each other in Christ, our participation in the world of the future.[79]

He comments: "We would do well to remember that this participation is what Christian ethics is about."[80] This insight, in my opinion, is not evidently Christian, but is more challenging as a way of giving ethics a new framework, different from both virtue and deontological ethics.

After a few years Owen published a book, which has been received well and highly appreciated by reviewers.[81] In it Owens recollects ancient and modern authors such as Cyril of Alexandria, Schleiermacher, Jenson, Milbank, and many others, adopts the philosophical concept of "practices" from MacIntyre, and writes two long chapters, one on Bonhoeffer and the other on McCabe. In the latter Owen provides the reader again with McCabe's anthropology and ethics and then presents a new deepening of Eucharist and incarnation. "The church is the community articulating . . . the world's future"; "this articulation happens primarily in church's sacramental life, and especially in the Eucharist, which makes present to the world Christ's body."[82]

78. Owens, "The Theological Ethics of Herbert McCabe OP," 590.

79. McCabe, *Law, Love and Language, etc.*, 172.

80. Owens, "The Theological Ethics of Herbert McCabe OP," 191.

81. Owens, *The Shape of Participation*. "The finest work of ecclesiology of the decade," says *Christian Century*.

82 Owens, *The Shape of Participation*, 126–27.

Admirers: Peter Serracino Inglott

Peter Serracino Inglott (1936–2012) was a Maltese philosopher and an influential advisor of local politicians. He used to meet McCabe during his stay in Oxford and also in Malta when McCabe was working as an external examiner there.[83] His biographer says that on the one hand he was impressed (but not convinced) by the Marxist "Oxford environment" of Terry Eagleton and Alasdair MacIntyre, the latter allegedly presented as a "disciple of McCabe who was writing a book about Marxism."[84] On the other end he admired the newness of McCabe's ethics, which rejected law as source of morality because goodness does not come from an act of will, and, rather, is a product of language; therefore, its field is wider than in the past when it was investigated just through a "small number of difficult moral cases." PSI summarizes McCabe's position this way: "the meaning of any natural action would only emerge if you see it in its total context, which has to be that of total world history, which one can't ever have."[85]

However, a critic notices that all those who met McCabe while working in Malta know well that he would not recognize himself "in the authoritarian version of Thomas Aquinas" held by Inglott, "captive of a dull conservative authoritarianism where those that deviate from the 'official' Thomas are condemned as so called progressive, not to say heretical."[86]

In any case, Inglott appreciated McCabe's teaching about how to speak of God: we can speak saying what God is not, and giving him analogical attributes, which are true but non-understandable. All the theological analogies show how the subject-predicate structure of human language cannot grasp the simplicity of God (i.e., that God's goodness is identical with his wisdom, will, and existence), and this is why God cannot be expressed in our language. There are, also, metaphorical attributes that are understandable but literally false, even though they populate any religious language.[87] We shall explore this further in the chapter about the knowability of God.

Admirers: Susannah Ticciati

Susannah Ticciati in her major work analyses in depth Denys Turner's philosophical theology and recognizes that it is "adumbrated in a succinct way

83. Massa, *PSI King-Maker*, 122.
84. Massa, *PSI King-Maker*, 159.
85. Massa, *PSI King-Maker*, 769.
86. Vella, *Reflections in a Canvas Bag*, 102.
87. Inglott, *Peopled Silence*, 163–64.

by Herbert McCabe";[88] also in the same book she refers to McCabe's view on incarnation. She appreciates his arguments about "the logical coherence of Chalcedon."[89] God is different from human beings, and does not reveal truth in terms of a set of propositions, says McCabe:

> The idea that Jesus, qua Son of God, constructed some special divinely authorized set of propositions such as the Christian creed is as anthropomorphic as the idea that God has a white beard. Whatever we can mean by speaking of God's knowledge, we know that it cannot mean that God is well informed, that he assents to a large number of true statements and Jesus's knowledge of history, as Son of God, was no difference from the existence of the world; it was not in the same ballgame with what he learnt as man.[90]

In his dissertation, Ethan D. Smith paraphrases Ticciati:[91]

> God is therefore a contrasting limit to humanity—even as these theologies develop "non-competitive" ontologies and models of agency—whereby the end of apophatic theology is always, to borrow the language of a recent constructive version of this theology—to "manifest the divine difference" from creatures.

This "divine difference" seems to be what Ticciati is so keen to stress. As Turner says—while reporting Ticciati's account of Barth's position—the so-called "natural philosophy" deplored by Barth may be misleading on this point. Barth's stand, followed by Ticciati, consists

> less in a hostility to rational proof on the sort of general epistemological grounds on which Kant opposed it than in a subtler and more complex objection; . . . for Karl Barth, the creation of the world *ex nihilo* is already and always has been itself within our election *ex nihilo* for, as Susannah Ticciati puts it, "election is God's gratuitous decision to create in the first place: a decision made in (and also by and for) Jesus Christ." . . . Susannah Ticciati therefore puts the case against "natural theology" succinctly and somewhat more subtly than does [Alvin] Plantinga. She writes, in Barthian spirit, that election is to be understood as more fundamental than creation. This gives rise to a historical

88. Ticciati, *A New Apophaticism*, 27.

89. Ticciati, syllabus for her 2006 module at KCL on "An Introduction to the Doctrine of the Person of Christ."

90. McCabe, *God Matters*, 58–59.

91. Ethan Smith, *The Praise of Glory*, 7.

ontology in which there is no point of stability other than God's faithful activity of questioning, which calls everything else into question. A rational proof of the existence of God would be such a stable point outside this activity of God.[92]

It is true that a Catholic theologian like McCabe still preserves a role for natural theology, that is, for a discourse about "God" independent from the Christian revelation, and therefore delivers a proof of God's existence and a treatise on God's attributes. However, the way he puts the proof and his careful attention to a proper understanding of analogical attributes brings the reader to perceive the "divine difference" (even though this perception springs from a timeless and "natural" framework drawn from the medieval philosophical attitude and not "historical" and, dare I say, existential attitudes, like in Barth). And this is the reason why a non-Barthian theologian like McCabe can be appreciated (and admired) by a Barthian theologian like Ticciati.

Admirers: Eugene McCarraher

Eugene McCarraher is an American left-wing academic who wrote a book about American liberal Christian intellectuals and is writing another one about the "theological history of capitalism." He is also an enthusiastic admirer of McCabe. He acknowledges that a long-lasting Western narrative has been the "disenchantment" of the world due to industrialization, whereas he wants to show that capitalism itself is a new "enchantment" that has to be dispelled.[93] Theology can be a key discipline in interpreting social phenomena like this and others without being intimidated by the secular social sciences:

> McCabe has had a simply incalculable impact on me. . . . I honestly can't remember exactly how I first came across McCabe's work. I know it was during the early '90s, when I was working on my dissertation, and I was reading the earliest works in Radical Orthodoxy (RO). . . . Because some of the RO work was being published in *New Blackfriars* . . . I may well have first encountered McCabe there. . . . [I]f RO led me to McCabe, McCabe led me away from RO. . . . RO was refreshing and stimulating, particularly the idea that theology can be a distinct and compelling form of social and cultural criticism. . . . But as I've watched how some of this has played out or not played out over the last

92. Turner, *Faith, Reason,* 8–9, 10.
93. McCarraher, "Mammon," 433.

decade, I've concluded that the theological renaissance these figures embodied not only has waned, but also has encouraged some very bad mental and political habits. For one thing, I'm tired of hearing "modernity" and "liberalism" treated as though they were the spawn of Satan.[94]

But McCarraher is a committed liberal and cannot stand this. McCabe, he observes, does not question the Enlightenment nor the fundamentals of liberalism, such as human rights, the independence of the judiciary, freedom of speech and press, and the balance of powers. McCabe grounded the relations between theology and politics in a "much more modest ecclesiology": the church provides something, like the sacraments, which speak of a future unity of humankind, not of the church itself; it "points beyond itself to the future where the church will no longer exist." Because of these reasons McCarraher says: "I swear that reading McCabe has often kept me Christian."[95]

Also, his evaluation of history is similar to McCabe's in its tone, that is, one more common in sermons than in scholarly essays. If we read McCarraher's criticism of the Christians who refuse the legitimacy of gay marriage, and compare it with John Milbank's writing on the same issue, in McCarraher's words we find McCabe's style,[96] not at all Milbank's.[97]

SCHOLARS

Scholars: Stephen Mulhall

Among the many scholars who have written about McCabe, without being clearly admirers and followers of his main ideas, I mention here only one: Stephen Mulhall.

Mulhall writes that at the 2011 Aquinas Colloquium at Blackfriars in Oxford:

---

94. McCarraher, "Meet the New Boss." However, despite this "incalculable impact", in his recent 816-page book *The Enchantment of Mammon* (November 2019) McCarraher never mentions McCabe.

95. McCarraher, "Meet the New Boss."

96. McCarraher, "Meet the New Boss."

97. Milbank, "Gay Marriage and the Future of Human Sexuality." As for McCabe, we do not know his opinion about gay marriage; however, he was clear in saying that there is not any evidence that homosexuality is against natural law ("Manuals and Rule Books").

> It was a surprise and a pleasure to discover . . . that there was such
> a thing as "Grammatical Thomism"—a practice of interpreting
> the theology of Thomas Aquinas as operating in ways that were
> internally related (or at least relatable) to Wittgenstein's later
> philosophical methods. This connection was of course evident
> in Fr. McCabe's writings; but I hadn't previously appreciated that
> those writings had come to be viewed (at least by some theolo-
> gians and philosophers of religion) as part of a more general
> movement or school of Thomist studies—one which was pre-
> sumed to include the work of Denys Turner (which I had previ-
> ously encountered) and of David Burrell (which I had not).[98]

He observes that although "the category appears to have been created
primarily by those who saw only error and darkness" in it, namely Francesca
Murphy, he appreciates its aims and the authors who belong to it. Eventually Mulhall wrote a book about this "school."[99] He is impressed by the idea
that the *Summa* could be read as "a grammatical investigation of the nature
and limits of (what McCabe would call) the human capacity to know and
name God" and that McCabe was part of "a broader interpretative project"
inspired by Victor Preller and carried on by David Burrell, Fergus Kerr, and
Denys Turner. Francesca Murphy is wrong for blaming this school for presenting "a theory aimed at translating metaphysical concerns [about God's
being] into concerns about the logic of religious language."

> For Wittgenstein, however, elucidating grammar and articu-
> lating the essence of things are not distinct tasks at all. On the
> contrary: according to his later writings, "*Essence* is expressed
> in grammar. . . . Grammar tells what kind of object anything is
> (theology as grammar)."[100]

Grammar focuses on words: for example, grammatical Thomists
analyze the words of Aquinas' "five ways." In particular, McCabe "offers
a reading of the Second Way which aspires to respect Thomas' pervasive
awareness that God is not a god, not an entity amongst entities, but rather
utterly transcendent to the world He created."[101]

Mulhall observes that McCabe characteristically is not interest in the
debate about the functions of Aquinas' "analogy" because McCabe thinks
that Aquinas himself was not interested in providing us any such theory.

98. Mulhall, "What Is 'Grammatical' about Grammatical Thomism?" 1.

99. Mulhall, *The Great Riddle: Wittgenstein and Nonsense, Theology and Philosophy* (2015).

100. Mulhall, *The Great Riddle*, 1–2.

101. Mulhall, *The Great Riddle*, 43.

When in *quaestio* 13 he mentions analogical names, he just intends to point to the openness to a variety of meanings that the words can get according to the different word games, in the same sense meant by Wittgenstein.[102]

ON THE INTERNET

Here I just notice, having read the first seventy weblogs reported by Google search in December 2017, that the admirers of McCabe belong to an unexpected variety of denominations: from the "interreligious, non-partisan" *First Things*, to the progressive Catholic *Commonweal*, to the progressive Orthodox *Eclectic Orthodoxy*, to the Mennonite *Jesus Loves You*, to the Baptist *Jason Goroncy*, to the Anglican *Kai Euthus* run by Mike Higton, and to the Methodist minister Richard Hall, who runs *Connexions*. Therefore, regardless of confessional identity, some admirers were impressed by both the ideas and the style of McCabe. Remarkably, through McCabe they started appreciating Aquinas from scratch: Jason Micheli on *The Tamed Cynic* praises and comments McCabe:

> As a Thomistic alternative to my normal Barthian tendencies, I'm observing Holy Week this year by reading the theological essays of Herbert McCabe. . . . A Dominican philosopher, McCabe has revolutionized my thinking about the faith and prompted me to get back in to reading Aquinas this past year.[103]

And the Uniting Church Australian theologian Ben Myers on *Faith and Theology* writes "Why I Am (Finally) Going to Read Herbert McCabe" where he reports McCabe's passages on Trinity and incarnation and observes that there is a strong convergence towards Barthian theologians like Jüngel.[104] And another Mennonite theologian, Tripp York, in the "McCabe Archives" on *The Other Journal* website writes "Jesus, stop suffering God. It's embarrassing and 'does' nothing," where he states that McCabe opened his eyes and showed how weak and broken was the Evangelical theology of Bonhoeffer about the suffering of God.[105]

The Orthodox Aidan Kimel starts criticizing the Evangelical "open theism" about a God who cannot predict the future, while himself relying on passages where McCabe writes about the transcendence of God, and eventually ends doubting the necessity of the Orthodox Palamas' distinction

102. Mulhall, *The Great Riddle*, 62.
103. Micheli, "Holy Week with Herbert."
104. York, "The McCabe Archives."
105. York, "The McCabe Archives."

between essence and energy and suggests to everybody a full immersion in the works of Aquinas.[106]

A proper investigation of the presence of McCabe on the web would require a long study on its own.

CONCLUSIONS

Via his published works and the presentations of them provided by disciples, kindred spirits, admirers, scholars, and bloggers McCabe handed down many ideas and much inspiration. The rest of this book will explore them in some depth.

First of all, McCabe spread a fresh and effective appreciation of Aquinas put in dialogue with modern thinkers and modern society's needs; this happened thanks to, among others, Turner, Davies, Eagleton, and also MacIntyre, who started appreciating Aquinas because of McCabe and now holds that Aquinas was the most important interpreter of Aristotle. When asked whether McCabe contributed to the Thomistic renaissance in the Anglophone world, Turner says:

> I do think that Herbert was very significant among a group of thinkers, mainly Catholic philosophers, who contributed to a revival of interest in Aquinas in the sixties and seventies. These would include, of course, Elizabeth Anscombe, Peter Geach, Michael Dummett, Anthony Kenny. . . . As to theology and the revival of interest in Aquinas, paradoxically the almost complete neglect of him in the documents of Vatican II helped, mainly by liberating Thomas from his entrapment in the confines of the neo-Thomisms of the seventy years or so from Leo XIII until 1962.[107]

What Turner says here seem to me true but still insufficient. Apart from Vatican II, we should add that McCabe did not belong to the conventional category of neo-Thomists: he was not interested in writing essays and monographs about Aquinas, and he was a liberal, radical, committed advocate of the progressive secular ideas of the 1960s about war, capitalism, feminism, love, workers' rights, colonialism, and so on, unlike almost all other scholars of Aquinas, even after Vatican II. He was able to make people

---

106. Kimel, "Open Theism, Eternity and the Biblical God." This is a neat example of how McCabe is able to make people, even priests who studied theology, aware of the lively importance of Aquinas' thought, towards whom previously they had only indifference if not contempt, and make them eager to read Aquinas.

107. Turner's email to me on 22 May 2018.

like Eagleton love Aquinas not out of erudite annotated studies about a particular *quaestio* and its seventeenth-century commentators, but because he applied Thomas' ideas to current political and social affairs.

Second, another legacy from McCabe is his completion of Aristotelian anthropology by means of Wittgenstein. This sort of non-reductionist "materialism" today—via, among others, Eagleton and MacIntyre—is much more widespread than it used to be in the past among both theologians and philosophers.

Third, mostly but not solely thanks to Turner and Davies, McCabe disseminated an overall strong apophatic approach to theology.

Fourth, McCabe provided us with powerful testimony of the life of a committed Catholic who was also a Marxist, without—however—any yielding to the totalitarian and atheistic part of the latter. We have this especially through Eagleton and McCarraher.

Fifth, McCabe gave us the insight that, paradoxically, both creationists and some atheists can share the same anthropomorphic God, as a supreme being who is part of the universe. This insight come to us via Eagleton, Turner, and also Davies' textbook of philosophy of religion.

Sixth, McCabe contributed to an increasing Protestant sympathy for Catholic theology: in fact, McCabe never polemicized against the Reformation as such, and, also, was very keen on the concept of God as "wholly other," an idea so loved by some Protestant theologians. Furthermore, he was also very critical of the Catholic church as an institution. We see this Protestant appreciation especially in Rowan Williams, Susannah Ticciati, and Roger L. Owens.

However, even though at least these six major ideas have been handed down to the theology of our time, McCabe himself and the complexity of his thought have not ever received a sustained study. As a consequence of this, his name is not included into the "good" canon of the second half of the twentieth century, unlike the names of Henri de Lubac, Karl Rahner, Rudolph Bultmann, Paul Tillich, Hans Urs von Balthazar, Edward Schillebeeckx, and many others.

Is McCabe underrated? Speaking of this last part of his life Eamon Duffy writes:

> [T]hese were also great years for McCabe as a teacher. Profoundly immersed in the thought of Aquinas, not as a dead authority but as a perpetually fertile questioner, "my colleague, Thomas Aquinas," McCabe transmitted this passionate engagement to others. His clarity of exposition was unrivalled and his understanding of Thomas coloured the attitudes of English

philosophers and theologians for two generations, beyond as well as inside the Dominican order.[108]

I think that this depiction is mostly true, but not entirely, because it is overoptimistic. For instance: were the people allegedly influenced by McCabe really both philosophers and theologians? Halden Doerge complains that McCabe is underrated at least by the theologians (since, at least some "philosophers"—Eagleton, MacIntyre, and Kenny—"acknowledge the significant influence of his thought on their own work").[109] Hauerwas holds the very opposite: "I think he had no influence among philosophers but he did among theologians."[110] Indeed, Doerge should have said, instead, "some English philosophers interested in theology." I do agree with him that McCabe had a "sharp dogmatic precision" that is "rare among theologians," that is, a sort of rigorous philosophical method:

> Either you have revolutionary theologians like Stanley Hauerwas who are something of a blunt instrument, despite all their brilliance, or you have systematically precise dogmaticians like George Hunsinger or Paul Molnar who lack innovation and original theological contribution. McCabe is in many ways the best of both worlds.[111]

However, I disagree with Doerge about McCabe's popularity among philosophers in general, let alone the Continental ones; even in the Anglophone world you would hardly meet any academic lecturer in a department of philosophy aware of McCabe's work.

Hauerwas, however, agrees with Doerge in complaining that McCabe is underrated. In ethics, for example:

> I have wondered if one of the reasons Herbert's account of ethics in *What Is Ethics All About?* did not have the influence it deserves is due to the effortless way he got right what is so hard to get right. His argument is so elegant and his examples so apposite one might be tempted to miss how he is trying to help us avoid theory-driven mistakes that make it impossible for us to see what is right before our eyes. Herbert was too erudite to need to display his erudition. . . . McCabe's ability to go to the heart of such issues without needless complexity may have

108. Duffy, "Herbert McCabe."
109. Doerge, "Herbert McCabe."
110. Hauerwas in my interview.
111. Doerge, "Herbert McCabe."

tempted some readers to overlook the revolutionary character
of his work.[112]

And in general, as well:

> That McCabe is not studied much in the academy, I think, is not
> because he was not an academic but simply because he makes
> people re-think too much. As far as Herbert's intellectual legacy,
> I wish it was stronger than it is. He was a seminal thinker al-
> though I think for personality reasons he was not appropriately
> recognized as such.[113]

I agree with him: even an English fellow Dominican friar, a contemporary of his and someone who knew him well, Fergus Kerr, when he has to
write a book about Thomism in the Anglophone world after WWII, quotes
McCabe only twice: once, on McCabe's quoting of Jane Austen on common
sense, and secondly in order to criticise McCabe's lack of interest in the
Thomistic debate on analogy. More than that, when Kerr approaches the
issue of "grammatical Thomism" (Aquinas read in the light of Wittgenstein)
he never mentions McCabe.[114]

In my opinion, McCabe is indeed underrated. Some reasons have been
presented already; I want to highlight that a major one is that almost none
of his works have been translated into other languages.

However, in this chapter and in the rest of my work I want to maintain
that, even though not sufficiently acknowledged, he has left a legacy. In my
chapter on the existence of God, for example, I will show how he was able to
revive the old "why-question." In fact, it was upheld by a few philosophers
in the past, such as Leibniz, Bergson, and Heidegger, but faded away later
on and, more particularly, was never inserted into the canonical interpretations of Aquinas by the Thomistic schools. Things have changed. Recently,
a learned Thomist, John Wippel, has edited an entire book about it (though
without mentioning McCabe).[115] And I will notice similar original achievements in presenting his positions about other topics and parts of systematic
theology.

Even in the three writers I called "disciples" there is not a structured
assessment of McCabe's legacy. They are grateful, they use some of his ideas,
but they do not explicitly present him as an author with his own system
of ideas and playing a particular role within his historical context, within

---

112. Hauerwas, "An Unpublished Foreword," 293.

113. Hauerwas, my interview.

114. Kerr, *After Aquinas*, 121, 239. Kerr, *Theology after Wittgenstein*.

115. Wippel (ed.), *The Ultimate Why Question*.

the debates and streams of the philosophical and theological thought of his time. Even the "quintessential" disciple, Terry Eagleton, does not do this. While he is presenting McCabe's ideas about God against Dawkins, they are presented as a timeless "Christian theological tradition"; whereas, in his different historical context (1960s–80s) McCabe did not attack any atheists. On the contrary, readers of his major book *God Matters* encounter atheism only to realize how much it is close to scientific research and to the committed endless quest of a sincere believer. And while Eagleton is advocating Catholic Marxism, he presents mostly a stand for social justice, which was indeed strong in McCabe, but which was also accompanied by a theory on love. The liberal/Marxist attitude of separating justice from love is typically understandable in Eagleton but was not McCabe's way.[116]

In Denys Turner the lack of a historical assessment about the cultural causes that provoked a revival of apophaticism by Victor White and McCabe prevents the reader from understanding why most Catholic authors of their times and afterwards were not apophatic and still are not, and, therefore, why many Protestant authors are still reluctant to give a legitimate role to natural theology. Moreover, since this assessment is missing, Turner, even though he uses several of McCabe's ideas while presenting Aquinas' revealed theology (on incarnation, Trinity, sacraments), does not show that this is not the prevalent reception of Aquinas today.

These two points are even more evident in Brian Davies' works. In his influential textbook on philosophy of religion the scarcity of mentions of McCabe prevents his readers from realizing that this system of philosophical theology is not "timeless" but is actually McCabe's and comes from a particular time and a particular cultural environment. As a consequence, the readers miss both the contrast with the historical mainstream of philosophical theology and the link to a well-developed revealed theology that McCabe indeed provided. In this book Davies does not hand down the systematicity of McCabe's thought and therefore a model for setting up proper connections between philosophical and revealed theology.

However, since all these authors belong to traditions—like Thomism and Marxism—where understanding the history of a question matters, they themselves and their readers should hopefully want to become more aware of the historical Herbert McCabe. The actual McCabe, in fact, was not only an intelligent preacher, an inspiring activist, and a powerful mentor, as they used to present him, but was also *a systematic thinker*. The main purpose of my book is, therefore, to fill a gap of the scholarship and present the

---

116. This is slightly paradoxical, since Eagleton's preferred quote from McCabe is right about love.

historical McCabe in this further dimension of his intellectual life, that is, his being a systematic thinker like—*si parva licet componere magnis*—his hero Thomas Aquinas.

Philosophical Theology

5

Why God?

When McCabe formulated the question "Why God?"[1] he did not mean to ask why God exists, that is, the reason for the existence of God himself. He did not intend ask *how*—from our human point of view—we can think and argue any demonstration of God's existence. Instead, he wanted to clarify the reasons why speaking of God is *important*.

It is possible to classify several kinds of situations/motivations experienced by those people for whom speech on God is important and several other kinds of situations/motivations experienced by those people for whom it is not.

It could be observed, as McCabe does,[2] that God is important also to those atheists who are consciously convinced, and committed to their conviction, because for them too, the question of the cause of the existence of the universe is an important one; furthermore, when they deny that the cause of the universe is some kind of Top Person who rules over everything because of his great power, they are as "atheist" as Aquinas was.

According to McCabe, God is important also to those "creative" scientists who, while facing new, radical, and courageous questions, challenge already existing knowledge; it is important also to all those who think that science will attain amazing new achievements that today we cannot even

1 McCabe, "Why God?" in *Faith within Reason*.

2. See McCabe, "Creation" in *God Matters*, 7.

imagine: this attitude, in McCabe's opinion, is equivalent to stating a belief in God.[3]

In addition, some philosophers—take Aristotle and Hegel—thought that speaking about God was important, because, even apart from the so-called "positive/revealed religions," it allows all our knowledge to be organized under a general principle of intelligibility.[4]

Obviously enough, God is important also to all genuine believers in Christianity and in other "positive" religions. They are believers because they have "faith/trust" in the adults of the previous generation, who in turn had inherited the same faith, and so forth, going back through intergenerational tradition, as far as the apostles (if we speak of Christianity), who in turn had had faith in Jesus, for what they were not able to get themselves, whereas, since he claimed he had indeed got a special insight, he was able to say, for instance: "I and the Father are one."[5]

In particular, McCabe explicitly gave two reasons that, in his opinion, can show to whatever person (believer or not, scientist or not, philosopher or not) that speaking of God is important. The first one, of a more intellectual kind, springs from a question that we can all ask ourselves, and sometimes throughout our lives we do actually ask: "Why is there anything rather than nothing?"[6] We are unable to give an answer to this question, because, in McCabe's opinion, only God can be the answer (albeit in ways we cannot imagine). Therefore, inasmuch as we are interested in the question, speech concerning God is important to us.

A second reason for God's relevance, of a more moral kind, is the following: in order to have a good life I have to acquire virtues, but I can do this only while inserted within an interpersonal context. Such a context, in turn, cannot be any one; it must be "in tune" with human nature and nature in general. However, "nature" itself cannot be just something that exists; it must be structured and aiming towards a good end. God, if God exists, is the cause of this good end, without which the human quest for a good life would be inane. Therefore, there must be, in McCabe's opinion, someone

3. McCabe, "Creation" in *God Matters*, 3.

4. Besides, not just to organize knowledge in itself, but—more in a practical way—the academic disciplines as well, according to Alasdair MacIntyre in his *God, Philosophy, Universities*, 175–76.

5. "Unless hearsay is finally anchored, as it were, in what is not hearsay but witness, there can be no reliable hearsay, only baseless rumour. I can really know what I am told only if there is or was someone who knows or knew without being told. Faith, which 'comes by hearsay,' has to depend on somebody's knowing." McCabe, "The Logic of Mysticism," in *God Still Matters*, 17.

6. McCabe repeats this question many times throughout his writings, for instance in McCabe, *God Still Matters*, 19.

who makes nature have a meaning (a striving toward an aim), who makes it a "story," not just a "span of time." This "someone" must be, therefore, a being endowed with a sort of intelligence, which is unlikely to be the same as that of human beings, but which is somehow analogous to ours.[7] (Though not "a being" *within* nor *alongside* the universe.)

On the other hand, which are the kinds of people/situations for which speech on God is not important? In McCabe's opinion, it is not important to us when we think we have *already* got science (for instance, Newton's) and thus there is not anything to be searched for any more. This attitude could be ours whether we are Third Reich citizens or we are committed Christians in the days of Galileo.[8] The real or "genuine" atheists are those people (all of us sometimes) who assume there is nothing conceptually problematic in thinking of God as a being inside the universe, the most powerful of all other beings, but anyway internal. Even though we hold that we are believers in God, if we do not see that that thought is problematic then, in McCabe's opinion, speech about God is not important to us. In particular (and this applies just to believers), speech about God is not important when we mistake him for a "god," that is, a powerful force friendly with us, one that helps us overcome our opponents, and is "on our side," that is, one that makes happen in history what we want.[9]

These ideas by McCabe, on one hand, incorporate a legacy from nineteenth- and twentieth-century existentialism: when we become "philistines" and content with both our certitudes and our usual behavior, we all forget the "leap of faith" of Kierkegaard and the "thrownness" of Sartre, and so the speaking of God becomes unimportant. These ideas of McCabe also incorporate that epistemological criticism of science's certainties, which starts with Socrates' "knowing of not knowing" and goes on to Popper's "criterion of falsifiability":[10] we all should know that sciences have advanced because scientists did not settle for already given solutions.

Moreover, these ideas of McCabe also include the tradition of philosophical/"natural" theology, which since the sixth century BC, passing through Aristotle and coming to Aquinas, intended to de-anthropomorphize our thinking of God: we should all be aware that conceptual thought

---

7. McCabe, *Faith within Reason,* 45–46. Here we perceive two Thomistic ideas in McCabe: the first says that the natural human desire of happiness, that is, of seeing God, cannot be inane: *Summa Contra Gentiles,* liber III, caput 57.4. The second one deals with "analogy" between creature and Creator.

8. McCabe, "Creation" in *God Matters,* 2.

9. McCabe, "The Involvement of God," in *God Matters,* 42–43.

10. See, amongst other things, Meynell "Faith, Objectivity and Historical Falsifiability" 145–48.

is necessary if we want to avoid transforming God into an idolatrous "god"; and conceptual thought in the first place must show the unsuitability of our imaginative representations of God.[11]

It is better to call this theology "philosophical" rather than "natural," because human reason is not affected just by the long duration of nature, that is human biology, but also by the much shorter one of history. Here I would say that ancient Greek "philosophy" already shows the historical development of this "natural": in just two centuries from Thales' water and Democritus' atom the concept of the *archē* of the universe (which is both only one and non-anthropomorphic) has transformed into Plato's Idea of Good, Aristotle's Unmoved Mover, which thinks of itself, and the provident universal Logos of the Stoics.

This tradition of philosophical theology has at least two components: that of scientific research, which tries to explain the material universe as a whole, as Aristotle does; and that of positive/revealed theology, which tries to clarify its dogmas by means of human rationality.

McCabe was not an academic and did not write very much. He dealt with typical topics of revealed theology, such as transubstantiation, the pre-existence and incarnation of God the Son, Easter Triduum, and Trinity. He also dealt with more philosophical topics such as anthropology, epistemology, ethics, and also philosophical theology, which includes what has, from Aristotle onwards,[12] been called "metaphysics."[13] In particular, he dealt metaphysics following its classic tradition, according to which philosophical theology "comes" to God and does not "start" from God. That is, it starts from intellectual and moral issues of both the individual and his or her society till it ends by stating that without that which we call "God" those issues and problems could not be properly explained.[14]

---

11. "Sed quia de Deo scire non possumus quid sit, sed quid non sit, non possumus considerare de Deo quomodo sit, sed potius quomodo non sit. Primo ergo considerandum est quomodo non sit; secundo, quomodo a nobis cognoscatur; tertio, quomodo nominetur": *ST,* qu. 3, proemium.

12. More precisely, since Andronicus of Rhodes edited and published Aristotle's works in the first century B.C.

13. See the second volume of *Elementi di Filosofia* by Sofia Vanni Rovighi, where the author clearly distinguishes general metaphysics from that part of it called "philosophical theology."

14. Movement is explained by an Unmoved Mover, contingency by an Absolute, Necessary Being, actions by an Ultimate End; and then we state that Unmoved Mover, Necessary Being and Ultimate end converge in a widespread tradition: "et hoc omnes intelligunt Deus" (*ST,* pars I, qu.2, art. 3). On this distinction between philosophical/natural and revealed/positive theology, see Rovighi, *Il problema teologico in filosofia,* 21.

Since philosophical theology "starts" from the world, in particular the human world, it is more suitable than revealed theology to be understood by those people who do not think God is important, in order to show them that "God matters," that is, that speech about God is important. Also, it is more suitable for an apprenticeship in reasoning and debating, minimizing the principle of authority. A former student of McCabe, Robert Ombres, recalls that at the start of his class of philosophy the students were told two basic rules: (1) in this classroom nothing is heretical, everything can be discussed freely; (2) never use the "-isms," do not shield yourself with "this stand was maintained by Kant" but express only what you yourself think.[15]

15. My interview with Robert Ombres.

6

Existence as Such

Is Ontology a Separate Discipline?

ristotle distinguished two meanings of *prote philosophia*: "ontology," i.e., the science of being as such, and *theologia* (later "metaphysics"), i.e., the science of those beings that are "beyond" physical
beings. Although Herbert McCabe quotes[1] Aquinas, who maintains the
importance of studying being qua being,[2] he does not think it evident that
such a study can exist, because all the other sciences already deal with those
"beings" that are the object of their study. For instance, a criminologist with
crime and a philatelic with stamps. As far as they are interested in that particular kind of thing, they are interested in their existence also. Therefore, it
seems ontology cannot be distinguished from the other sciences: in fact, it is
not only true that *de facto* their objects exist, but it is also true that sciences
are purposely interested in the existence of their objects.

It is true that it could be objected that ontology is interested in beings
not because they are qualified as so-and-so, but just because they are beings. However, there is not any act of abstraction (that is considering just
an aspect of a thing, leaving aside the others) that allows us to reach the
concept of "being" as the largest genus that comprehends all the beings; in

---

1. McCabe, "Metaphysical Preliminaries" in *God and Evil*, 16ff.
2. Aquinas, *Commentary on the Metaphysics of Aristotle*, Book IV, lect. 1, n. 532.

fact, whatever aspect we leave aside is a being as well.[3] "Being" is not the most general characteristic of all things, different, for instance, from "crime" which is more general than "theft" and "murder."

> There is, however, an important difference between the two cases. The more general characteristic, being a crime, can be opposed to not being a crime in the sense of being something other than a crime, whereas the so-called general characteristic of being cannot be opposed to not being in the sense of being something other than a being.[4]

Therefore, we can be trapped and think that the "beings" exist in the same dimension of "not-beings," but this is an illusion. Moreover:

> If we compare the statements "I can see trees" and "I can see nothing," it is clear that while "trees" serves to signify what can be seen, "nothing" does not have this function. It functions rather in the manner of an adverb than as an object of the verb. Similarly, if we compare "Flossy is a purple cow" with "Peter is a human being," it will be clear that while the first can be split into two independent statements "Flossy is purple" and "Flossy is a cow," the second cannot be split into two independent statements "Peter is human" and "Peter is a being." It is instructive to compare "Peter is a human being" with "M. Poujade is a political nonentity." Just as the latter does not entail "M. Poujade is a nonentity," so the former does not entail "Peter is a being."[5]

That is, McCabe warns us of how peculiar the concept of "being" is: (1) because it is already implicitly contained in any other concept (say "human"), and therefore it is not a further attribute that could be predicated of things ("Peter"), and (2) because its contrary ("nonentity") cannot be predicated of things. Things can be thought just insofar as they exist. When we say the Brandywine does not exist, this simply means that we are not giving the Brandywine an attribute that qualifies it, different from when we say that the Brandywine is a river.[6]

"Being" cannot be contrasted with "nothing," unlike the way in which "white" can be contrasted with "black." That being stated, with what can we contrast it? How can we know anything about it? McCabe, together with

---

3. Aquinas, *Questiones Disputatae de Veritate*, qu. 1, art, 1.

4. McCabe, "Metaphysical Preliminaries" in *God and Evil*, 18.

5. McCabe, "Metaphysical Preliminaries" in *God and Evil*, 20.

6. McCabe, "Metaphysical Preliminaries" in *God and Evil*. The Brandywine is a river flowing through Tolkien's fictional Middle-Earth.

Aquinas, maintains that "being" cannot be contrasted with anything, and, together with Kant,[7] argues that while "something" can be conceived insofar as it is limited by other "somethings," "everything" instead cannot be conceived because it should be limited by that "nothing" which we do not have any concept of. When we use the word "nothing," we use it relatively: for instance, if we say that in the cupboard there is nothing, we mean that there are not any large or small objects, but we know there is dust and air.[8]

TO EXIST IS TO HAVE AN ESSENCE

Invoking Aquinas, McCabe maintains that to be is not different from not to be: there are differences only between things that exist.[9] Therefore, invoking Aristotle, McCabe argues that for any particular thing, "being" means to be a thing *of a certain kind*, that is to have an "essence."[10] For instance, when a horse is not a horse any more, it ceases to exist as well.[11] All essences exist; it would be meaningless to speak of an essence that does not exist: to say that Harry is a human being amounts to saying that Harry exists.[12] It could be observed that this stance by McCabe is a sort of linguistic interpretation of Aquinas that many Thomists could not agree with:

> In saying, then, that existence belongs to the essence, St Thomas is saying that reality is not made up of facts, or phenomena, or collections of phenomena, or of "something I know not what" behind appearances, but of topics of discussion. . . . For each kind of thing there is its appropriate language (it has an essence) and this language can be used to make true or false statements, statements with point (it exists). . . . Thomas does not attempt to answer the question "What is the relation of language (or thought) to reality?" As Wittgenstein clearly saw, there is no language in which to answer this question. Instead St Thomas asks: "How can we talk about this, and about that . . . ?" To ask this is to ask for essences, and, in his metaphysics, puzzles about

7. "Transcendental Dialectic" in Kant's *Critique of Pure Reason*.

8. McCabe, *God Matters*, 5.

9. McCabe, *Faith within Reason*, 65.

10. McCabe, "Metaphysical Preliminaries" in *God and Evil*, 20.

11. McCabe, "Metaphysical Preliminaries" in *God and Evil*, 21. This is the Aristotelian "substantial change," because of generation and corruption.

12. McCabe, "Metaphysical Preliminaries" in *God and Evil*, 31.

the relation of language to reality are eliminated by the principle that existence simply belongs to essence.[13]

At first, we experience the properties of things: for instance, a thing is white and walks. Then, from the properties we go up to the essence: in order to be white and to walk, that thing must be of a defined kind (have an essence), which allows it to have those properties. When we say *what* that thing is, we say also *that* that thing exists. It is not necessary that this "thing" is material like a horse. It can be just an entity in the mind (i.e. an idea), such as the "idea of table," the "idea of Renaissance," or the "idea of unicorn."

On the one hand, an essence is tautological: it would be self-contradictory to say that human beings are not animals. On the other hand, the properties imply the existence of something in a world: if there is a world where sparrows can be, most sparrows must be able to fly most of the time.[14]

An essence is the *"what* it is" of a thing, but it is not the same as the "universal," if with this word we mean *id quod potest predicari de pluribus* and, therefore, cannot be an individual. Some essences individualize because of the union between form and matter within them: for instance, because of their very essence human beings are individuals; insofar "the essence is that according to which the thing is said to exist,"[15] one of the things that makes human beings exist is that they are individuals. (By contrast, in the essence of God and the angels there is not any composition of matter and form and therefore they are not individuals.)[16]

Fido is a dog because its essence, which makes it exist *as a dog*, has been produced by natural causes; while producing its essence they produced its existence as well: if you beget a dog, it certainly will exist. When we describe this generation or production, we do not need any quality called "existence." So, when we say that God is the "cause" because of which things exist, we have to understand that he is a cause *sui generis*: God does not "insert" existence into things, as if existence was a quality of things and we could make the impossible distinction between existing things and non-existing things. Things exist because their essences are produced by their proper natural causes. Aquinas thinks we have not any single concept of existence, and for things "to exist" depends entirely on what they are.[17]

13. McCabe, "Metaphysical Preliminaries" in *God and Evil*, 28–29, 33–34.

14. McCabe, *Faith within Reason*, 54.

15. Aquinas, *On Being and Essence*, ch. 2, n. 6.

16. McCabe, "Metaphysical Preliminaries" in *God and Evil*, 29.

17. McCabe, *Faith within Reason*, 61.

ONTOLOGY CAN BE RECOVERED

Nevertheless, says McCabe, Aquinas was not completely against ontology, i.e., the science of being as such: according to him, in fact, it is possible to speak of the existence of things. However, he speaks of existence when he deals with statements: stating something is a logical act of the mind different from conceiving something; since stating has to do with truth and falsity, it goes beyond the conceptual. We can make true statements and false statements, and "existence" allows us to distinguish that act of the mind which is to conceive from that other act of the mind which is to state, precisely because "existence" is not a concept among other concepts. According to Aquinas, "existence" can be mentally grasped even if we cannot have any concept of it. McCabe thinks that Wittgenstein would have observed that it can be "shown" but cannot be "said."[18]

Moreover, according to McCabe, Aquinas had another reason not to be completely hostile to ontology as the science of being as such. In fact, even if it is true that it is meaningless to consider the many different things looking for any common characteristic called "existence,"[19] it is still possible to investigate the various meanings of this word, most of all the different meanings by which substances and accidents are said to exist.[20] It is true that, if you say "George is a human being," you do not say anything different from saying "George exists," but, if you say "George is white," you are saying something different: that is, that George exists *thus*.

McCabe maintains the doctrine of categories is important to Aquinas because it enables us to answer the question "What is being contrasted with X?" "Being" cannot be contrasted with "not being," whereas it is possible to contrast existence in a primary sense (substance or being *simpliciter*) with existence in a secondary sense (accident). The secondary sense of "being" depends on the primary one, even though it is not reducible to it.[21] An accident (e.g., being red) cannot exist by itself, but only as an attribute of a substance (e.g., a ball).[22]

Aquinas observes that the transcendental words (one, being, good, true) vary their meaning according to the different categories, and upon how all the accidents relate to the substance. This is his doctrine on "anal-

---

18. McCabe, *Faith*, 61–62.
19. McCabe, *Faith*, 60.
20. McCabe, "Metaphysical Preliminaries" in *God and Evil*, 3.
21. McCabe, "Metaphysical Preliminaries" in *God and Evil*, 25.
22. McCabe, "Categories" Appendix 1 in *God and Evil*, 181–84.

ogy," be it "of attribution"[23] or "of proportion,"[24] which McCabe doesn't focus on at length; he just observes that this doctrine allows him to link the existence of things to the peculiar existence of God.[25]

Another point worth clarifying is that existence is not a genus: genus is "quasi-material" because it waits for being specified into this or that species and into that or this individual, whereas existence is "quasi-formal" because it tells us that something has already achieved its specification and individualization.[26] Accordingly, McCabe underlines that he is interested in a "pluralistic view of the world": we cannot speak of Reality or the World as absolute, because there are many things and many different kinds of things, and each of them provides a different context of knowledge.[27] There are philosophers who think the world as the ultimate reality, a sort of "wall" on which the shapes of things are drawn; those philosophers try to go beyond the differences and find the common reality that things are expected to share.[28] Here, perhaps, McCabe is thinking of Spinoza, Hegel, Schopenhauer, and Marx. Anyway, he says that Aquinas, unlike them, did not think things are ultimately part of the same world. The only thing they share is that they all owe their existence to one Creator, which is not part of the world.

On the one hand, to Aquinas that a world exists is less obvious than that God exists, and, on the other hand, that God exists is less obvious than the things that exist in their diversity. It is like paintings by Picasso, which are so different from one another that it is impossible to catalogue them in one common genus (one world), and so they connect with each other just because they all owe their existence to the creative act of the painter.[29]

Coming back to the beginning, that is the legitimacy of ontology (the science of being *qua* being), McCabe observes that Aquinas does not cancel it, despite his firm denial of any general concept of existence: "When a horse ceases to be a horse it simply ceases to exist. It might seem at first sight that here what might perhaps be called the 'positivist' strain in St Thomas has eliminated metaphysics and the study of being altogether"; but we still have to clarify the concept of being because "as soon as it occurs to us to

---

23. McCabe, "Categories" in *God and Evil*, 186.
24. McCabe, "Aquinas on Trinity" in *God Still Matters*, 38.
25. McCabe, "Categories" in *God and Evil*, 186.
26. McCabe, *God Still Matters*, 23.
27. McCabe, "Metaphysical Preliminaries" in *God and Evil*, 21.
28. McCabe, "Metaphysical Preliminaries" in *God and Evil*, 33.
29. McCabe, *God Still Matters*, 24.

distinguish being human from, for example, being upside down, or being heavy, certain complications set in."[30]

CONCLUSIONS: FROM ONTOLOGY TO METAPHYSICS/THEOLOGY

Above I attributed the word "linguistic" to McCabe's interpretation of Aquinas' doctrine on "being." In this last citation McCabe uses the word "positivist." Both words come from the philosophies of the nineteenth century and early twentieth century (with its philosophy of language and neo-positivism), whose legacy probably affected McCabe more than other Thomists.

From twentieth-century Thomism McCabe follows the teaching of Étienne Gilson, who maintains that Aquinas thought it impossible to achieve a concept of being as such and the human mind can perceive "being" just by means of the logical act of statement, whereas most contemporary Thomists follow Maritain, disagree with Gilson, and in Aquinas' works find several concepts of "being": a "vague and confused concept," an "abstract concept," and an "intensive concept."[31]

As for analogy, McCabe follows both Aristotle and Aquinas, in the sense that he maintains that being has a meaning that is analogical and not univocal (unlike Duns Scotus and Francisco Suarez); however, unlike contemporary mainstream Thomism, McCabe does not dwell on the analysis of analogy, and, while translating the *Summa Theologiae*, comments:

> in the opinion of the present translator, too much has been made of Saint Thomas's alleged teachings on analogy. For him, analogy is not a way of getting to know about God, nor is it a theory of the structure of the universe, it is a comment on our use of certain words. . . . His real concern is to maintain that we can use words to mean more than they mean to us.[32]

According to McCabe, what Aquinas calls "existence" is the "gratuitousness" of things. What is such a gratuitousness? It is not that individual things might have not existed (in the sense that they would not have been part of this world if their proper natural causes had not produced them), but that the world *as a whole* could have not existed.[33]

---

30. McCabe, "Metaphysical Preliminaries" in *God and Evil*, 21.

31. See by Mondin, "Il problema della conoscenza dell'essere," 93ff.

32. McCabe, "Analogy," in Aquinas *ST, vol. 3*, 106.

33. McCabe, "The Logic of Mysticism" in *God Still Matters*, 20.

7

Proving the Existence of God

PROOFS OF THE EXISTENCE OF GOD

Even in the last century thinkers sought a ration proof of God's existence.[1] They did it in different ways: Kurt Gödel and Harvey Friedman address only other logicians, Jacques Maritain addresses people who are interested and trained in philosophy, C. S. Lewis speaks to reflective people without any special cultural background. Herbert McCabe sometimes presented his argument on God's existence as Maritain did, and sometimes as Lewis did, depending on the different occasions of his writings.

McCabe clearly states that for Christians it is meaningless to express their faith in Jesus Christ without any sort of a previous understanding of what they mean to say while speaking of "God."[2] In fact, Christians maintain that Jesus Christ is God indeed. Therefore, philosophical theology is a task worth being undertaken.

McCabe's main proof for God does not belong to the category of "moral" proofs, which Lewis' proof belongs to,[3] that is, those proofs meant

1. Gödel, "Ontological Proof" (1941); Friedman, *A Divine Consistency Proof for Mathematics* (2012); Maritain, *Raison and Raisons* (1947); Lewis, *Mere Christianity* (1941–44); .

2. McCabe, "God and Creation," 386.

3. Even though, as we have already seen, in his article "Why God?" McCabe provides a "moral" argument also, which is, for that matter, quite similar to Lewis' when

to reach the existence of God as the final answer to a quest for the meaning of life; nor does it belong to the "pragmatic" proofs category (such as those by Blaise Pascal and William James), which are meant to reach God in order to support our hope and will to live; nor to the "(onto)logic" kind of proofs that were given by Anselm of Canterbury, Descartes, Leibniz, and seek to reach God starting from the *idea* of God we have in our minds. McCabe's proof belongs to the "cosmological" category as well as the proofs given by his intellectual hero Thomas Aquinas. Just like Aquinas, McCabe also wants to distinguish his proof from the "(onto)logical" one.[4]

QUESTIONS

McCabe's attitude is that of a person who, on one hand, trusts human reason (albeit moderately because of his awareness of its limits), and, on the other hand, confesses a special experience: the Aristotelian "wonder" stemming from the Socratic acknowledgement of human ignorance. While undertaking a scientific inquiry, we start asking ourselves, for instance, why our dog Fido exists (where he comes from), and, then we continue asking why there are dogs (whence they come):

> Now of course it is always possible to stop the questioning at any point; a man may refuse to ask why there are dogs. He may say there just *are* dogs and perhaps it is impious to enquire how come—there were people who actually said that to Darwin. Similarly, it is possible to ask this ultimate question, to say as Russell once did: the universe is just there. This seems to me just as arbitrary as to say: dogs are just there. The difference is that we now know by hindsight that Darwin's critics were irrational because we have familiarised ourselves with an *answer* to the question, how come there are dogs?

Whereas, McCabe observes, we have not "familiarized" ourselves yet with the question "why is there anything at all rather than nothing whatsoever?" Although we do not know how to answer to such a question, this does not mean that it cannot be asked.[5]

The question itself is not new in the history of philosophy; William Gerber provides a list of the authors who formulated it and (in different ways) tried to answer it: including William of Sherwood, G. W. Leibniz,

---

the latter refers to the "natural law" and uses a metaphor drawn from music (see Lewis, *Mere Christianity*, 13–14).

4. McCabe, "The Logic of Mysticism" in *God Still Matters*, 15–16.

5. McCabe, *God Matters*, 5

Voltaire, Jonathan Edwards, William Paley, William James, Henri Bergson, Andrè Gide, Julian Huxley, Martin Heidegger, Ludwig Wittgenstein, George Boas, Thomas S. Knight, Robert Nozick, and David Ruelle.[6] I would add the name of C. S. Lewis who wrote: "But why anything comes to be there at all, and whether there is anything behind the things science observes— something of a different kind—this is not a scientific question."[7]

McCabe relies on the idea of *creatio ex nihilo* as it was interpreted by Aquinas: the *nihil*, the "nothing," is not a sort of substrate from which God shapes things (unlike we see with Plato's Demiurge in *Timaeus*). To say that "God creates from nothing" means "God does not create starting from anything."[8] The "nothing" is not a "something" (*pace* William of Sherwood), but it is a "non-something." On the one hand, therefore, the "something" has a priority over what can be called its privation (the "non-something"), but, on the other hand, since everything (the universe) is created (i.e., it comes from "nothing") we can also say that for this aspect the "nothing" has a priority over the "something," as John Wippel observes while commenting on Aquinas:

> Non-existence is prior to existence in a created thing in the sense that if the creature were simply left to itself without being caused by God, it would not exist. The priority involved in this usage is a priority of nature, but not necessarily one of time.[9]

Thus, McCabe is influenced by this manner of setting up the question about the existence of God—that is, starting with an attitude of wonder when realizing that something exists when it could have been nothing. Even though he does not find the exact words in Aquinas' writings, McCabe thinks that the core idea of this question is embedded in his Five Ways;[10] therefore, he maintains the Five Ways are an intellectual strategy to show the epistemological validity of this question, since its validity is not evident at all.[11] McCabe thinks that Thomas gave us as a legacy his conviction that there is always a valid question when its answer can be either true or false.

6. Gerber, *Anatomy of What We Value Most*.

7. Lewis, *Mere Christianity*, 19.

8. Aquinas, *ST*, 1a, qu. 45, art. 1.

9. Wippel, "Thomas Aquinas on the Ultimate Why Question," 737–38.

10. Both these statements (i.e., that the very wording of the question is not present in Aquinas' writings, but that the core idea is) are maintained by John Wippel throughout a detailed analysis of Aquinas' texts; see "Thomas Aquinas on the Ultimate, Why Question," where Wippel demonstrates that we can find the exact wording for the first time in the writings of Siger of Brabant, a few years after Thomas' death (ibid., 731–32).

11. McCabe, *God Matters*, 40.

Therefore, first of all we need to put the question, and then we have to give it a true answer.[12]

According to McCabe, we can arrive at this question through a gradual process: if I ask myself whence this dog, Fido, comes, I can answer that he comes from his parents, those dogs I have sometimes seen, and he does not come from Rover's parents, who are different dogs; moreover, I can say that Fido is a dog because a species of mammals, called dogs and featuring characteristics different from those of the giraffes, exists as a part of the vast community of living beings, and the living beings exist because of certain biochemical causes that, in turn, come from a certain physical state of the world. However, our radical "ultimate question" is not asking why Fido is *this* dog rather than any other individual dog, nor is it asking why Fido is *a dog* instead of a giraffe, nor why he is *a living being* and not a rock; our question is asking, instead, *why Fido exists at all* rather than being nothing.

Now we see more clearly the logic and the outcome of this way of arguing: just as when we ask why he is a dog we can put him in the context of dogs, then, in the very same way, when we ask why Fido exists rather than not existing, we can put Fido *in the context of everything*, of the world or universe. This is what McCabe names the "question about God."[13]

McCabe thinks this question, beyond its "modern" wording, summarizes Thomas' Five Ways, by which he wanted to tell us two things: that the question asking why the universe exists is a valid question, and that we do not know the answer; and this amounts to saying (a) that God exists, but also (b) that God is an incomprehensible mystery.[14] Thus, we formulate the ultimate question while using inadequate tools, that is words whose meaning has to be stretched and extended beyond what we are able to understand.[15]

ANSWERS

According to McCabe, to maintain that this question is valid (that is, it is not absurd, because an answer is logically permitted) is the same as affirming that God exists. In fact, God is whatever can be an answer to this question,[16] or, better said, it should be specified that God *would* be an answer, because, since we do not know what God is, we have not got an answer to this

---

12. McCabe, "A Sermon for Saint Thomas," in *God Matters*, 235–37.

13. McCabe, "Creation," 5.

14. McCabe, "The Involvement of God," in *God Matters*, 40.

15. McCabe, "Creation," 5.

16. McCabe, "Creation," 5.

question.[17] If the argument about God was a clean and simple one that we could solve in terms of familiar concepts, then, whatever we were speaking of, it would not be *God*.[18] A God who was comprehensible in those terms would not be worth worshipping. Therefore, we stretch forward that answer even though we are not able to reach it:

> It is clear that we reach out to, but do not reach, an answer to our ultimate question, how come anything instead of nothing? But we are able to exclude some answers. If God is whatever answers our question, how come everything? Then evidently, he is not to be included amongst everything. God cannot be a thing, an existent among others. It is not possible that God and the universe should add up to make two. . . . If God is the cause of everything, there is nothing that he is alongside.[19]

Therefore, according to McCabe, "God" is the answer to that question, even though "God" is not *part of* "everything," nor is identical with *the sum total of* everything. In fact, in God and in things we cannot find any common characteristic, i.e., they do not share the characteristic of "existence":

> N things + God would be N + 1 beings or existents. But not so. To be existent is not a nature. An existent is not a kind of thing. . . . There is not enough common ground between them for you to add God to everything. God is not part of everything. If God made everything, God is not a thing.[20]

Moreover, just because God is not a part of everything, he cannot be the object of a further question shaped after the "ultimate" question:

> And I should add, I suppose, that it cannot be possible to ask of him, how come God instead of nothing? Not just in the sense that God must be imperishable, but that it must make no sense to consider that God might not be.[21]

CRITICAL RECEPTION

Although McCabe did not invent an original proof of the existence of God, he proposed it in such a lively and interesting way that it has had a lasting

17. McCabe, "The Logic of Mysticism" in *God Still Matters*, 50.

18. McCabe, "Creation," 6.

19. McCabe, "Creation," 6.

20. McCabe, "God and Creation," 389.

21. McCabe, "Creation," 6.

influence among later theologians. Special software and much time would be needed in order to provide the empirical evidence on how much this "ultimate why question" (as it is sometimes called today) has spread throughout Anglophone theological scholarship subsequent to the publishing of *God Matters* in 1987. Although most of this scholarship does not quote or explicitly mention McCabe, it substantially follows him in underlining how the contingency of single contingent beings has to be distinguished from the contingency of everything, and how the answer to the "why question" is conceptually incomprehensible. This is a characteristic of McCabe's legacy.

Despite the elusiveness of this quantitative research, two entire books subsequent to *God Matters* in 1987 have a title shaped after the "why question" (whereas I was not able to find anyone before that year).[22]

However, we find a direct example of McCabe's influence in the writings of Terry Eagleton[23] and in the writings of Brian Davies.[24] We find explicit discussions of McCabe's proof in Andrew Gleeson,[25] Francesca Murphy,[26] and Denys Turner.[27]

EVALUATION

Even though the "why question" is not literally explicit within Aquinas' writings, it is more similar to his Third Way than to his other four. Aquinas' Third Way is, in fact, the only one discussed by McCabe. It is the so-called *"ex contingentia mundi"* proof.[28] It is a proof more peculiar to the modern

22. Rundle, *Why There Is Something Rather Than Nothing* (2004); Wippel (ed.), *The Ultimate Why Question: Why Is There Anything at All Rather Than Nothing Whatsoever?* (2011). It is worth noticing that in both these books McCabe is never mentioned, nor are mentioned those authors who personally had known him and sometimes wrote about him, such as Denys Turner, Brian Davies, David Burrell, Stanley Hauerwas, and Alasdair MacIntyre.

23. Eagleton, "Lunging, Flailing, Mispunching," *The London Review of Books*, 19 October 2006.

24. Davies, "Introduction," in McCabe, *The McCabe Reader*.

25. "An impersonal reading of the question will produce an impersonal answer, and such an answer just is an answer inside the world of un-mysterious causation and the forms of cosmological argument McCabe-Davies spurned" (Gleeson, "God and Evil," 343).

26. Murphy, "The Why-Proof Revisited," in *God Is Not a Story*, 194.

27. Turner, *Faith, Reason and the Existence of God,* 29ff.

28. Denys Turner holds the same opinion: it is not the "thisness" of a contingent thing (e.g., Fido) that drives us to God, but it is the total sum of all the contingent things (which is itself contingent) that drives us to an X which maintains it within existence. See Turner, *Thomas Aquinas, a Portrait,* 140.

age—from Leibniz onwards we see a progressive rise of philosophical interest in it—and it incorporates an existentialistic taste (it is somehow bent to reverse the atheistic assumption present in Sartre's *L'Être et le Néant*). McCabe does not focus on the First Way, which Aquinas maintained to be the clearest ("*manifestior*"), that is, the proof that starts from the "change" we can observe in some things in the world, and directly comes from Aristotle and his scientific concerns.

Although in the twentieth century Henri Bergson, Martin Heidegger and C. S. Lewis had already used this argument, after a few decades McCabe was successful in giving it a new life, and in the years following 1987, in influencing a group of theologians who more and more frequently have focused on this question about God. More in particular, since in the Anglophone world McCabe has a reputation as a scholar of Aquinas, he influenced other Anglophone Thomists and made them undertake a philological research of the wording or at least of the philosophical spirit of this question throughout the vastness of Thomas' works (Wippel and Turner being examples).

Is this proof a persuasive one? As for atheists, Denys Turner observes, they may object that this argument is too weak because

> you [the theist] say that your question "How is it that anything exists?," yields the answer "God"; and you say "God exists," but only to add: "in no knowable form of existence." . . . What sense can there be to the question when on your own account there is so little sense or content to the answer?"[29]

To this objection of the atheist it could be replied that:

> There is something which the theist affirms—asking the question "Why anything?" just is its affirmation—but it is something affirmed about the world, namely that the world is created; . . . saying that the world is created is . . . how to talk about God.[30]

As for the believers, Brian Davies comments:

> Central to McCabe's thinking is the claim that we have philosophical reason to suppose both that God exists and that we do not know what God is. This, of course, might seem an odd conclusion to arrive at. If one does not know what something is, then how can one produce arguments for the thing existing? Must not such arguments rely on a knowledge of what the thing would be if it existed? McCabe, however, takes the view that our

29. Turner, *Faith, Reason*, 235.

30. Turner, *Faith, Reason*, 236.

very reason for believing that God exists effectively *implies* that
we are seriously ignorant concerning God's nature.[31]

Because of its formulation being modern, existentialist, apophatic
(demythologizing), and, last but not least, brief, this proof has permeated
through to many in our society, so that, if I am not mistaken, today it is
perhaps the most common of all the proofs, at least among the theologians.

---

31. Davies, "Introduction" to McCabe, *The McCabe Reader*, loc. 204.

8

The Knowability of God

TRADITION AND MENTORS

Aquinas often underlines that the human mind, whereby we mean both reason and faith, is not able to know the *nature* of God: since *we cannot know what God is in himself*, we should search for what he is *not* more than for what he is.[1] We cannot know him directly, but only by the representations that come from the perfections existing in his creatures. Those representations provide us with the so called "names of God."[2] However, McCabe observes that this philosophical position has been obscured and put in the background by many Thomists, so that the readers of their handbooks are not aware of it.[3]

As for McCabe, he avoided this confusion because he had received this apophatic emphasis from his teacher at Blackfriars studium in Oxford, Victor White,[4] who nowadays is better known because of his correspondence with Carl G. Jung, but whose major theological book is entitled *God the Unknown*.[5]

---

1. Aquinas, *ST*, I, qu. 3, proemium.

2. Aquinas, *ST*, I, qu. 13, art. 2.

3. McCabe, *God Matters*, 40.

4. See an accurate presentation of his intellectual life in Nichols, "Victor White," 53ff.

5. White, *God the Unknown and Other Essays* (1956).

We can trace a sort of "tradition" of apophatic Christian thinkers throughout the centuries: Clement of Alexandria, Pseudo-Dionysious, Thomas Aquinas, Meister Eckart, and Saint John of the Cross. Also, in the second half of the nineteenth century, within Catholic theology, there was the inception of neo-Thomism. This renewed study of Aquinas gradually brought up a rediscovery of that author's apophaticism, that is of a sharp distinction between the human mind and God.

However, this development was not immediate. If we read the 1914 *Twenty-Four Theses* written by the most authoritative Thomist philosophers of that time and approved by the proper Vatican commission, on the one hand, we see there is not any hint at all of the apophatic "via negativa/re-motionis," and, on the other hand, there is an explicit claim that we human beings do have a certain notion of God's essence.[6] A few years later, we get the passages on the knowability of God in two handbooks of neo-Thomistic philosophy, which were quite widespread in the Catholic colleges of the first half of the twentieth century, one written by Cardinal Mercier[7] and the other one by Reginald Garrigou Lagrange;[8] while reading these passages we can realize how much the apophatic power of Aquinas' texts had not yet been clearly perceived by their exegetes.

In particular, in the 1960s in the Anglophone world the Catholic colleges prescribed the handbook written by Richard Phillips,[9] as we are told by an eyewitness, Fergus Kerr.[10] In this book, reading the chapter "The Nature of God," we do not receive a clear-cut teaching: on the one hand, Phillips accurately reports that Aquinas is as far from agnosticism as he is from anthropomorphism and that we cannot reach any "quiddative" knowledge of God; but, on the other hand, he writes that we cannot be entirely ignorant of the nature of God if we want to give some sense to the proofs of his existence. Moreover, Phillips looks for a "formal constituent of the Divine Nature" and, without further verbal cautions, finds it in "subsisting existence."[11]

Indeed, before WWII within neo-Thomism a new stream was emerging, that of Maritain, Sertillanges, and Gilson, which afterwards came to be called "Existential Thomism," became the majority followed only after the

6. *Acta Apostolicae Sedis*, VI (1914), 383–86; VII (1916), 157–58.

7. Mercier, "The Nature of God—The Metaphysical Essence of God," 62.

8. Garrigou-Lagrange, *God, His Existence and Nature*, vol. 1, 228; vol. 2, 3.

9. Phillips, *Modern Thomistic Philosophy*, vol. 2, metaphysics.

10. Kerr, *After Aquinas*, 20.

11. Phillips, *Modern Thomistic*, 303–7.

1960s and showed more awareness of human reason's limits. Étienne Gilson underlined the apophatic spirit of Aquinas' philosophical theology:

> [We know only what God is *not:*] the only way of circumscribing his nature is therefore to remove successively from our notion of him all the modes of existing which cannot be his. . . . [T]o say what God is is *omnino ignotum* [everything unknown] . . . is to affirm that all knowledge, perfect or imperfect, of the essence of God is radically inaccessible here below.[12]

Gilson criticized Cajetan (whom he contrasted with John of Saint Thomas), often argued with Garrigou-Lagrange, and esteemed Antonin D. Sertillanges,[13] who for his part had written even more radically: "we do not know in any way, by any means, to any degree what God is. . . . [A]ll that can be said about God is false."[14]

We know that Victor White, Thomist mentor of McCabe, "was especially indebted to Pére Antonin-Dalmace Sertillanges' *Sant Thomas d'Aquin et son Oeuvre*,"[15] and McCabe, for his part, used to say he did not want to be called "Thomist" but the Thomist he quotes most (and gratefully) is Gilson.

Therefore, it is not a generic reading of Aquinas that influenced McCabe via White, but a particular one, one that underlines the unknowability of God. Although human reason allows us to build a philosophical theology, we need to clearly define its limits:

> [I]t is impossible to know God's essence, nature or "whatness." . . . [S]ome Thomists watered [down] this idea and said that it is possible to know the divine nature in a sort of "non-quidditative" way, . . . but Pere Sertillanges stressed that Aquinas was categorical: we do not know the divine nature at all! . . . [W]e can know that God is, even though we cannot know what his existence means.[16]

However, White maintains that this acknowledgement of reason's limits is not an irrationalistic and fideistic opening; rather, it makes the theologian feel like a travel companion of the scientists. As nowadays sciences discover increasingly new aspects of nature that make it more mysterious

---

12. Gilson, *The Christian Philosophy of St. Thomas Aquinas*, 87, 107.

13. Murphy, *Art and Intellect in the Philosophy of Étienne Gilson*, 61.

14. Sertillanges,*Somme théologique de S. Thomas d'Aquin* (1947), Dieu, II, 382–83; *La Quinzaine*,64 (1905), June 1st, 412. Quoted in Bonansea, "The Human Mind and the Knowledge of God."

15. Nichols, *Dominican Gallery*, 63.

16. White, *God the Unknown*, 16, 18.

and the most familiar ideas about universe (space, time, matter, etc.) are subverted, so the same happens for our knowledge of God.[17] The theologian is also a travel companion of any serious atheist: "Much apparent atheism can be motivated by a genuine, if not fully conscious, appreciation of and reverence for the divine transcendence."[18] This kind of Thomism came down to McCabe via White.

MCCABE ON HOW TO STUDY GOD

As for his "apophatic" philosophical theology, McCabe's main purpose was "not concerned with trying to say what God is but in trying to stop us talking nonsense."[19] Therefore, it is necessary to avoid mistakes, which, in this case, are not "factual" ones but rather "nonsense," that is, affirmations that are logically inconsistent with those ideas we are able to conceive about God starting from our observation of worldly reality. For example, if we hold the idea that God is pure act, then we cannot think of him as changeable; moreover, if he is unchangeable, he cannot suffer. Therefore, if we hold at the same time his unchangeability and his passibility, we speak nonsense. However, such (nonsensical) affirmations are not usually perceived as inconsistent, because our desire for representing God by images is a steady drive within us, also as powerful is our desire for knowledge, so that we can fall into maintaining that we know when in truth we do not know.

However, "Images are not substitutes for hard thinking," McCabe replies. Nevertheless, while taking account of both our most common daily experiences and Aristotle's epistemology, he also adds that we are animals and therefore we are *forced* to use images in order to conceive even the most abstract thought. For instance, when we try to conceive *thoughts* about creation we are forced to represent *images*, say of the potter who moulds the pot, and—in this case—the image is very misleading, because both the potter and the pot are worldly items and therefore interact with each other, whereas God: (1) is not an item of the world, (2) cannot be external to or alongside the world (he is not "alongside" because he is not "other" in the same way in which the things in the world are "other" to one another), (3) we imagine God as a Top Person or Big Boss in the universe, while, instead,

---

17. White, *God the Unknown,* 24.

18. White, *God the Unknown* 47.

19. McCabe, *God Matters,* 316. We could notice that this characteristic McCabe sentence is modeled after one fashionable among the Anglophone analytical philosophers.

he does not belong to the universe and—on principle—does not interfere with it.[20]

Therefore, since our mind has a radically sense-based structure, when we have to speak of God, our priority must be to state what God is *not*. Here, we see, Aquinas, White, and McCabe distance themselves from Pseudo-Denys, who held that both affirmations and denials equally fall short of God.

In characteristic modesty McCabe concludes:

> In the end, I suppose, I am only trying to say two not very original things: that the only God who matters is an unfathomable mystery of love because of which there is being and meaning to anything that is; and that we are united with God in matter, in our flesh and his flesh.[21]

THE FUNDAMENTAL PREMISE: "STARTING FROM THE WORLD"

Let us focus now on how this deductive, apophatic, and Socratic theology deals with the knowledge of God.

According to McCabe (and Aquinas), in the same way as the proof of the existence of God is *a posteriori*,[22] that is, it does not start from an alleged idea of God but from our experience of the world and of some problematic issues (change, contingency, finality) it contains, so also our inquiry on the nature of God starts from the world: "we know how to talk about God, not because of any understanding of God, but because of what we know about his creatures."[23] The validity of our questions about the world, which is based on the validity of our knowledge of the world, gives validity to our questions about God and our knowledge of him:[24] "what governs our use of the word

20. McCabe, *God Matters*, 15, 14, 46, 18, 59.

21. McCabe, "Preface" to *God Matters*. Here, by the word "flesh," McCabe means that we are not united to God by our understanding of him, but, instead, by our bodily and historical lives, sharing his story because he incarnated in history, the only one existing history by which we all are influenced from our birth till our death.

22. My Italian neo-Thomist mentor, Sofia Vanni Rovighi, used to repeat often a sentence from her neo-Thomist mentor, Amato Masnovo: "in philosophy, God is always a predicate and never a subject."

23. McCabe, appendix "Knowledge," in Aquinas, *Summa Theologiae*, vol. 3, *Knowing and Naming God*, 99.

24. McCabe, *God Matters*, 3.

'God' is not an understanding of what God is but the validity of a question about the world."[25]

This is the fundamental premise: in order to know God, or, better said, to be able to talk of God by true statements, we need to first understand worldly beings, as Aquinas (quoted by White) says: "although we do not know what God is, we nevertheless employ his effects of grace and nature . . . using an effect instead of a definition of the cause."[26]

Although the universe relates to God as its cause, it does so *just from the point of view of the creatures as effects* (the world, human beings). What could this mean? It means a difference between creation as a whole and all the other causes within the universe: the latter to some extent depend on the effects as well as vice versa. For example, the Sun (cause) heats the Earth (effect), but the fact that the Earth is heated implies something that happens in the Sun (loss of heat) and also a context of reciprocal closeness in space and time. Whereas these two elements do not apply to the former (i.e., to creation considered as a whole in relation to God, its cause).

Therefore, our ideas of God relate to God just because he is the "cause" of us. They do not say what God is *in himself*. Denys Turner comments on this point, saying Aquinas suggests that we are not allowed to conclude that what God is and what God means is confined to our knowledge of those effects; then he refers to McCabe's metaphor[27] and modifies it: my experience and knowledge of an effect caused by my computer (to be able to copy/paste texts by word processors) do not make me understand what a computer is.[28]

On the worldly/creaturely language we use speaking of God, McCabe references Aquinas and writes:

> Thomas is comparing the very odd difference between knowing how to use a word and knowing what it means when used of God, to the difference between the etymology of a word and its meaning. The etymology is what makes us use it, but this needs not to be the same as what it means; similarly, the perfection to be found in creatures is what makes us apply to God, but this, he thinks, needs not to be the same as what it means in God.[29]

Then, still quoting Aquinas, he provides a concrete example, coming from those deductive consequences we can draw from the simplicity of God: the different attributes which we give a man (he is wise, intoxicated)

---

25. McCabe, *God Matters*, 6.

26. Aquinas, *ST*, I, qu. 1, art. 7, quoted by White in "Prelude," 45.

27. McCabe, "Aquinas on Trinity," in *God Still Matters*, 37–38.

28. Turner, *Faith, Reason*, 173–74.

29. McCabe, "Knowledge," 105.

are heteronymous because, albeit they refer to the same individual, they mean several aspects that are unlike one another,

> but this cannot be the case with God; the words we use of him cannot be heteronymous because they mean different aspects of him, for there are not different aspects to God. What these words mean in God is entirely one, nevertheless they have different meanings. This is because the meanings of the words— what controls our use of them—is their meaning in application to creatures. When we use them of God, we are trying to mean more than this.[30]

Therefore, McCabe holds that the rules that control the meanings of the words (of whatever word!) always come from our earthly sense experiences; both language and thought stem from these experiences in order to describe the world and communicate such descriptions between us human beings who are ourselves part of the world. Thus, in order to speak of something that is not part of the world the starting point is a thorough awareness that we are obliged to use a language that was completely made for mundane purposes, and, therefore, if applied to this new purpose, an inadequate language.

What strategies should we follow to be able to use an inadequate language (the only one we have) and, at the same time, to make statements about God? In the next sections we will analyze three strategies: two (*via negativa* and analogy) for true statements and one (metaphor) for "fictional" statements, that are literary false but fit and are consistent for our imagination.

VIA NEGATIVA

Augustine said "God is best known in not knowing him (*melius scitur nesciendo*) and also "If you think you have grasped him, it is not God you have grasped" (*si comprehendis non est Deus*), because God is "completely other" (*aliud, aliud valde*).[31] Aquinas, after having proved the existence of God, says we cannot know what God is, but rather what he is not.[32]

However, it is not easy to realize that the attributes given to God by Aquinas and the tradition after him (such as simple, perfect, good, highest good, infinite, eternal, one) are actually *negations*: non-composed,

---

30. McCabe, "Knowledge," 105.

31. Respectively: Augustine, *De Ordine* XVI.44; *Sermo 117*; *Confessiones*, 7.10.16.

32. Aquinas, *ST*, I, qu 3 proemium.

non-lacking, non-caused, non-univocal cause, non-finite, non-changeable, and non-plural. If these negations were understood as affirmations, it would seem to us that we know what God is rather than what he is not, just as our minds could "see" the simplicity, the perfection, or the immutability, whereas in reality human minds can only experience what is composed, lacking, and changeable. In reality, we give God these attributes to specify that that "X" factor—which is needed in order to take away some contradictions from our mundane experience (e.g., change)—cannot be conceived as if it itself had those contradictory characteristics (the "X" factor cannot be changeable). For example (as in the First Way), change within one given thing is not contradictory only if there is *another* thing that moves the former, but, since the chain of moved things and movers cannot be infinite, there must be something that moves without change; if this "something" (this "X" factor, that is, God) had change within itself, it could not work as a contradiction-solver.

This negative way of speaking of God is a sort of "getting used" to understanding that this "X" is *other* from the world; we become accustomed through many consecutive analytical removals of the mundane characteristics.

Moreover, God does not explain the events of the world in the way that causes in the world explain events because he is not a cause that works inside the world; there does not exist any fact or phenomenon inside the world that can make us say that it is caused by God, because, if it was so, God would be an item of the world and a part of its chain of causes and effects. On the contrary, if God is the reason everything exists, he is not part of everything:[33]

> "God made everything" or "God makes everything" sounds harmless enough at first, but let us look at some of the implications. In the first place, if God made everything, God cannot be included in everything. God can't be one of the beings that go to make up everything. So, everything-plus-God is not any greater than everything just by itself (or themselves).[34]

What McCabe tells us here is worth recalling, because, while understanding that God is *not* part of the world, we realize also that he is not a *particular* cause in it, and, therefore, he cannot explain any specific effect or phenomenon within the world: all the particular effects/phenomena in the world are explained only by the natural and social sciences, and never by theology.

33. McCabe, *God Matters*, 6.
34. McCabe, "God and Creation," 388.

While following the *via negativa* (*via remotionis*), we avoid making false statements about God, but we do not succeed in knowing what God is: interestingly, McCabe observes that some readers of Aquinas, who write that God never changes, could think that God is static, and, if they read that God cannot suffer, they could think that God is uncaring. However, McCabe objects, this is a mistake similar to that one we could make if we thought that, since God is not a fan of Glasgow Celtic, therefore he is a fan of Glasgow Rangers.[35] Namely, McCabe suggests that God could be neither a Glasgow football team fan nor a football fan at all, but we are not allowed to deduce any one of these conclusions from the mere negative sentence "he is not fan of Glasgow Celtic," because all of them are possible in principle.

KATAPHATICISM

McCabe and other kindred theologians—unlike Kant—maintain that to be "agnostic" (or, better said, "apophatic") about our knowledge of God's nature does not inhibit affirmative theology. In particular, McCabe follows Aquinas,[36] who in turn adopts Pseudo-Dionysius' framework:[37] in order to speak of God there is not only the *via negativa* (*via remotionis*), even though it is primary, but also the *via causalitatis* (based on the proofs of the existence of God) and the *via eminentiae*, which develop by analogical predications, as summarized by McCabe's mentor Victor White:

> [B]esides (not without) the *via remotionis* there are: *via causalitatis*, and *via eminentiae*. . . . [T]he *via eminentiae* is the kataphatic theology. . . . [A]ll affirmations we can do about God are not such as our minds may rest in them, we give God names always taken from creatures, they can be applied to God and applied to him they have a meaning which we cannot grasp, though it has some relationship (analogy, based on causality) to the meaning with which we are familiar from our experiences of creatures.[38]

According to Aquinas, if we absolutize the apophatic way, we destroy it: Moses Maimonides is wrong when he says that the sentence "God is good" just means "God is not evil," because this does not explain why we

35. McCabe, *God Matters*, 41.

36. Aquinas, *ST*, I, qu. 3 proemium; I, q. 3, a. 3; q. 13, a. 12 ; *Contra Gentiles*, lib. I, c. Xiv.

37. Pseudo-Dionysius, *De Divinis Nominibus*, c. i, sect. 6, in G., III, 595; c. i, sect. 41, in G., III, 516, 590.

38. White, *God the Unknown*, 20–21.

give God only some names instead of many possible others; moreover, also those philosophers who think that that sentence means just "God is the cause of the goods" are wrong because, for instance, God is cause of the bodies but is not a body.[39]

Aquinas goes on saying that, after having said what God is not (he is not composed, not lacking, not changeable, not plural), we have to deal with how God is in our human knowledge, and McCabe comments:

> it is highly significant that almost the whole of Question 12, which is about the way we know God, is devoted to a discussion of the beatific vision; such knowledge of God as we have in this life is so exiguous as to be hardly worth discussing.[40]

Generally speaking, McCabe says that to know what God is not is the precondition of saying what God is: our apophaticism is the non-avoidable premise of our kataphaticism. For instance, he argues that at first we need to say that God is not material, and only afterwards we can say that he is intelligent, even though we are not able to understand what his intelligence means.[41] Moreover, he observes that all the attributes predicable of God form a multiplicity in our mind only, but not in his, because in him they identify with one another in the same way as his existence identifies with his essence.[42]

THE NAMES OF GOD: METAPHORS AND ANALOGIES

Gilson, while summarizing Aquinas' thought, says that, in the case of God, any definition is impossible and we can just give him "names," but names are not definitions; to define anything we need a genus under which we define, but this is impossible in the case of God, because, had he a genus, he would have an essence distinguished from his existence; moreover, every difference should not be already included in that genus as such, but, since God is subsistent being itself (*ipse esse subsistens*), then every difference is already included.[43]

Which names are we to use of God? Aquinas maintains that we humans beings draw our knowledge from composed bodily things, so that

39. Aquinas, *ST*, 1, qu. 13, art. 2.

40. McCabe, "Knowledge," 104.

41. McCabe, *God Still Matters*, 25–26.

42. McCabe, *God Still Matters*, 25–26.

43. Gilson, *The Christian Philosophy*, 96.

when we speak of God we can give him both the name "Good" to mean his subsistence (since, for us, only composed things are subsistent) and the name "Goodness" to mean his simplicity, because we speak of simple beings by means of abstract words.[44] In both cases, since the names we use derive from creatures, they do not express God's essence, unlike when we use, for example, the word "man," which does express the very nature of human beings. These names of God express his subsistence and perfections, but do not express his essence (*modus essendi*).[45] They are "proper" and not metaphorical with regard to what they mean, but they are not proper regarding the manner whereby they mean it:

> . . . the names applied to God—viz. the perfections which they signify, such as goodness, life and the like, and their mode of signification. As regards what is signified by these names, they belong properly to God, and more properly than they belong to creatures, and are applied primarily to Him. But as regards their mode of signification, they do not properly and strictly apply to God; for their mode of signification applies to creatures.[46]

McCabe underlines the distinction between metaphorical and proper (even though analogical) names: a metaphor is compatible with its negation ("God is a rock" is compatible with "God is not a rock"), whereas analogy is not ("God is good" is not compatible with "God is not good," though you can say: "God is not good *in the same way* (*modus significandi*) we are").[47]

Since we cannot help speaking of God by "borrowed" names, we should look at him as if he were always dressed "by second-hand clothes" and be aware that those clothes do not reveal what or who he is. To avoid mistakes, according to McCabe, to name the Christian God it would be better to use a metaphorical name such as "father," because in this word it is clear both that the thing we mean (*res significata*) is not the proper one, and we hold a lively and understandable meaning (*modus significandi*), which does not happen with names as "good" and "wise."[48]

---

44. Aquinas, *ST*, I, qu. 3, art. 2.

45. Aquinas, *ST*, I, qu. 13, art. 1. "The evidence we may have for saying that the swiftly moving shadow in the gloom was a cat may have been the miaow: but 'that was a cat' does not mean: 'that was a miaow causer,' but rather: 'that was a feline quadruped.' So with the names of God. God's causality legitimizes our naming her by the names of her effects. But what we name is a being in whom is possessed in transcendent abundance all the perfections of the beings caused." Turner, *The Darkness of God*, 24.

46. Aquinas, *ST*, I, qu. 13, art. 3.

47. McCabe, "Analogy," appendix 4 in Aquinas, *Summa Theologiae*, 106.

48. McCabe, *God Still Matters*, 3.

Analogical names have neither a literal meaning nor a metaphorical one, so we have to distinguish them carefully from these two other kinds of attributes.

What is an analogy? Let us start by underlining that analogies speak the truth differently from metaphors. Metaphors are not literally true but are useful—McCabe argues—because we are bodily and imaginative beings.[49] In fact, they are mostly used in fictional literature, which appeals to us because of its imaginative strength:

> When you say "God is a warrior" and "Goliath is a warrior," the word warrior is being used in exactly the same sense. What makes "God is a warrior" metaphorical is not a variation in either the meaning or the *modus significandi* (way of meaning) of "warrior" but the whole role of the sentence in which it occurs. . . . The difference between "God is a warrior" and "Goliath is a warrior" is more like the difference between fiction and fact than it is like the difference between, say "This curry is very good" and "The weather is very good," a case of analogy.[50]

What is an analogy, then? It is a ratio that links four terms into a comparison: the goodness of God relates to God in the same way that human goodness relates to humans.

A theologically important case of analogy is creation: to create means "to make," but in the case of *creatio ex nihilo* this is making in a way we do not understand at all. Although we do not understand what being "the maker of the world" means, nonetheless, to say that of God is not a falsity, whereas it is a literal falsity to say that God is a "mighty fortress" or a "cup of tea." Often, we do not know how the predicates we give to God are compatible with one another, however, this is not identical with saying that they are "incompatible." In this case, we just do not know how "maker of the world," "good," "eternal," "simple," and "perfect" are compatible with one another, whereas we know that "mighty fortress" and "warrior" are literally incompatible.[51]

While metaphors *can* be incompatible ("this small voice," "the shaking cedars"), when we use analogy we *cannot* say both "God made the world" and "God did not make the world."[52] The verb "to make" and the verb "to create" point to the same reality (*res significata*), but we use the latter to mean a new *modus significandi*, a new way of meaning "to make." To achieve

49. McCabe, *God Still Matters*, 27–281.

50. McCabe, "God and Creation," 387.

51. McCabe, "Aquinas on the Trinity," in *God Still Matters*, 38–39.

52. "McCabe, Aquinas on the Trinity," in *God Still Matters*, 38–39.

this, we must undertake a long intellectual process whereby we add many qualifications to the word "make," and all of them point in the same direction. It is the process itself that matters, it points to something we cannot predict, and, at its ending, there is no (provisionally) final product that might be separated from it, no clear concept of what the verb "to create" means.[53]

McCabe is not interested in the mammoth Thomist debate on analogy, a discussion that is centuries old and has piled up several complex and different interpretations of that concept from many commentators: (analogy of) extrinsic and intrinsic attribution, proportion, extrinsic and intrinsic proportionality, inequality, and such like. Especially in the twentieth century, after Jesuit Eric Pzywara's book *Analogia entis* was published in 1932, among both Catholic and Protestant theologians the scholarly literature on this topic quickly grew swollen.[54] Therefore, McCabe, while explicitly treating Thomas' idea of analogy, quite quickly stops dealing with this debate and its history.

> [F]or Thomas analogy is not a way of getting to know about God, nor is it a theory of the structure of the universe, it is a comment on our use of certain words. . . . [H]is real concern is to maintain that we can use words to mean more than they mean to us—that we can use words "to try to mean" what God is like, that we can reach out to God with our words even though they do not circumscribe what he is.[55]

If we analyze this passage two points can be noticed. One is that McCabe focuses on a transformative use of language: we are obliged to use pre-existent words to signify new meanings, not in order to shade the initial meaning into a faint genericity, but to intensify it. According to McCabe, Aquinas thinks that there is something that

> we can only call goodness in God—goodness is the best word available for signifying this although it does so imperfectly. . . . [H]e attaches great importance to the idea that such words apply primarily to God. The point of this seems to be that when we "try to mean" God's goodness by using the word "good" of him,

---

53. McCabe, "God and Creation," 388.

54. For a detailed analysis of the different meanings of analogy throughout the centuries (and also on how Karl Barth both criticized and used this concept), see Mondin, *Il problema del linguaggio teologico dalle origini ad oggi,* 171–240, 324–30.

55. McCabe, "Analogy," appendix 4 in Aquinas, *Summa Theologiae,* 106.

you are not straying outside its normal meaning but trying to enter more deeply into it.[56]

The second point is that McCabe refuses any interpretation of analogy that entails a general "structure of the universe," that is what was indeed proposed by Przywara.

THE POWER AND LIMITS OF REASON AND FAITH

Many people, both scholars and non-scholars, maintain that although natural reason cannot provide us with a knowledge of God, at least Christian faith can. Here we should question this claim while following what Aquinas, White, and McCabe say about it.

As McCabe's mentor Victor White recalled, there are two theologies: the revealed one, which is theology in the proper and strict sense of the word, and philosophical theology, also called natural theology. The validity of philosophical theology is held mainly by Catholics; for instance, Joseph Ratzinger maintains that the God of Aristotle is the same God of Jesus; although the latter is more profound and pure and elevates and purifies the former, nonetheless does not contradict it: "grace does not destroy nature but perfects it" (*gratia non destruit, sed elevat et perficit naturam*).[57]

McCabe actually follows this line: the "God of philosophers" of Augustine and Aquinas is the same as the God of Abraham, Isaac, and Jacob, the Creator God as he is meant, at least after Isaiah.[58] The philosophical comprehension of God is a necessary precondition for Christology: "to put it at its simplest, we cannot ask the question: 'In what sense is Jesus to be called Son of God?' without some prior use for the word 'God.' And, of course, the New Testament did have such a prior use."[59]

Turner comments that, according to Aquinas, the power of reason is revealed at its utmost when it acknowledges its own limits because by means of reason we understand that God is unknowable and demonstrates the existence of a mystery.[60]

---

56. McCabe, "Analogy," appendix 4 in Aquinas, *Summa Theologiae*, 106.

57. Ratzinger, *Il Dio della fede e il Dio dei filosofi*, Kindle edition, loc. 105.

58. McCabe, *God Matters*, 42–43.

59. McCabe, *God Matters*, 42; Davies comments saying that prior to speaking of Jesus we must speak of creation ("Herbert McCabe," 15).

60. Turner, *Faith, Reason*, 48, 79.

Anyhow, human reason, when aware of its limits, matches revealed religion—which it complements but never vies with—and does not become a sort of deism or rationalism:

> There used to be an idea (invented, I think, by Pascal) that the God of philosophers was a different kind of being from the God of Abraham, Isaac and Jacob. Now of course the God of the philosophers that Pascal had in mind may very well be different from the God of Abraham, Isaac and Jacob, but the God of my philosophy (and here I am at one with St. Thomas) is not well known enough to be different from Yahweh of the Old Testament. Philosophy tells us almost nothing about God, certainly not enough to set up a rival religion.[61]

However, can religious faith itself provide us with a better knowledge of God than that one provided by human reason and its philosophical theology? McCabe's answer is: yes and no. Yes, as for the true statements we can say about God; no, as for our understanding of them and, thus, our understanding of what God is. Yes, because our experience of redemption endowed on us by Jesus makes us say, e.g., more quickly, more easily, and more firmly the true proposition "God is good." No, because we do not understand the *modus essendi* of God's goodness. For a Christian a main confusion comes from the two natures—divine and human—of Jesus Christ: when we think to know what God is in himself because we know what (the fundamental qualities of) Jesus Christ is, we are wrong, since what we know and understand is just his human nature and not his divine one, as we will see below.

Aquinas holds that faith as well—and not just reason—is unable to give us a knowledge of God's nature:

> Although by the revelation of grace in this life we cannot know of God "what He is," and thus are united to Him as to one unknown; still we know Him more fully according as many and more excellent of His effects are demonstrated to us.[62]

In a persuasive way Victor White comments:

> Thomas thinks that even by revelation and faith we cannot know the essence of God, . . . we just know more and better effects (*plures and excellentiores effectus*), but never in this life is there an exception to the rule that we do not know what God is.[63]

61. McCabe, *The New Creation*, 2.

62. Aquinas, *ST*, I, qu. 12, art. 13, ad 1.

63. White, *God the Unknown*, 23. Moreover, "we attribute to Him some things

As we have already seen, from the effects we can argue that "something" similar exists in the cause, albeit in a super-eminent way, but, because of the very *modus essendi* of this "something," we have no concept of it, and so we are unable to know what God is. However, from "more numerous and better" effects (that is phenomena and events) such as Jesus' life, resurrection, redemption, church, life within grace, we can more easily attribute to God that set of perfections (simplicity, goodness, infinity, omnipotence) at which by philosophical means alone we were already able to arrive, even though with more difficulty and less clarity.

McCabe reminds Christians that from the Council of Chalcedon onwards they have held that God takes part in creation not just because he is the Creator, but also because in the incarnation he is mysteriously united to a created nature.[64] Because of that we assume that every scientific research on Jesus' life we undertake by our naturally bestowed reason will make us achieve an always greater knowledge of his human nature only. Moreover, what we could achieve by our supernaturally bestowed faith is our firm statement as believers that in Jesus there is present a divine nature alongside his human one.[65] However, as believers, we must acknowledge that that divine nature is thoroughly and utterly unknown to us:

> God is the ultimate mystery, that we are peering into the dark. In Christ, Aquinas says, we are joined to God as to the utterly unknown. . . . The revelation of God in Jesus in no way, for Aquinas, changes the situation. By the revelation of grace, he says, we are joined to God as an unknown, *ei quasi ignoto coniugamur.*[66]

What does this "joined to God" mean if it rules out knowledge?

> The revelation lies in responding in faith to the offer of love. This is why the revelation in Jesus, and in the scriptures that speak of him, does not remove any of our ignorance about God. We do not get to know more about him, we encounter him, we are in communication with him. . . . So far as God is concerned what we are offered in the Church and its scriptures is not a further information but a share in his life.[67]

---

known by divine revelation, to which natural reason cannot reach, as, for instance, that God is Three and One" (ibidem).

64. McCabe, *God Matters*, 48.

65. McCabe, *God Matters*, 71.

66. McCabe, *God Matters*, 195, 41.

67. McCabe, *God Matters*, 19.

Possibly and eventually, McCabe argues, we will improve and refine our knowledge, but this increased knowledge will be just of ourselves; this knowledge is really nothing else other than ethics, that is the due meditation on that "natural law," which is not a privileged commitment of Christians but was also highly considered by ancient Jews and Greco-Roman pagans as well. This is solely as regards humankind. As for God, instead,

> our faith seems not like an increase of knowledge, but, if any-thing, an increase of ignorance. We became more acutely aware of our inadequacy before the mystery as we are brought closer to it.[68]

What does White's and McCabe's interpretation of Aquinas' texts suggest to us, especially if we compare it with that of Garrigou-Lagrange?[69] Denys Turner clearly maintains that in Aquinas there is not any cataphaticism of faith as opposed to an apophaticism of reason, whereas many theologians today actually propose this very dualistic approach and, thus, cannot grasp a truth both paradoxical and profound: no one, be he a believer or not, is able to know God's nature.[70] McCabe says something more: the believer is bestowed with a stronger consciousness of the mystery of God than the non-believer is, and, then, it is more unlikely for him to identify the Cause of All in some phenomenon of the universe, be it the human spirit (Hegel), the World's Will (Schopenhauer), or the Big Bang.

CONCLUSIONS

An important contemporary issue to which we should apply McCabe's theological guidelines is the so-called Intelligent Design theory. In it the attribute "intelligent" is applied to God in its literal human meaning, and, doing so, the followers of that theory seek to dismiss Darwin, at least as an explanation for the origins of life. However, an apophatic-minded theologian can show that all the best Christian theological tradition would have considered such a view to be a nonsense; thus, the theologian can endorse the most radical scientific palaeontology, which claims that life on this planet is radically contingent and disconnected from any human predictive scheme.[71]

68. McCabe, *God Matters*, 20.

69. Thus: "to arrive at a knowledge of God, according to what properly constitutes the Deity, there must be a supernatural revelation" ("What Formally Constitutes the Divine Nature," in Garrigou Lagrange, *God, Its Existence and Nature*, vol. 2, 9).

70. Turner, *Faith, Reason*, 48, 51, 76.

71. Distinguished Darwinian scholar Stephen Jay Gould (who was not a believer)

Also, what McCabe says on faith could be helpful for at least two reasons. When he says that faith does not diminish our ignorance of God's nature, he refuses the fideist errors of those people who despise human reason (and therefore human dialogue) while pretending—by faith alone—to be able to know what God thinks, wants, and plans. Secondly, when he says that faith increases the awareness of our ignorance about God, McCabe stands for a new dignity of believers in their relationships with non-believers, because the former can introduce themselves to the latter as people who do not claim any privileged access to an otherwise inaccessible knowledge.

---

in many of his works demonstrated the radical contingency and unpredictability of life. On his philosophy of natural history see his book *A Wonderful Life,* and its companion *Full House.*

9

God as a Cause and Creator

THEOLOGICAL EBB AND FLOW

The ancient era Niceno-Constantinopolitan Creed (one of whose concerns was Gnosticism)[1] and the Middle Ages Council of Lateran IV (one of whose concerns was Chatarism) stated the doctrine of creation in order to confute pessimistic dualism; in nineteenth century Vatican Council I stated this doctrine to confute two modern versions of pantheism, Hegel's idealism and Marx's materialism. This Christian doctrine of creation, when set up against dualism, maintains that the world is *good* because it originates from the only One God. The same doctrine, when set up against pantheism, maintains that God infinitely transcends the world: therefore, human beings' dignity is safeguarded both from dualist pessimism and from illusory optimism; against dualism it rejects any devaluation of the material world, against pantheism it maintains that the world, albeit good, is not an *absolute* good, because it is "created" by God. The world is neither God's expansion (pantheism) nor his alienation (dualism).[2]

In the twentieth century from the 1950s till the 1980s, because of Karl Barth's influence among Protestants and the "nouvelle théologie" of

1. See Clayton, "Creatio ex Nihilo and Intensifying the Vulnerability of God," 18.

2. de La Pena, *Teologia della creazione*, 82–83, 108–9, 136–37. I said "expansion" thinking of Hegel and his system, where the world of "nature" and "spirit" are developments of the immanent original "idea"; I said "alienation" thinking of Manichaean God of Evil who creates the material world.

Chenu, Congar, De Lubac, and others among Catholics, this doctrine was so much moved to the background that in 1986 Joseph Ratzinger denounced this neglect, saying that creation had become a topic absent from preaching and theology.[3] In fact, in those decades Christian thinkers were mostly influenced by philosophical positivism: to them to build a biblical theology meant to show how much the Christian message was minutely historical and not dependent on the "abstractions" of "Greek" metaphysics that was followed by medieval thinkers. According to them, the Old Testament could show the history of salvation by which God led the people of Israel, while the New Testament showed the path of redemption followed by Jesus' disciple. Therefore, theologians could respond to atheistic Marxist philosophers that Christianity also was focused on the collective history of humankind and to atheistic existentialist philosophers that Christianity also was interested in the life history of the individual persons.

However, while those atheistic philosophies, Marxism and existentialism, have declined throughout the subsequent decades, a new philosophical attitude, more scientistic, has become relevant, sometimes coming from atheistic scientists, such as Stephen Hawking and Richard Dawkins. Today atheistic thinkers focus on natural sciences to find arguments that could deny the existence of God, and their attitude is perhaps a relevant cause of the rise of a new theological trend recovering the theme of creation. Since the late 1990s Christian theologians have turned back to metaphysical themes of ancient and medieval tradition. For instance, Rowan Williams argues that there is a recent increase in interest for creation because of (1) cosmological theories from astronomy, (2) growing awareness of environmental issues, leading us to seek unity between humanity and the world, and (3) increasing interest in the human body, which was not dealt with by the theology of redemption, whereas creation before the fall speaks of nature and bodily life.[4]

Present-day theologians are coping with these new challenges by focusing on metaphysics. Paul Haffner, while saying that sciences in the twentieth century showed that the improvement of knowledge brought an improvement in awareness of the complexity and mystery of nature, refers back to classical metaphysics and highlights what creation is not: procession inside an eternal nature, emanation, transformation (change).[5] Spanish scholar Miguel Pérez de Laborda establishes his treatise on creation in a metaphysical

---

3. Ratzinger, *In the Beginning*, ix.

4. "On Being Creatures," in Williams, *On Christian Theology*, 3.

5. Hoffner, *Mystery of Creation*, 6, 2.

way as well.[6] In fact, there is a widespread challenge to be faced, as Marit A. Trelstad notes, exemplified by, for example, Lawrence Krauss' *A Universe from Nothing*. That book is a deliberate attack on the theological theory of the *creatio ex nihilo* because, according to Krauss, the quantum field should demonstrate that the universe does not need God and, also, that the "nothing" does not exist.[7]

McCabe, on the one hand, treated the creation theme in accordance with the post-war theology that I have mentioned above, that is, as an auxiliary concept derived from the major concept of Christ's redemption; in his book *The New Creation*, written during the years of Vatican Council I, he deals with sacraments and says:

> First of all, God revealed his secret plan in the way he guided their [Hebrews'] history. The Word of God is first of all heard in the creation and government of the Hebrews; it is only later that is extended to the world as a whole. . . . [I]n the Church the new creation is already realised, though in a hidden way; . . . the church is the new creation. She is not just a group of people within the world, she is a new world.[8]

Later, in a lecture given in Cape Town, "God and Creation," he argued:

> [I] myself do not see how God could be said to give meaning to the world, or to be the final meaning or purpose of the world, unless God were the one who made it in some sense. But it is not unimaginable that some people might have a word meaning "what it's all about," or "the point of everything," or "what makes the world not meaningless," and yet never have reflected on the world as created or made. And I think we might very reasonably say they were nonetheless talking about God.[9]

In this passage McCabe, on the one hand, acknowledges the reasons of biblical theology and of those secular philosophies that are concerned with "what makes the world not meaningless," and, on the other hand, recommends a further reflection on the "world as created and made." Moreover, elsewhere, he argues that we may be saved by faith alone, but we do not live by faith alone, we live also by communication, society, language, intelligence, and affection; it is a specially Catholic feature "to defend the rights of the nature in which we were created" and reject any view that exalts grace at

---

6. Pérez de Laborda, *La ricerca di Dio*.

7. Trelstad, "The Fecundity of Nothing," 47.

8. McCabe, *The New Creation*, 8, xii, 43.

9. McCabe, "God and Creation," 387.

the expense of nature.[10] In fact, such a spiritualistic "theology of grace" is not engaged with cosmology and, thus, is both uninterested in and incapable of refuting what atheist physicists say;[11] that theology forgets that

> some philosophers have argued that there is no need for a God because it is quite conceivable that the world should have emerged from nothing. Why shouldn't it?[12] The fundamental error is not the crude one of supposing that things are spun out of a material called "nothingness," but of supposing that creation is the act of supplying the "vacant inter-stellar spaces" with inhabitants. . . . A historically interesting variant of this view is that of Newton who thought of absolute space and time as a "sensorium of God."[13]

If these "some philosophers" could achieve a widespread consensus among the general public, any faith relying on grace alone eventually would be held to be just a spiritualistic and Manichaean flight from the world.

To confute these philosophers, according to McCabe, it is worth going back to the concepts of cause and being in their various meanings, both scientific and metaphysical, as at first Aristotle and later Aquinas did.

Since several of McCabe's writings on creation go back to the 1980s, including the first chapters of his most influential book *God Matters* (1987), we can ponder the hypothesis of whether he was a sort of precursor of that theological ebb and flow beginning in the 1990s that I have outlined above.

IS CREATION A CONCEPT FROM REASON OR FROM FAITH?

Before approaching McCabe's metaphysical treatise on creation, I briefly report some voices from a particular theological debate: is human reason alone, without any support by faith in Christian revelation, able to deal with the creation theme, or can this theme be dealt with only by faith?

Aquinas, commenting on Peter Lombard's *Sentences*, maintains that creation can be proved by reason,[14] and in *Summa Theologiae* says that it is

---

10. McCabe, "God," in *God Still Matters*, 9.

11. As opposed to the other one that follows the maxim *gratia perficit naturam non destruit*.

12. McCabe, "Causes and God," In *Faith within Reason*, 65.

13. "The Creator and Evil," in his licence in sacred theology dissertation McCabe, *God and Evil*, 93.

14. Aquinas, *S Sent* d., q. 1, art. 2.

"necessary" to state that everything originates from God, as, in his opinion, Plato and Aristotle had maintained. However, he structures *Summa*'s first part dealing with creation only *after* having treated a typical topic of revealed theology, that is the Trinity.

Vatican Council I, instead, firstly deals with creation and only afterwards with revelation and faith, even though, as Denys Turner observes, the Council says nothing explicitly about the possibility of proving even the existence of God apart from any Christian faith and theology.[15]

Among more recent theologians and philosophers, Sofia Vanni Rovighi argues, after Aquinas, that creation is demonstrable because God is the *ipsum esse subsistens* (the subsistent act of "to be" itself) and therefore all the rest has just a participated existence.[16] On the contrary, Ruiz de la Pena thinks that creation should be considered mainly as a mystery of faith.[17] Pérez de Laborda holds an intermediate opinion, that is, that the idea of creation as conservation of the universe and non-dependent from a beginning in time is only subsequent to Jewish-Christian revelation, and was conceived by Christian philosophy but not by Greek philosophy; to prove this, he quotes some of Aquinas' texts (*ST* I, 44, 2; *SCG* II, 37) where Thomas says that creation is the third and last step in the history of philosophy.[18] Janet Martin Soskice says something similar:

> the doctrine of creation ex nihilo is a biblically inspired piece of metaphysics—not a teaching of Hellenistic philosophy pure and simple, but something that arises from what Greek-speaking Jews found in their scriptures.[19]

Pérez de Laborda and Soskice, thus, suggest that human reason is not timeless, it is "historical": the creation theme is indeed philosophical, that is, it is reachable by reason without faith, but our concrete capacity of reasoning is the result of a precise historical development, that is, the outbreak of the three monotheistic religions, which spread new points of view and new inspirations throughout society and mentality in some peoples, also affecting, as a consequence, the minds of individual thinkers.

As for McCabe, on the one hand, he says that in the New Testament we move from seeing God first of all as Creator to seeing him first of all

---

15. Turner, *Faith, Reason,* 37.

16. Vanni Rovighi, *Elementi di Filosofia,* vol. II, 174.

17. de la Pena, *Teologia,* 122–23.

18. Pérez de Laborda, *La ricerca di Dio.*

19. Soskice, "Creation and the Glory of Creatures," 10.

engaged in loving Christ.[20] On the other hand, in order to understand who Christ is, we previously need an idea of "God," and, without the Jewish faith and its question about creation, the New Testament itself is not intelligible.[21] However, it is not just a matter of faith coming from the Hebrews; in fact, McCabe also adds that God made me and the whole world and for this very reason we know that God exists. Therefore, "[t]his kind of reflection is a matter of philosophy, and like any other interesting philosophical question, it a matter of great controversy."[22]

We have already seen one aspect of this controversy while dealing with God's existence and knowability: to state that God's existence is demonstrable by reason does not imply that human reason is able to conceive a concept of God, that is to know what God is. In a similar way, McCabe observes on the concept of creation:

> We do not understand what creation means. We merely point towards it in the process of qualifying to death the notion of God-making-the-world. For the world to be created is for it to exist instead of nothing. And we can have no concept of nothing. We can have no concept of creation (any more than of God), but this will not, I trust, prevent us from talking about them.[23]

Among the things that we can talk about, one is—as we shall see in more detail later on—that God as Creator does not leave any trace of his creative work within creation.

I conclude by observing that, as for the debate I outlined here about the sources of the idea of creation, McCabe takes sides in favor of human reason, but he does not speak of the "historical nature" of it as far it is influenced by and embedded in the centuries-long diffusion of monotheistic religions that I hinted at above. However, McCabe maintains that philosophy, just as with the nature of God theme, can state that creation happened and happens, but it cannot understand what it is. On what the Creator God is, we are ignorant, and neither reason nor faith can remove this ignorance of ours.[24]

---

20. McCabe, "God," in *God Still Matters*, 8.

21. McCabe, "The Involvement of God," in *God Matters*, 42.

22. McCabe, *The New Creation*, 2.

23. McCabe, "God and Creation," 394.

24. McCabe,"Freedom," in *God Matters*, 19. We will see later on in this chapter what we could know about ourselves if we held the universe is created.

CAUSES

Following Aristotle and Aquinas, McCabe maintains that causality is not about events but about things, each of which has a form and a subject: "A inserts F into B," where A is the efficient cause, F the formal cause, and B the material cause (the subject). What F is depends on the nature of A, what the effects looks like depends also on the nature of B: a sharp rise of temperature shows itself quite differently in petrol and in ice. According to Aquinas, the relationship between cause and effect is not just "empirical" (in the Humean meaning of a collection of observations of past events): in fact, we think that there is some *necessary* connection between them, and we would be amazed if the effect did not appear. According to this view, things have certain natures and so have certain activities that are natural to them; puzzles arise when a thing behaves unlike how we expected it would, and you can solve the puzzle only by pointing to previously un-noticed elements.[25]

After Aristotle, McCabe argues "When an event surprises us we ask about its cause": as when we see a bishop rising into air and floating, we seek the cause of this quite unusual phenomenon. Expectations about the behavior of things derive from a knowledge of their "nature." Searching for causes and nature are in some way opposed: when something is natural, we do not think that seeking a cause is necessary. We ask about causes when the things seem to behave unnaturally. When you are surprised, you look for a cause and then realize that, besides A and B, you have also C, D, and E and you understand that the grouping ABCDE will naturally produce the thing that surprised you at first. This is what finding a cause means: seeing that such-and-such a thing is, after all, quite natural.[26]

Moreover, McCabe observes that what makes us seek a cause is not only our desire for an explanation, but that there are some other reasons for seeking a cause, notably the desire to control the events. A great many of the uses of "cause" in our language are based on this technological sense: whatever we have to do to bring about an effect. It is in this sense we say that the pressing of a switch causes the light to go on or that a cracked rivet caused the aircraft to crash. However, these are not explanatory causes because it is only in an unmentioned context of other things that they can be called explanations; they are called causes because they are picked out as the most easily controlled factor in the situation.[27]

---

25. McCabe, "Causes," appendix 2 in Aquinas' *ST*, vol. 3, 106.

26. McCabe, "Causes and God," in *Faith within Reason*, 48, 49, 51.

27. McCabe, "Causes and God," in *Faith within Reason*, 56.

A way to describe that particular cause which is the act of creation is by using the concept of analogy. McCabe says that a natural cause within the world always involves some kind of *change* (from one state to another) whereas in the creation of the world there is no change, for there is no state prior to creation. In the act of creation, we can speak only of the difference between existence and non-existence, if *esse* (essence) were a sort of form. We can say of the Creator *some* things that are said about causes within creation (e.g., that the cause is the reason for the effect), but we must never forget the infinite difference between divine causation and created causes; the latter cause change, the former does not. We must admit that we do not have a purified concept of cause to be applied to God as Creator and we have simply the word with an analogical meaning.[28] McCabe says that when we use the word "creation" we have in mind the concept of cause, which is contextually dependent, and in fact, according to Aristotle, can be an action, an essence, a matter, or a purpose. Then it could be said that "creation" is "a word we use when we wish to apply an essentially contextually dependent word without any context."[29]

Therefore, McCabe prepares his treatment of creation by analyzing the concept of cause. This is a meaningful choice of his, because he could have approached creation by underlining other concepts: "power," "love/gift," "exertion of goodness," "renewal," "freedom," "providence," "fatherhood," and others. I think the main reason for this choice is the line followed by Aquinas, who, in fact, as soon as he approaches the problem of creation, states that creation is an "efficient cause" as well as "exemplar" and "final,"[30] and in this way he refers to the ancient pagan tradition of Plato and Aristotle. Aquinas and McCabe after him do this to prepare a treatment of creation which could be universalistic, that is acceptable (at least in part)[31] to non-Christians as well as to Christians.

Moreover, while underlining that the proper concept of cause is not the "modern" one (which sees causes in terms of the law of probability) but is related to the "nature of things," as ancient and medieval thinkers held, McCabe distinguishes the search for causes kindled by wonder and aimed at explanations from the search for causes as a means for controlling the events; doing so, he suggests that a mind focused on controlling things

28. McCabe, *God and Evil*, 104.

29. McCabe, *God and Evil*, 101.

30. Aquinas, ST, I, qu. 44, art. 1, 3, 4. Moreover, in art. 2, while saying that God creates matter, Thomas indirectly also refers to the fourth Aristotelian cause, "material cause."

31. I say "in part," because in *ST*, I, qu. 45, art. 6 Thomas says that creation is accomplished by the Trinity.

might misunderstand that particular cause that is creation, because in this case any control of the events is impossible.

So, what can we say about creation as an "analogical" cause which produces effects "inadequate" to itself?

TRADITION

On the one hand, in ancient Greece the four main philosophical schools (Platonic, Aristotelian, Epicurean, Stoic) never dealt with creation out of nothing, and, on the other hand, the three monotheistic religions do speak of it, more or less explicitly. However, the philosophical thought that accompanied these religions formalized its arguments only in the Middle Ages. Aquinas himself, in five different works,[32] attributes this idea to "some other philosophers." R. E. Houser wrote a very learned essay that presents many different opinions of twentieth-century scholars about these "aliqui philosophi" (among whom Plato, Aristotle and Plotinus are mentioned), and eventually singles out Avicenna as being the proper person.

The concept of creation out of nothing had contend with the centuries-old Neoplatonic tradition and its "chain of being"—which depicted the universe as a hierarchical structure where the One "emanates" from itself a first entity, which in turn emanates a further entity, and so forth, along a direction that proceeds from "spiritual" beings to "material" beings. Denys Turner showed clearly how these two doctrines clashed with each other in the important Neoplatonic Christian philosopher Pseudo-Dionysius.[33]

McCabe follows Gilson and explicitly says that *creatio ex nihilo* was never conceived by ancient Greek philosophers. But he never makes any references to the Neoplatonic hierarchical "chain of being," thus holding an even more radical position than Aquinas himself, who had already partly abandoned the idea of hierarchy in creation.[34] McCabe, thus, because of his literary and philosophical culture, knew well that the ancient Greeks strongly maintained the idea that human beings are "contingent" (they used to be called "the mortals"), and also they thought there were some things

---

32. One of them is *ST*, I, qu. 44, art. 2. See the summary of this passage made by Houser, "Avicenna, *Aliqui* and the Thomistic Doctrine of Creation," 1.

33. Turner, "Cataphatic and the Apophatic in Denys the Areopagite," in *The Darkness of God*, 31.

34. "Aquinas put farther in the background the idea of the great chain of beings because it does not fit relating God to creation. . . . [T]he chain of beings puts other beings as creators and so it does non sharply distinguish God from the world, moreover emanation is anthropomorphic because it replicates the ascent of human mind in knowing." Burrell, *Knowing the Unknowable*, 17, 16.

that do not die (e.g., the stars, the gods). However, the Greeks did not appreciate that even these "immortal" things are not bestowed with any "privilege" in comparison with the "contingent" things. Even what is able to last "for ever" (that is, to endure through an infinite amount of time) shares the same ontological status of radical dependence with all the other beings. The same point could be made about what scientists today would call a universe without beginning. Even such a universe would not cease to be ontologically contingent at each and every moment of its infinite existence.

CREATION AS A CAUSE ACCORDING TO MCCABE

In today's ordinary language the word "creation" (as well as to create, creative, creativity) is widely used, even if often without any connection with the idea of God, and I think that this happens because of the legacy of the nineteenth-century Romantic movement, when many intellectuals spread the idea that the artistic "genius" was bestowed with "divine" attributes.

As for McCabe, instead, creation is something peculiar to God; it is a cause that is not "a particular kind of cause"; while every color is a particular color, the same does not apply to creation, because the idea of cause is not a "genus."[35] Creation resembles an "efficient cause" because we can think of it only as a "making": however, we must think also on all those aspects for which "to create" is different from "to make": "Just as the only way to get at the resurrection is to go through the crucifixion, so the only way to 'understand' creation is to attend to the whittling away and death of 'making.'"[36]

God is cause of the existence of the world and all the things in it, as he gave them existence; but this image is misleading. If it were true, the word "existent" should enter in the description of the things classified (as opposed to non-existing things), but in reality we speak of the Creator God as a cause of existence *as though* the things could be classified like that.[37] Between Creator and creatures there is the tension between essence and existence, whereas between creature and their natural causes, which are themselves creatures, there is the strain between potentiality and actuality.[38]

Aquinas says that, in contrast to making, creation does not imply any real change from potentiality to actuality; nevertheless, our mind thinks it

35. McCabe, *God and Evil*, 102.

36. McCabe, "God and Creation," 388; and he continues saying: "Most theological mistakes come from carelessly thinking that we have now 'grasped' what our terms mean, that we no longer need to work them out again for ourselves."

37. McCabe, *Faith within Reason*, 61.

38. McCabe, *God Still Matters*, 20.

"as if" it was a change, because our mind is inadequate and thus we cannot understand what this particular kind of making means.[39] One kind of making we understand is "to generate": when dog Fido is born, it does not change, in fact, prior to its birth (or conception) there is not any Fido apt to change; however, both the active and passive features in its parents do change and, moreover, the world changes, since previously the world only had the potential to include Fido. Also that making which is the product of human art brings changes, and in certain respects it is a better analogy for creation than generating—as we have already seen[40]—because, just as happens in creation, human art shows the inadequacy (dissimilarity) of the effect to its cause: in fact the sculptor lives and his statues do not, whereas both the parents and their offspring are living beings.

One difference between creation and causality among creatures is therefore that the latter works within a world where every effect is potential: potentiality is there because other things already exist.[41] As for this particular making that is creation, McCabe follows Aquinas and says:

> So, creation is making, but not making out of anything. When X is created there is not anything that is changed into X. Creation is *ex nihilo* (not out of anything). Creation, then, is not a change in anything; there was nothing to be changed.[42]

What can this mean? He adds that a created giraffe is just a giraffe. If a giraffe is born (or conceived), this fact is *not* its creation. The conception/birth of a giraffe is just an example of what Aristotle called substantial change (a giraffe previously "potential" to the world, that is before being conceived/born, and then "actual" in the world after its conception/birth). The conception/birth of a giraffe *is* a change, whereas creation is not, because creation is the real fact that makes the giraffe exist both as potential and actual in the world; in fact, it makes the world itself exist. Therefore, it can be said that between "created world" and "world" there is not any difference. In other words, creation is *ex nihilo*, that is, not out of anything that exists and can change. As McCabe, recalling Gilson, observes: there can be "a coming into existence which is not a generation but a coming into existence which not only makes no difference to the thing itself but even makes no difference to

39. Aquinas, *ST*, I, qu. 44, art. 2.

40. See section "Causes" in this chapter.

41. McCabe, *God and Evil*, 97. Therefore creation is neither a passive potency (in things that are changed) nor an active one (in the causes of their change), as Rowan Williams says: "creation is not an exercise of power, because power is acted by A on B whereas creation does not have power on anything" ("On Being Creatures," 68).

42. McCabe, "God and Creation," 389.

a world, which amounts to no difference at all."[43] Moreover, *ex nihilo* (not out of anything) is actually the world, which is created together with what it contains, that is "everything."[44]

Thus, according to this doctrine, God is not inside the world, he is not the pantheistic "order" of the "universal logos" mentioned by the Stoics and Hegel, nor is he an entity that "adds" to the world, because such an addition would make the human mind conceive the dualistic pattern of two parallel realms. What is he, then?

Apart from being "not out from anything" and making "everything," creation is a "relationship" and, as Aquinas and after him McCabe say, such relationship is not real *in God* (McCabe says: "just as the relationship of 'being looked at' is not real in what you are looking at"), whereas it is real in creatures. This statement implies another and odder one: that creatures are "prior" to creation, quite the reverse of how we commonly imagine the creative act. However, Aquinas argues that in reality (not in knowledge) creatures are "prior" to creation itself, just as a substance is prior to its accidents. Creation could be said to be "prior" to creatures only if we consider the effect of this relationship, that is that creatures are causally dependent.[45] According to McCabe, this relationship between creatures (which could have been nothing, not just "potential" to the world) and God (who cannot not be) is what creation *is*, so different from the concept of "making" we started with .[46]

To take us more deeply into the mystery of creation, McCabe presents and criticizes what he calls "the metaphysics of contingency" (which he refers to late Scholasticism, in particular to Francisco Suarez).[47] According to this metaphysics of contingency, things are thought as being able to be and not to be, and creation is seen as the passage from the mere possibility of things to their actual existence, and this would be the difference from the Creator who cannot not be; whereas the distinction between necessary and contingent things for Aquinas is *within* the world, between what is composed by matter and form and what is not (e.g., angels): the former are able not to be, the latter are not, they are necessary. For Suarez, creatures are things that can be or not be, for Aquinas the creatures are such because of their distinction between essence and existence.

---

43. McCabe, "God and Creation," 389.
44. McCabe, "God and Creation," 388.
45. Aquinas, *ST*, I, qu. 45, art. 3, ad 3.
46. McCabe, "God and Creation," 394.
47. McCabe, *God and Evil*, 93.

What does this mean? McCabe says that for Aquinas it is not contingency that demands the action of a creator, for that it is sufficient that things have natural causes—this is indeed why we call them causes; "rather, it is the fact that the existence of contingent beings is accounted for by their causes that demands the action of a creator."[48] This "metaphysics of contingency" thinks God does the same job of other causes but what he gives is "being" just as the other causes give the things their determinate "characteristics." This is wrong, says McCabe. In fact, Aquinas thinks that God as Creator does not make any change or difference in the world, "for to exist is not to be different from not existing. All the differences are formal and can be adequately accounted for by created causes."[49] If someone objected that, for instance, a unicorn "does not exist" and therefore is different from, say, a lion, which does exist, we should reply that the unicorn also does exist, even though not as a living animal but as a poetic invention that was really produced by some poets and still is present in many human minds.

The underpinning point of such metaphysics of contingency is that it is impossible that prior to the world there was nothing: this doctrine thinks that instead there was God prior to the world, because it refuses the idea of a primordial nothing. Prior to the world there must have been not nothing but God. However, against this doctrine there are some philosophers who think that before the things there was not God, there was *nothing*: why should not the world have come from nothing? McCabe observes that Aquinas holds a third position: he disagrees with these philosophers because he thinks that it is inconceivable that the world came from nothing, but, in agreement with them and in disagreement with the metaphysics of contingency, he thinks that, nonetheless, this is exactly what happened or happens. There was or is nothing and "God is not invoked to fill any gap left by the absence of anything else."[50] As McCabe specifies, God does not do any work that the other causes can do; to say that God created the world does not eliminate the "intellectual vertigo" that we feel when we think about the beginning of things. Recognition of the action of God does not remove the mystery from the world.[51]

It seems to me that what McCabe tells us by this elusive three-fold scheme (metaphysics of contingency; atheist cosmology; Thomist doctrine of creation) is that we think of God only if there is a creation and human

---

48. McCabe, *God and Evil*, 93–94, 96.

49. McCabe, "God and Causes," in *Faith within Reason*, 65.

50. McCabe, "God and Causes," in *Faith within Reason*, 65.

51. McCabe, "God and Causes," in *Faith within Reason*, 65–66.

beings in it as well;[52] the existence of God without creation is unthinkable, but, creation being given, we are able to know that God does not depend on it, and, moreover, that God is not any "immortal and necessary" entity to be contrasted with us who are mortal and contingent. Therefore, we should not put ourselves within that unfavorable comparison, typical of the ancient pagan mind, which used to contrast mortal men to the immortal gods.

GOD AS CREATOR

Aquinas thinks that God necessarily wants his own goodness, but does not necessarily create; even if he did not create, he would be perfect all the same.[53] On this point Sofia Vanni Rovighi argues that creation is free because, if the world was necessary, then God could not exist without a world, therefore the Absolute would be God-with-the-world and so within the Absolute there would be all those defective features, such as change, which show non-absoluteness, and we should say that the Absolute is not absolute, which is a contradiction.[54] Moreover—says Brian Davies while commenting on Aquinas—God wants his own goodness, but he can seek his goodness without willing me to exist, so my existence is in no sense something that we can deduce from a knowledge of God being Creator. God does not create because he needs to communicate his goodness to creatures, but, while creating, his intention is to communicate his goodness.[55]

McCabe embraces these Thomistic premises and adds something "apophatic": the fact that God had created the world does not tell us anything about God's nature; rather, his being Creator tells us what God is *not* (he is not a natural cause), just as Jesus' crucifixion tells us what human beings are not (they are not made for power and success).[56] Thus, there is a great difference between saying that God is wise and saying that God is Creator; in the first case we speak of the essence of God, in the second case the reality is only in the creature and there is just a verbal change in God.[57] In order to know that God exists it is not necessary to know he is Creator, because both Aquinas and McCabe think that creation is an "efficient cause," but God's existence can be demonstrated also thinking of God as a "final

52. Because human beings are able to think and produce statements about God.

53. On this point, see how John Wippel discusses several Aquinas' texts (from *ST, SCG,* and *De Veritate*) in his "Thomas Aquinas on the Ultimate Why Question."

54. Sofia Vanni Rovighi, *Elementi,* 174.

55. Davies, *The Thought of Thomas Aquinas,* 148.

56. McCabe, *God Still Matters,* 32.

57. McCabe, *God Still Matters,* 43.

cause," that is, the ultimate purpose or end of the "life" (changes) of the universe.[58]

Following the *via negativa*, since we know that God does not change, his being Creator does not add anything to him.[59] For example, God does not change if Margaret Thatcher is created: it was not true in 1920 to say that God was the creator of Margaret Thatcher (since she was born in 1925), however, even so, after her birth there was no change in God; it became true of him that he was creator of her because of some reality *in her*. Furthermore, in particular, God does not learn anything from creatures, nor does he share human beings' hopes while they live throughout history, nor does he share their sufferings and therefore, *in this sense*, he does not feel com-passion towards them: in fact, learning, hoping, and suffering would be all changes within God.[60] Therefore, being Creator of the world is not part of what it is to be God; when we say that God does not change we do not mean that he is always the same all the time, because he is eternal, out of time: to attribute stasis to him is as mistaken as to attribute change to him.[61] All the changes that happen in things (e.g., Jack is saved) do not happen in God: if Jack—a contemporary of ours—was not saved this is only a change in God *from our point of view*, because in this case it would not be true to say that God was the saviour of Jack. Moreover, if God saved him, it is only in twentieth century that it is true to say that God is the saviour of him, not in the nineteenth century.[62] "To say" means "to think," that is a human activity, within time. Therefore, when we say that God might not have done some things, this statement is just from our point of view.

Following Aquinas, Brian Davies gives us an image intended to depict the absence of any real relationship in God as a Creator: I go to visit Australia and so I know it, but the fact that Australia is known by me does not put anything into Australia, and if somebody knows that Australia is known by me, he or she is not better informed about Australia than other people that have never been to Australia.[63] We are dealing here with really

58. McCabe, "God and Creation," 387.

59. McCabe, "The Involvement of God," *God Matters*, 44.

60. McCabe, "The Involvement of God," 44, 42, 44–45.

61. McCabe, *God Still Matters*, 43.

62. McCabe, *Faith within Reason*, 20–22.

63. Davies, *The Thought of Thomas Aquinas*, 76. I think that this analogy fails in part because, if somebody knows that Brian Davies visited Australia, this knowledge adds something to the idea of Australia in that person's mind; in fact, he now knows that Australia has some features that make it reachable by an American Dominican friar. Whereas, in the case of God, to know that he created Mrs Thatcher does not add any knowable features to our idea of God (because he is unknowable), it merely adds

difficult concepts. David Burrell says that we always have the temptation of distinguishing God in this world in the same way as every distinction we are used to making, but if we do this two opposite mistaken ideas arise: (1) contempt for the world in favor of another "divine world," a sort of realm of God which "truly is," as separated from our world, which does not have a true reality (Plato); (2) over-appreciation of our world, considered as the Absolute and so including God (Hegel).[64]

I think that Burrell means that we must not apply to God those concepts that we apply to natural causes, that is, he is not a cause "external" to the world (in contrast to the Sun, which is an external cause of the growing plant), nor he is a formal cause "internal" to the world (in contrast to the soul of an animal, which shapes and coordinates the lungs, heart, legs, etc.). According to Burrell, the right distinction, instead, "appears" in the world as we know it, but does not express a division present in the world.[65] In my opinion, here Burrell means that God as Creator, if he is truly something that "appears," is a kind of "knowledge,"[66] a possible awareness in the human mind that human beings and the rest of the world are just "creatures" that are dependent on some "Other" (the Creator). However, such an awareness does not have—as an objective referent—either any other existent realm or thing, or any "soul" (substantial form, central agency that coordinates the parts) of this world.

Within this asymmetrical relationship between Creator and creature we have just seen treated by Aquinas, Davies, and Burrell, McCabe, for his part, underlines the final cause: God seeks his own goodness, and creatures, made by God, seek God as their ultimate aim: God is a second-order maker who gives the purpose to the things. Like a human manufacturer, he is not similar to what he makes, and as such the ultimate good is the ultimate maker; he is our ultimate aim because he is Creator and all things aim at their perfection, but in God there are all the perfections. Each creature aims at God, that is, while tending towards its own goodness, it tends to God as its maker. God contains all the perfections in "a higher way, in the way they are in the intention of the maker"; these perfections are in the maker before in the things, but "before" does not mean "prior in time," it means that the created perfections depend on their being in the intention of the maker.[67]

---

something to our idea of the world (we now know it was potential to Mrs Thatcher).

64. Burrell, *Knowing the Unknowable God*, 17.

65. Burrell, *Knowing the Unknowable God*, 17.

66. I acknowledge that it could be objected that Burrell is not so quick to identify the appearance of God in the world as a sort of "knowledge" while he is discussing our attitudes to existence.

67. McCabe, *Faith within Reason*, 117–18.

To state—as Aquinas and McCabe do—that this relationship is not real in the Creator, that is, that it makes all the difference for the creatures (their very existence) whereas "being Creator does not add anything to him," primarily means that God does not have any needs. In fact, Thomas says that to act because of a lack belongs only to imperfect agents, therefore, not to God; he alone is *maxime liberalis* (completely generous), because he does not act for his utility but just for his goodness.[68] David Burrell comments: God as Creator (and not as First Being or Prime Mover) is shown by grace.[69] Rowan Williams argues that this is liberating because, since God does not need me in order to become God, so I never need to define myself as a person who needs to meet God's needs.[70]

McCabe goes into more depth: he criticizes our imagery by which we reify God, making him as similar to the world, as the potter who shares the same dimension of existence with the pot. And McCabe's criticism points to something that we are not used to. This happens because we often confuse images with thoughts, so, since we have images, we believe that we have thoughts, and, therefore, we believe we already hold some sort of knowledge. McCabe, instead, moving beyond any images of similarity, underlines the difference between Creator and creatures: God cannot make a creature with the same nature as himself for the same reason that he cannot make a square circle, therefore, an "uncreated creature" would be a contradiction.[71] What does this mean? One thing is that we experience only creatures and never what is uncreated, so that we never experience the Creator. A second thing is that the Creator is limited by the principle of non-contradiction, he is not an arbitrary agent. A third thing is that he is the One, since there are not any other uncreated entities ("uncreated creatures").

Given this radical difference between what is created and what is uncreated, God as Creator cannot be thought of as existing *before* creation—he cannot be something that existed before our universe and then made it. Therefore, creation cannot be conceived as what makes the difference between God alone and God with creatures; it would be more accurate to say that creation is what lies between nothing at all and creatures, but, since we cannot conceive nothing at all, we cannot conceive creation.[72]

Since we cannot hold a proper concept of creation, we are obliged to build an imaginary pattern representing the Creator God and the created

68. Aquinas, *ST*, I, qu. 44, art. 4.

69. Burrell, *Knowing the Unknowable God*, 15.

70. Williams, "On Being Creatures," 72.

71. McCabe, *Faith within Reason*, 21.

72. McCabe, *God and Evil*, 101.

universe alongside each other: "the model of God as another being over against us belongs (probably necessarily belongs), like the sacraments and all religious cult, to the era of man's alienation."[73]

Thus, on the one hand, McCabe thinks this model necessary only because human life is warped. On the other hand, according to McCabe, by the "death of 'making'" and by the insights of the *via negativa,* theology should oppose the identification of such "another being over against us" with any particular entity within the universe, be it the "matter" of Marxism, the "science" of positivism, the "beauty" of certain Romanticism, or the "race" of twentieth-century irrationalism.[74] McCabe says that to worship anything in the universe (which by definition is not God) is to dehumanise the human being; we should worship only our Creator. This was an Israelite discovery that was a turning point in history and implied some knowledge about human beings: they are the worshippers of the Creator.[75]

I think that, if we put such a phrase ("worshippers of the Creator") into the context of all of McCabe's philosophical theology, we can maintain that the Aristotelian definition of human beings as "rational animals" gets enriched with other aspects: human beings are creatures that through their reason focus their feelings and the actions of their lives on a particular awareness, the awareness of being radically dependent, always and for all, not just on other people and other natural items/events, but also *together with* other people and nature. To be creatures means to be dependent on a network of beings that are dependent as well, because this network—that is the system of the universe—is itself non-self-granted; and to be "worshippers of the Creator" means to be aware of the creaturely status of the universe.

A CREATED UNIVERSE

Although McCabe follows the traditional "first cause/secondary causes" model, he explains it more clearly than is usually done: it is no more the "chain" model with its first "ring," but it is a relationship between the cause of the existence of the universe as a whole, and the particular causes acting

73. McCabe, *God Matters,* 170.

74. In the earlier decades of twentieth century there was the outbreak of the myths of land and blood that focused on the (confused) idea of race. This stream of thought can be called "irrationalism" because those authors such as Alfred Rosemberg (*The Myth of 20th Century*) and Julius Evola (editor of *The Protocols of the Elders of Zion*) used to despise modern reason, science, and classic philosophy.

75. McCabe, *God Still Matters,* 56.

within the universe. In this sense the Big Bang also would be a secondary cause, not a first cause. McCabe makes a comparison between the truth that we get from hearsay by some person and the existence that comes from a natural cause (for example, a child from his or her parents): as hearsay relies on a first-hand witness, so existence coming from any natural cause relies on the existence of the whole universe, whose cause is God.

After Thomas, McCabe says that *esse* is not a form but it is the *actualitatis omnis formae*: "there are movers but God accounts for the movers being movers, he accounts for causes being causes, for necessary beings being necessary, for purposes being purposes."[76] Natural agents bring things into existence because they are instruments of God's causality; we can say that the fire boils the water, but we can also say (with a different tone of voice) that it is God who boils it; "everything which is brought about by natural causes is brought about by God; and there are some things, like human free decisions, that are not brought about by any natural causes but only by God."[77]

What is created (i.e., what exists because the whole universe exists) does not have any "created" characteristics that could enable us to detect any activity by the Creator. There is no quality like "to be a creature": the fact that things are created does not leave any trace in them, in the same way as happens when a thing is thought.[78] "To be created" identifies with "to exist from nothing," and an existing thing does not have different qualities in comparison with a non-existing thing.[79] Creation would be impossible if it made a difference to something: for instance, if creation made any difference, it would be impossible for God to create a Nicaraguan Okapi because he should create a *"created* Nicaraguan Okapi" which would be different from the *mere* Nicaraguan Okapi, and, if he wanted to create a created Nicaraguan Okapi he could only create a *"created* created Nicaraguan Okapi."[80] Whereas, apart from creation, all the other causes make differences in the world (for example, a hurricane leaves detectable traces of its action), but God does not: he makes things precisely as they are, the world as it is.

This is the "autonomy" of all and any creatures. Each creature is autonomous insofar as it is itself and not conditioned by other creatures.

76. McCabe, *God and Evil*, 96–97.

77. McCabe, *God and Evil*, 18–19. The last remark refers to God being truth, and free actions being such only if they stem from true knowledge about the good of the agent.

78. McCabe, "God and Creation," 389.

79. McCabe, *Faith within Reason*, 65.

80. McCabe, *God Matters*, 70.

You can say that a hurricane has been there but you cannot say God has been there, since there are no traces of God; therefore, William Paley's "Argument for Design" is wrong because no traces of creation (order, ingenuity, etc.) can be detected; you can no more say that the world that exists has to be made by God than you can say *this* sort of world must exist.[81]

Like existence itself, "being created" does not add anything to a thing, it cannot enter into the *description* of anything, we could never say, "if this is created then it must be like this and not like that." This truth does not interest only logicians and metaphysicians but also theologians, because if the person of Jesus is uncreated this fact does not make any difference either: being uncreated does not add any feature to the person of Jesus.

Just as we cannot infer anything about Fred from Fred being created, so we cannot infer anything about Jesus from Jesus being uncreated; to be divine is not to be a kind of being, just as to be a creature is not to be a kind of being (the word "nature" is used only analogically in the phrase "divine nature"), whereas, to be a man *is* to be a kind of being and this is the kind of being that Jesus was and is.[82] Therefore, to try to find differences within things from the concept of creation can produce only mistakes, both in sciences and in our idea of God.

According to McCabe, "what we say about the world compels us to make certain statements about God, but no statement about God entails any statement about the world."[83] From Creator God we do not get *any* information about nature; if we got it, it would be just our minds' projections onto nature. Creation is different from the origin of the universe: for example, the Big Bang is fascinating but *irrelevant* to creation. When we say that God created the world there still remains the scientific question about *what kind* of world it is and *how it began*, if ever.[84] In fact, Aquinas would have been quite puzzled about the suggestion that the study of the Big Bang concerns creation: he thought that creation is not confined to a unique time in the beginning—given the fact that there was a beginning—but it is *what continuously sustains the world in being*.[85]

God is not a causal explanation of the events in the world: to explain the world's events it is enough to know the natures of thing. However, we need an explanation for *the existence of the world itself:* that is, how it is that there is any causal explanation within it. God is not mentioned in scientific

81. McCabe, *Faith within Reason*, 75.

82. McCabe *God Matters*, 70–71.

83. McCabe, *God and Evil*, 68.

84. McCabe, *God Matters*, 7–8.

85. McCabe, *Faith within Reason*, 101.

explanations, but *we need God in order for scientific explanation to be able to exist*.[86] In fact, Thomas holds that creation is not "hidden" within natural operations, because, instead, creation is the very premise for all causality present within nature.[87]

Therefore, it is important to avoid mistakes in our knowledge of creatures (i.e., in our natural sciences), because they result in mistakes of faith. Aquinas already said that mistakes in natural sciences generate mistakes in faith: for example, a "positivistic" approach to science makes us think that God is material and a mechanistic approach can lead us to suppose that God emanates the world by necessity.[88]

On the one hand, we have seen how McCabe perceives the worship of the Creator as an aspect of being creatures—i.e., that it is the human consciousness of universal solidarity with all the other radically dependent beings. When the universe raises the question "why is there anything rather than nothing?" creation is the name we give to God's answer to this question;[89] because it is dependence (coming out of nothing) and not contingency (not lasting forever)[90] that qualifies creatures. The fact that a creature has a limited life-span is not the relevant criteria to distinguish it from God, in so far as necessary beings do not have a limited life-span and can still be distinguished from God.[91]

On the other hand, we have also seen another feature of being creatures, that is, autonomy (which is not to be confused with self-sufficiency). This is a sort of reply to Ludwig Feuerbach's theory on alienation, which sets God as rival to man and the world; instead, Rowan Williams—I think being influenced by McCabe and having in mind this main idea by Feuerbach—summarizes the previous arguments this way: we act properly as creatures when we do not think that it is worth leaving people and things in order to dedicated ourselves to a God who is a rival of them.[92]

86. McCabe, "Causes," 102.

87. Aquinas, *ST*, I, qu. 45, art. 8.

88. Aquinas, *Summa Contra Gentiles*, book II, chapter 2.

89. McCabe, *God Matters*, 7.

90. At least according to debatable McCabe's definitions, an angel is "necessary" (i.e., he cannot not be) and so he is not "contingent" (that is, something which *can* not be) and therefore he lasts forever; but an angel is a creature, so he gets his necessary (everlasting) existence from an Other. Thus, McCabe, following Aquinas, distinguishes created from uncreated necessary beings, "necessity" from "absolute necessity."

91. McCabe, *God and Evil*, 99.

92. Rowan Williams, "On Being Creatures," 73. Autonomy can stem from non-competition; in fact, since God is thought much more powerful than man, if there was competition there would not be human beings' autonomy from God, like between small children and their parents. I will deal with autonomy in the following section.

DEPENDENCE AND AUTONOMY

We should understand the relationship between these two aspects—dependence and autonomy—while avoiding any contrast.[93]

Rowan Williams reflected in depth on dependence: we have both a good reason (our experience of unhealthy past dependences) and a bad reason (our illusion of being self-sufficient) to be suspicious of it. In order to get a role and therefore to be independent, we risk depending in a problematic way on particular persons and institutions; whereas, a healthy dependence is one that makes us love our individual self because we acknowledge it exists "for another," even though we are aware that every particular "other" cannot fulfil our expectations. The classical doctrine of creation says that before being engaged with other people, we exist because God knows us and relates to us.[94] This idea of God here, I think, points to the unforeseeable multiplicity of particular dependences towards other equally dependent creatures. "Unforeseeable" because we do not know God's plans, as McCabe says: by creation we mean the dependence of all that is, even though we do not know what it depends on.[95]

While other creatures limit, or, at least, influence us, God does not do this. Even though he is united to us as other creatures cannot be,[96] nonetheless this intimacy does not influence us, on the contrary it *makes us be ourselves*. That God continuously operates within creatures does not mean they have not their own actions, but that every creature is what it is because of God.[97]

McCabe thinks that it is easier to appreciate this in human beings and their actions than in other creatures. The more our actions are free, that is not conditioned by other creatures, the more a "window" on the Creator God opens; in fact, then, we are acting exactly because we are ourselves.[98] My action is free when it stems from my motives and reasons and is not caused by anything else; however, it is caused by God because God is not

---

93. For a lengthy explanation of how radical autonomy is not only compatible with radical dependency, but even logically implies it, see Clavier, "Sartre and Sertillanges on Creation."

94. Clavier, "Sartre and Sertillanges on Creation," 69–71.

95. McCabe, *God Matters*, 10.

96. For example, if another person feels compassion for me, he or she both is to some extent united to me and suffers together with me; whereas God is completely united to me (since he makes me exist, even if suffering) but he does not change and thus does not suffer (McCabe, *God Matters*, 45).

97. McCabe, *God Matters*, 7.

98. McCabe, *God Matters*, 14.

anything else, is not a rival agent in the universe; the creative causal power of God does not operate on me from outside, it is what makes me me.[99] The idea that God could interfere with my freedom springs from a idolatrous concept of God: in a hierarchy of less and more powerful causes God should be at the top; however, the more a cause is powerful the more it interferes with the other causes, in this case my freedom. However, God does not make the greatest difference, greater than say an earthquake or the explosion of a star, because he makes *all* the differences, i.e., creation (that is, the existence of the universe), which means that he does not make any differences at all:[100]

> as man becomes more and more self-creative, God does not fade out of the picture, he fades in. The pictures of God, however, fade out. The God who makes us instead of us making ourselves is replaced by the God who makes us make ourselves. . . . The creative power is just the power that, because it results in things being what they are, cannot interfere with creatures. . . . Creation is simply and solely letting the things be, and our love is just a faint image of that.[101]

I comment on these passages saying that we achieve this freedom from other creatures' pressure as far as we have true ideas aimed at reaching real goodness; freedom is a sort of self-regulation that reveals ("a window opens") our dependence on a God who is Truth and Goodness. So, God "fades in," not ontologically but in our understanding: if we think that God is Truth and Goodness, the true ideas we conceive that move our will towards real goodness make us free, that is "ourselves" (not forced by other creatures), and this fact "opens a window" onto the creative action of God, who makes us be ourselves. As Ratzinger suggests, the doctrine of creation means a true humility that is grateful for life and the other goods, of being dependent in love, as opposed to the kind of humility that despises existence, human beings, and the world (i.e., Gnosticism).[102]

God, McCabe says, is the power upon which the other powers depend for their efficacy; if such a power does exist, then the world that we take for granted must be given in a much richer and more mysterious way; in fact, if the world were simply granted, to exist for me would mean just to be A and not B, i.e., a particular kind of thing. Whereas, if the world is created and not

---

99. McCabe, *God Matters*, 13.

100. McCabe, *Faith within Reason*, 76.

101. McCabe, *God Matters*, 170, 108–9. See Brian Davies' comments in "Introduction" to *The McCabe Reader*, 18–19.

102. Ratzinger, *In the Beginning*, 99–100.

granted, to exist means that the entire system of being-a-particular-kind-of-things exists, of which I am a part.

We at some time have a very strong feeling of the gratuitousness of things, a sense of gratitude for there being a world.[103] Christians believe that even if a person was not loved by other persons, he or she is nonetheless loved by God because God "is the unconditional everlasting love which sustains us in being" and, therefore, God is but a "label" for whatever makes sense of our gratitude for existing, to which we say "thank you."[104]

Thus, as far as a creature is good, it is not hindered or diminished by other creatures, as we can see more clearly in free human actions. This is its autonomy. However, as far as a creature exists and is good, it depends on God who is Being and Goodness; and this is its dependence. Human beings, when they acknowledge this dependence by their conscious gratitude, show more clearly this union of autonomy and dependence than other creatures.

A NEW CREATION

Saint Paul's idea of Christ inaugurating a "new creation" is affirmed by Mc-Cabe and connected by him with creation. Baptism is a new birth, a participation in the new creation of the resurrection of Christ; it makes us enter the church, which is a new creation: "She is not just a group of people within the world, she is a new world."[105] The church is founded by Jesus and, like him, is a created reality: so long as we are asking historical questions about Jesus, we shall come up with answers to the effect that he was a man and not an angel. However, we do not only examine Jesus historically, we also listen to him, "and it is in this rapport with Jesus that we explore a different dimension of his existence—rather as when we say that the world is created we are considering a different dimension of it from the one we look at as physicists."[106]

Even if in a convoluted way, here McCabe, on the one hand, relates historical study of Jesus' life to scientific study of the universe, and, on the other hand, relates creation to the redemptive power of faith in Christ. If

103. McCabe, *God Still Matters*, 20–21.

104. McCabe, *Faith within Reason*, 167.

105. McCabe, *The New Creation*, 40, 43.

106. McCabe, *God Matters*, 71. If it was objected that this language does not fit well with saying that being created "makes no difference," it could be replied that, if the language is unfit, the concept is not: the perspective of creation is different from that of the physicists, because, for instance, when the theologians say that creation is the cause of the world as such they do not mean that it makes any changes *in* the world, whereas the physicists think that all the natural causes do make such changes.

this is true, then, creation and new creation share something: the relationship between creatures and God, as distinct from the relationships among creatures. What is different, however?

McCabe thinks that the modern atheism of Nietzsche and Marx is right in saying that God cannot love creatures because of the inequality between them; for Nietzsche and Marx God the Creator of the world is just a vast omnipotent baby unable to grow up and to abandon himself in that true love that requires equality; they say that to accept this God is to accept a sort of slavery. But McCabe observes that these atheists omitted to notice that we are no longer *just* creatures, because, by being taken up into Christ, we are raised into share in divinity.[107] The fact that God cannot love us is not because we are sinners, but because we are creatures; "sin is nothing but our deliberate settling for simple creature-hood," closing ourselves off and rejecting the gift of God's love, the risk of divinity.[108] However, the missions of Jesus and the Holy Spirit deify us and so they perform the ultimate liberation of people, the "liberation from God", the liberation from *mere* creature-hood, so that we could stand in front of him as Jesus does, as *equals* in an exchange of love.[109]

Therefore, it seems that the difference between creation and new creation is that the former lacks equality (the relationship is real only in the creatures, as Aquinas says), whereas the latter does have this equality, which is the necessary premise for reciprocity.[110] However, new creation is not an improvement of creatures, as it would happen to a man, for example, who became more handsome, intelligent, generous, brave, or long-lived: "A creature with grace is not just a higher kind of creature. . . . Grace does not make man a better kind of creature, it raises him beyond creature-hood, it

107. McCabe, *God Matters*, 21; McCabe, *God Still Matters*, 6. It could be objected that Nietzsche's and Marx's critique has already been tackled while clarifying that God is not the Powerful Boss / Omnipotent Baby of the universe, because he does not belong to it. To this possible objection I would reply that, on the one hand, the foundational idea of De Lubac (a "pure nature" does not exist; nature has been always contained within grace) has been consistently developed by the Jesuits I refer to while introducing the third part of my work (McCabe's Revealed Theology), not by the Dominicans. On the other, even if creation and redemption are two aspects of the same gracious act of God, redemption attains our human side; it is how—thanks to Jesus—we realize at the same time *both* that we are creatures *and* we are children.

108. McCabe, *God Still Matters*, 7–8.

109. McCabe, *God Still Matters*, 181.

110. If it was asked whether in "new creation" the relationship between Creator and creature will be real in the former too, it should be replied that it will be: we will become like Christ (his body actually, says Saint Paul) and the Trinitarian processions are real relationships among all the persons of Trinity.

makes him share in divinity."[111] That is, equality with God is not achieved by a creature through progressive improvements of its nature, it is not a sort of Lamarckian (that is, hierarchical) evolution, but, rather, it requires the end of any hierarchical structure. According to McCabe, hierarchy is very ancient and belongs especially to our prelinguistic ancestors, it is ingrained in our bones but with human beings it is "slowly subverted by love"; hierarchical structures are not necessarily evil and are better than individualistic anarchy, but they are not love: "we will shed them as we have already shed our tails."[112]

CONCLUSIONS

Towards the end of his 1980 lecture "God and Creation," McCabe states:

> We do not understand what creation means. We merely point towards it in the process of qualifying to death the notion of God-making-the-world. . . . We can have no concept of creation (any more than of God), but this will not, I trust, prevent us from talking about them.[113]

However, as we have appreciated in this chapter, McCabe talks quite extensively about creation. Here I summarize some concepts.

A general premise is that, unlike "making," creation does not make changes; therefore, it is neither an active nor a passive power, and it allows the things to be themselves in their reciprocal relationships. Simply because of this, creation does "everything": perhaps it could be said that creation makes *all* the relationships among beings, without any exception, whereas natural causes make just *some* relationships.

From this premise comes the disproof of those scientists who think that traces of God's creative act should be found but they are not, and, therefore, they think that creation is simply a mythological way for speaking of the Big Bang. Furthermore, from it also comes the disproof of those Christian creationists who think that traces of God's creative act should be found, and they are.

An important concept is that in God there is not a real relationship with the universe, whereas there is a real one in the universe. Therefore,

---

111. McCabe, *The New Creation*, 3. We can notice an interesting parallelism with his doctrine of creation: Creator God leaves no traces in creation, Redeemer God leaves no traces in redeemed humans.

112. McCabe, *God Still Matters*, 4–5.

113. McCabe, "God and Creation," 395.

it cannot be assumed either that God is "prior" to the universe or that the universe can be "added" to God to make a set of two. From this concept comes the disproof of dualism, according to which there are two "things" (two comparable ways of being), God and the universe (one superior and the other inferior); and also comes the disproof of pantheism according to which God is the "organism" and the particular beings are just its "organs": in other words, pantheism claims that only the universe exists but that it is self-animated and self-sufficient. McCabe's doctrine of creation, instead, tells us that only one "thing" exists, but it is not self-sufficient.

To be a creature means to exist from nothing (not like when we say that a horse "exists" when it is conceived/born, because before conception/birth it was already existing even though just potentially). Since there are no differences between an existing horse and a non-existing horse (because the non-existing horse does not exist and thus it is not a term for comparison), creature-hood/existence is not a feature that is suitable for making distinctions (say between me, this grain of dust, Satan, and the theorem of Pythagoras). On the one hand, when we call a being "creature" we mean that it is "dependent," as are all beings, since the universe could have not existed; on the other hand, being a creature means to be "autonomous," since the universe works only by its internal laws.

Another important concept is that creation is not a power, whereas everything in the universe is both relatively powerful and relatively powerless, exercising some power and being affected by some other power. If God creates the universe without exercising any power on it, the message we get is that the complex system of powers in the universe relies on something that is not power. The uncreated Being, which is divine, is not something hierarchically superior to what is created; the "theosis" caused by divine grace does not improve a creature as if it brought it to a higher level of a staircase, but, rather, makes any kind of hierarchy dissolve.

10

The Problem of Evil

DISTINCTION IN CREATURES

In the previous chapter I said: "as far as a creature is good." However, the reality is that evil does exist in this world. As David Fergusson says, the greatest difficulty for a theory of creation is to explain the existence of evil in the world; there is strong scriptural evidence that the attempt to show how evil will be eventually defeated spread before the attempts to explain how it had come into earth.[1] In fact, the first task is more urgent and the second one is more difficult. Brian Davies, while commenting on *Summa Theologiae*, writes:

> the world contains things of different kinds. Are these things distinct because of God or something else? In Ia.47.1 Aquinas unsurprisingly says that the existence of distinctions in creatures derives from God. As creator it is God who primarily accounts for the distinctions between them. . . . Can we think of a distinction between things that is especially pervasive? One might say that we can since it is obvious that some things are good and that other things are bad. With this thought in mind, Aquinas proceeds in Ia.48 and 49 to consider evil and what accounts for it.[2]

1. Fergusson, *The Cosmos and the Creator*, 77, 83.
2. Davies, *Thomas Aquinas' Summa Theologiae*, 113–14.

Following Aquinas, McCabe relates the problem of evil to the doctrine of creation: it follows from creation not causing change that it is impossible to create well or badly. Since without creation there is not even the potentiality of things, we are not allowed to ask: does this created thing conform to the requirements for this kind of thing or not ? What could have happened is not only that this thing would not have existed, but also that the entire world itself would not have existed. And we can speak of defective things only if there is a world in which they can actualize their potentiality well or badly.[3] Brian Davies comments McCabe's position this way:

> So, McCabe never invokes the Freewill defence when writing about God and evil. Instead, his strategy is usually to emphasize (a) that everything good is caused to exist by God, (b) that evil is a lack or privation of being and is, therefore, not creatively caused by God, (c) that in the case of naturally occurring evil there is always an explanation in terms of concomitant good, and (d) that attacks on belief in God which presume that God has some moral case to answer miss the point that God is not, like people, a moral agent subject to moral duties or obligations and is not something we can intelligibly think of as possessing human virtues and vices. Again, we see the importance for Mc-Cabe of his notion of God as creator.[4]

THE PROBLEM STATED

From a Western point of view, we have had reflections about evil, seen as a "problem" (i.e., how to understand the co-existence of God/gods together with the evil of this world), since Antiquity. We can go back to Old Testament books, such as *Genesis* and *Job*, and to Greek tragedies, such as those by Aeschylus, and then to Plato's philosophy. It was Epicurus who stated:

> Is God willing to prevent evil, but not able? Then he is not omnipotent. Is he able, but not willing? Then he is malevolent. Is he both able and willing? Then whence cometh evil? Is he neither able nor willing? Then why call him God?[5]

While summarizing twentieth-century debate on the topic, Brian Davies conveniently observes that the real problem is goodness—that is, the discussion of its uncertain nature—rather than evil, whose real presence in

---

3. McCabe, *God and Evil*, 104.

4. Davies, "Introduction" to *The McCabe's Reader*, 21.

5. Reported in Lactantius, *De Ira Dei*, caput XIII.

this world is never disputed by recent authors,[6] none of whom claim, as some in the past have done, that it is "appearance" and not reality.

In these writings we can distinguish several literary genres: C. S. Lewis and his novel *This Hideous Strength*, Jean Paul Sartre and his novel *Nausea*, Hanna Arendt with her journalistic reportage *Eichmann in Jerusalem: A Report on the Banality of Evil*, the historical-philosophical pamphlet by Hans Jonas, *A Search for God after Auschwitz*, the religious pastoral exhortation by Pope John Paul II, *Salvifici Doloris*. Among these genres, there is the academic-philosophical essay, and this genre is the one quoted by McCabe in his writings on the problem of evil, such as works by Antony Flew[7] and J. L. Mackie.[8] His choice was this one, in my opinion, because in this genre the authors are concerned to provide an account of previous philosophical tradition, in a systematic and "complete" way, and, therefore, to McCabe it worked as a bridge to Aquinas.

McCabe's philosophical mentors were Dorothy Emmet at Manchester University and Victor White at the Dominican Study in Oxford. The former, an admirer of Whitehead and a cautiously moderate follower of the analytical philosophy of her times, was not interested in this topic. When she deals with it briefly, she says: evil in the world lies in the character of things being mutually obstructive, organisms must prey upon one another, and the more complex, the more transient they are (e.g., a man compared with a rock); evil cannot be absolute because it is parasitical, if a good thing vanishes, also the evil of that thing vanishes; moreover, she reports that Whitehead thought that there is a redemptive value to suffering.[9] The first two ideas, as we will see later, were McCabe's as well, whereas not so the third one.

Victor White was a great friend of Carl G. Jung, but their friendship broke down because of their disagreement about the problem of evil, since White maintained the *privatio boni* theory, which Jung denied.[10] As we will see, this theory is McCabe's main argument.

---

6. Davies, *The Reality of God and the Problem of Evil*, 4.

7. Flew, "Divine Omnipotence and Human Freedom."

8. Mackie, "Evil and Omnipotence." "It is no exaggeration to say that nearly all subsequent work on the problem of evil by philosophers writing in English addresses the problem as Mackie formulated it. What is not yet widely known, however, is that the English Dominican Herbert McCabe, who died in 2001, came up with a reply that, in my opinion, is the best so far." Liccione, "On Evil and Omnipotence," n.p.

9. Emmet, *Whitehead's Philosophy of Organism*, 268–70.

10. See *The Jung-White Letters*, edited by Lammers and Cunningham, xxxii, 384.

METHOD

Some scholars have underlined how McCabe, rather than attempting to explain the presence of evil in this world, prefers to dispute the logical errors of those thinkers who, starting from the ascertainment of evil, either refuse God or badly understand his attributes.[11]

The problem of evil, before being an obstacle, is a resource, McCabe says: in fact, if we do not pass through pain and evil, we cannot enter God's mystery; if someone is not put on trial by this problem, he or she does not have the possibility of recognizing God's love. However, we should not be confounded by the philosophical muddle about God and evil.[12]

What we can do is not much: just offer a little bit of clarity amongst some logical muddles. First of all, we should refuse the "mist" of that relativism that denies evil's objective existence and says that everything depends on subjective points of view.[13]

Secondly, we should be aware that, if we denied the existence or the omnipotence of God, we would not eventually achieve much; if you deny his existence you do not have to say any more that God is good, but you should nevertheless continue to acknowledge the mystery of evil (why this world is so bad?); and if you deny his omnipotence, you have added another problem, because you have invented this powerful (albeit not omnipotent) wicked creature who could prevent a lot of evils (albeit not all of them) but does not do that; all you have achieved is to eliminate one logical puzzle, but awe and resentment at evil will be worsened. In fact, you could say that comic-book heroes like Superman are powerful, albeit not omnipotent, but at least they are good because they save the poor victim of abuses, when they are aware of those abuses, whereas God doesn't, and so he is wicked.

Instead, it is possible to clear logical hindrances, such as those in Epicurus' formula, without denying God's existence and his full omnipotence (not limited by anything, not even by so-called human "free will"):

> To have said this (that it makes no sense to speak of God as competent or incompetent, as morally good or morally evil) is already to have answered the "problem of evil," which is formulated on the assumption that such talk makes sense. . . . We have seen that the formulation of the problem of evil with which I began is a typical metaphysical muddle. That is to say, it contains phrases that seem to make familiar sense but that on

11. Liccione, "On Evil"; Davies, *The Reality,* 246.
12. McCabe, "Evil," in *God Matters,* 25.
13. McCabe, "On Evil and Omnipotence," in *Faith within Reason,* 79.

examination turn out to be senseless because they employ words outside their proper context. The problem of evil is stated by asking questions about God that can only intelligibly be asked about creatures.[14]

However, solving such a "logical puzzle" or "metaphysical muddle" is not enough to make us see how and why evil flows from God's goodness:[15]

> my remarks upon the problem of evil will not remove any of the vertigo we feel when we contemplate the world of pain and misery entirely in the power of an infinitely good and powerful God.[16]

Every gain of clarity (e.g., that God, being unchangeable, cannot be blamed for not being morally good), though limited, has its importance, as we will see later, but, as C. S. Lewis writes, when in our lives we face great evils, extra-theoretical facts are more important: a bit of courage more than much knowledge, a bit of human sympathy more than much courage, and a bit of divine love more than all.[17]

Whereas McCabe, although in some pages, such as those on death, seeks to "console" his readers, that is, to show how pessimistic ideas or images on death do not stem from any evident truth,[18] nevertheless, most times he is not interested to soften the reality of evil. Therefore, I agree with John Haldane when he writes:

> McCabe's opening formulation of the problem of evil included mention of God's failure to intervene when evil occurs, but his solution is to the more limited problem of reconciling the existence of evil with that of God, which leaves the question of alleviation unaddressed.[19]

At the end of his essay "On Evil and Omnipotence" McCabe himself declares he had "disentangled a puzzle," but "[w]hen all is said and done, we are left with an irrational but strong feeling that if we were God we would have acted differently. Perhaps one of his reasons for acting as he did is to warn us not to try to make him in our own image."[20]

---

14. McCabe, *God and Evil*, 111.
15. McCabe, "On Evil," 79.
16. McCabe, *God and Evil*, 111.
17. Lewis, *The Problem of Pain*.
18. McCabe, see the chapter "Life after Death" in *The New Creation*.
19. John Haldane's review of McCabe's *God and Evil*.
20. McCabe, "On Evil and Omnipotence," in *Faith within Reason*, 93.

That is, some unvanquished complaints about evil still remain: for example, we can think of God as infantile because he does not understand our suffering, or that we are infantile, as Job thought, and then come to a deeper vision of God; in fact, the first "atheist" reaction can be part of the second one.[21] McCabe comments:

> I do not want to say that God is innocent, nor to explain how his activities have been good; I just want to refute the charges against him; I hope I prove that he is not guilty but also I expect you will be puzzled like me about his innocence: it will remain a mystery why he has done what he has done.[22]

CORE THESES

Responding to complaints/charges towards God because of evil, in his essay "Evil" McCabe imitates the judiciary style of a hypothetical lawyer. Three defences are not open to God's defence attorney: (1) that he is not omnipotent; (2) evil is not real; (3) at least some evil is caused by the free will of people and not by God.

On the other hand the attorney wants to argue: (1) everything good in the world is brought about by God; (2) some evil—"evil suffered"—is a necessary concomitant of a material natural world, which is good, and so God has brought it about in the sense that he brought about that good; (3) "evil done" (sin) is not brought about by God in any sense: he could have prevented that, but he is not guilty of neglect.[23]

TWO EVILS

McCabe cares for a distinction:

> Evil suffered is what comes to a thing when it is damaged or diseased or knocked around in one way or another. Evil done is peculiar to responsible beings. It means wickedness.[24]

"Evil suffered" comes from "outside," both from things and people, whereas "evil done" comes from "within," and only from people.[25] This dis-

21. McCabe, "Evil," 25.
22. McCabe, "Evil," 26.
23. McCabe, "Evil," 26–27.
24. McCabe, "On Evil and Omnipotence," 80.
25. McCabe, "Evil," 30.

tinction refers to that of Augustine and Aquinas between *malum poenae* and *malum culpae*.[26] McCabe argues that "evil suffered" is a sort of zero-sum game, because, if a lamb is killed by a wolf, the lamb's evil is met by the wolf's good, if a man is killed by an illness, his evil is met by the good of the flourishing bacteria:

> if it can be shown that evil suffered has a necessary function in the material world, then clearly it is not incompatible with the goodness of God—unless, like Manichees, you think that matter as such is evil, and this would be very difficult to show. . . . There is a natural order in events. One of the prices for such a natural world is suffering, a price exacted not by God but by the way things are in a material world.[27]

In "evil suffered" there are two sides: one suffers and the other gains something; it could be said that God acts in the suffering side to the extent he acts in the gaining one; for instance, he acts in my perishing inasmuch he acts in the bacteria which infect me. "Evil done" (sin) is different because in it, when I sin, I mistreat myself and nobody gains from this attack. Other beings can inflict physical and psychological damages on me, but no moral defects, because, if they did that, those defects would not be misdeeds but only misfortunes; another person can make me mad, but he is not able to make me sin. Moral evil is a self-inflicted imperfection. Therefore, since no one is perfected while sinning, there is nothing in sin itself where God acts (even though there could be good consequences stemming from sins).[28] I will discuss presently McCabe's distinction.

Although in several passages McCabe seems to identify "evil suffered" with pain, the two concepts are to be distinguished: a being can suffer an evil (a defect of its nature) without feeling pain, as it happens not only to inanimate things but also to human beings when they do not perceive—either by senses or by thoughts—a physical or psychological evil that affects them. This happens because pain is the *perception* (it does not matter whether true or false) of a present evil and not just the mere presence of that evil.[29] This wrong identification hinders any comprehension of the relationship between evil suffered and evil done in human beings. For example, a psychological trauma I have suffered since I was a small child because of lasting

26. Even though this one is larger because it does not deal just with human beings: every 'poena' is a defect in some being's form, every 'culpa' is a defect in some being's operation (see *ST*, I, qu. 48, art. 5).

27. McCabe, 'On Evil and Omnipotence,' 82.

28. Ibidem, 88.

29. *ST*, I-IIae, qu. 35, art. 1.

abuses from my parents produces an evil suffered that, if I am not aware of it and thus I do not feel pain, probably will make me commit in turn other bad actions ("evil done"). C. S. Lewis, in fact, effectively described pain as that particular kind of evil that is "disinfected," "sterilised," because it does not tend to "proliferate," unlike other evils.[30]

Furthermore, the lamb-wolf example concerns only one group of "evil suffered," that one involving interactions among living beings throughout a natural food chain, but it is not suitable to meteorite impacts and the dinosaurs' extinction or to those people slaughtered in Auschwitz, that is to all those cases when the loss suffered by a subject does not show clearly any true gain by other subjects.

Moreover, McCabe himself sometimes explicitly says that human "free acts" are very few because most times our freedom is diminished by other creatures—usually other people—who impose more or less strong psychological pressures on us. However, he never discusses whether in this world any completely free human acts really exist. Is this "freedom" nothing but an ideal model? McCabe does not seem to follow Augustine, who says that, after the fall, human beings *non possunt non peccare*, that is, they cannot avoid sinning and are thus unable to experience real freedom.[31] On this point, McCabe agrees with Victor White, who, although he had studied Jungian psychoanalysis and had been very impressed by the idea of "mental illness," nevertheless kept a distinction: psychotherapy deals with misfortunes, confession deals with misdeeds.[32] This implies that the psychotherapist can ignore the bad actions (a more or less free "evil done") of his patients and the confessor can ignore the mental illnesses (more or less heavy "evil suffered") of his penitents.

I think that this distinction between evil done and evil suffered was so important to McCabe for two reasons. The first one, more formal, is that Aquinas states that God is not a cause of *malum culpae*, whereas he is a cause of *malum poenae*.[33] I say "more formal" because, as we will see later, while developing his reflections on the problem of evil, McCabe forgets any distinction between the two evils in their relationships with divine causality. The second reason, more substantial, is his concern in defending the goodness of the material world from any spiritualistic and "Manichaean" charge.

30. Lewis, *The Problem of Pain*, 117.

31. Augustine, *On Correction and Grace* 12, 33.

32. White, *God and the Unconscious*, 166.

33. Aquinas, *ST*, I, qu. 48, art. 6.

MANICHAEISM?

One Manichaean point that McCabe is keen on is its idea of life as a dramatic strife, against any easy "Pelagian"[34] optimism: "we help to create heaven by failing to make it."[35] He says that, according to John's Gospel, the world cannot be improved but has to be destroyed: salvation is *from* the world; today perhaps we can understand better this gospel because we are more aware of the complex interconnections of evil, a whole system of human exploitation[36] in the meaning of our lives, because now the meaning of life lies in what power we can exercise.[37]

However, from the Manichaean panoply McCabe does not take any contempt of matter.[38] The rational animal does not attain its own proper evil (moral evil, sin) because of the materiality of the world:

> In the case of a human being the naturalness of vital activities like eating and the preservation of life depends in turn on something higher. Sometimes it will be natural to satisfy the appetite for food; sometimes it will be equally natural to starve to death; for "natural" in this case means "in accordance with reason" or "with a view to the *bonum universale*" (universal good).[39]

How is it possible to integrate these two elements (no to any contempt of our material world, yes to a "warfare" between good and evil within the moral sphere)? Jung had given two suggestions to McCabe's mentor Victor White, who too one-sidedly entrenched himself on the concept of evil as *privatio boni* and had accused his Swiss friend of holding a "quasi-Manichaean dualism": (1) we should take into account the existence of the devil; (2) we should avoid confusing the metaphysical plan with the psychological one:

> This *privatio boni* business is odious to me on account of its dangerous consequences: it causes a negative inflation of man, who can't help imagining himself, if not as the source of the Evil, at least as a great destroyer, capable of devastating God's beautiful creation. This doctrine produces Luciferian vanity and

---

34. McCabe, "Christ and Politics," in *God Still Matters,* 174: a liberal and moderate person could be called "Pelagian."

35. McCabe, "Christ and Politics," in *God Still Matters,* 181.

36. McCabe, "Christ and Politics," in *God Still Matters,* 168–69.

37. McCabe, "Mammon and Thanksgiving," in *God, Christ and Us,* 136.

38. McCabe, "Christ and Politics," in *God Still Matters,* 168–69. In his gospel, John may reject "the world," but by the word "world" he does *not* mean the earth, nature, the material things around us. He refers to human societies that are embroiled in sin.

39. McCabe, *God and Evil,* 86.

is also greatly responsible for the fatal underrating of the human soul being the original abode of Evil. It gives a monstrous importance to the soul and not a word about on whose account the presence of the Serpent in paradise belongs! The question of Good and Evil, so far as I am concerned with it, has nothing to do with metaphysics; it is only a concern of psychology.[40]

Jung criticizes White because of the exaggerated importance he gives to human "free will" as the main cause of moral evil, without taking into account "structural" evils, both unconscious and super-personal (not by chance Jung mentions the "Serpent" present in the description of original sin), and, moreover, he underlines how the typical Manichaean metaphysical dilemma (evil matter/good spirit) should not be taken into account at all, because evil is something that concerns only our experience of human life (psychological issue), which is an indissoluble unity of so-called "matter" (the human body) and so-called "spirit" (the human soul).

To summarize: when engaging the problem of evil White was in favor of both *privatio boni* and free will; Jung was against both *privatio boni* and free will; McCabe was in favor of *privatio boni* and against free will.

THE PRESENCE OF EVIL

One typical Jewish-Christian concept that tends to integrate those two elements and, thus, to get away from Manichaean dualism is the existence of the devil and of his deeds. The devil is a creature, not the god of evil, but he is a non-human wicked creature who affects nature, and in particular human nature. He is a "spirit" and therefore not related to the alleged badness of matter. However, this creature worsens the world, even in its material aspects, and, therefore, for instance, in McCabe's philosophy, can provide an escape from the too narrow optimistic view of the zero-sum relationship between lambs and wolves. We could observe that, on this topic, McCabe takes sides with Jung more than with White. But, also, that he contradicts his zero-sum view related to a "natural" world where there are "good" predators and "good" prey. In fact, the devil, despite being just as natural a creature as a lion, is not good at all and does not "gain" from his evil deeds.

McCabe observes that every sickness is to be fought because it comes from the power of Satan; the patient is somehow in the hands of Satan. A person can be morally improved while fighting against a sickness but that happens precisely because it is his enemy, because it degrades him, and

---

40. Carl Gustav Jung, reported by Figueiredo, *C. G. Jung, Father Victor White and Privatio Boni.*

Satan's power is devoted to the degradation of man and to his unhappi-
ness. Every cure against sickness is a setback for Satan's realm:[41] "it is part of
the Christian mission to wage war against his [Satan's] power on earth; the
Christian ministry of healing is part of this war."[42]

Who is Satan? From previous passages we could think that McCabe
holds the traditional doctrine about a personal autonomous existence of the
devil. In other passages, however, he seems to suggest that Satan is built up
by human sin:

> Sin is something that changes God into a projection of our guilt,
> so that we don't see the real God at all; all we see is some kind
> of judge. God (the whole meaning and purpose and point of
> our existence) has become a condemnation of us. God has been
> turned into Satan, the accuser of man, the paymaster, the one
> who weighs our deeds and condemns us. . . . It is very odd that
> so much casual Christian thinking should be worship of Satan,
> that we should think of the punitive satanic God as the only God
> available to the sinner.[43]

The sinners are not aware of being sinners and they find many ways
to excuse themselves. In hell the conversation is about the mistake made by
God because they are really good persons; the boredom of this conversation
is the pain of hell, but the thing that makes hell to be hell is that God cannot
be seen: they only see that vengeful god who is Satan.[44]

McCabe does not seem sure as to what Satan is. However, whether he
is an autonomous creature or a structure of human sin, in any case the devil
holds a power over the world that cannot allow us to be optimistic: it is an
illusion that we can bring about a just world order, because the world is still
in the power of the Prince of this World. Satan has fallen from heaven on
earth and the faithful Christian can expect nothing but persecutions by his
agents.[45]

On one point, however, McCabe does not doubt: human life is much
more tragic than humanism holds. Although the moral philosopher recognizes that there are moments when a person, to keep his or her morality,
must choose to die and so must be heroic, nonetheless self-control (from
Aristotelian ethics) is concerned with life whereas Christian self-denial is
concerned with death. All of us should die in Christ, regardless whether

41. McCabe, *The New Creation*, 81, 84–85.

42. McCabe, *The New Creation*, 87.

43. McCabe, "Forgiveness," in *Faith within Reason*, 156.

44. McCabe, "Forgiveness," in *Faith within Reason*, 156.

45. McCabe, "Christ and Politics," in *God Still Matters*, 87.

publicly, as the martyrs do, or privately; the same giving up of life is asked of all of us.[46] Because of the distortion of creation made by sin, the passage from perishable flesh to the new divine life is not a smooth movement from the old to the new: "in a fallen world sacrifice implies dying to the profane order to belong to the sacred." All men are asked to give up their lives: there is no casual death but only a choice between martyrdom and betrayal.[47] Our hope is different from optimism, because there is not an automatic mechanism by which we are bound to progress regardless of how we struggle.[48]

GOD'S OMNIPOTENCE

In addition to Satan and the tragedy of human life, another aspect that distances McCabe from liberal humanism is his view on what God's omnipotence is and its relationship to human "free will."[49]

Out of the three horns of Epicurus' dilemma, McCabe states that evil is not illusory, and that God is fully omnipotent; therefore, as we will see later, he must discuss the concept of God's goodness.[50] Brian Davies observes a paradox: both atheists such as J. L. Mackie and theists such as Jürgen Moltmann share the idea that God is not omnipotent.[51] Whereas McCabe strongly disagrees: wherever something is, there God is; whenever something acts, then God acts.[52]

In general:

> Someone, who can only prevent an evil by committing another evil, lacks the means of preventing the first one; such a person is indeed not wicked for tolerating the evil. Nevertheless, to be in a position in which one can only prevent an evil by committing another is to be of limited power, for it is always possible to imagine another way of preventing the evil, which a more powerful being could use. It is always possible to imagine that

---

46. McCabe, *New Creation*, 75–76.

47. McCabe, *New Creation*, 125, 127.

48. McCabe, *God, Christ and Us*, 19.

49. A liberal point of view underlines the responsibility of Christians; everyone is free to make his own free decision; the world is not an awful place; this is the idea of liberal progressive Christians. McCabe, "Original Sin," 166–67.

50. See Yaure, "The Problem of Evil," 104.

51. Davies, *The Reality of God,* 26.

52. McCabe, "On Evil," 86.

a miracle might occur. If we are to excuse God's inactivity on these grounds, we are admitting that his power is limited.[53]

In particular, the "free will" defence—adopted by many philosophical theologians, such as Alvin Plantinga—applies general Hegelian ideas to the case of human beings: God, in order to obtain a higher good (human freedom) tolerates those evils that stem from their bad actions. On this point, McCabe agrees with atheists such as Mackie and Flew and argues that this defence is "worthless."[54] In fact:

> in determining whether something is free or not (whether, for example, a man is acting freely or under compulsion, whether external or internal) no reference is made to God. Someone who does not know that God exists can make this judgement as well as someone who does. It follows that to be free does not mean to be independent of God.[55]

McCabe rejects the free will theory because he thinks that God is able to do everything, whereas if there was so-called free will, understood in a libertarian sense, God would be unable to control the activities of human beings and this would be a limitation of his omnipotence. God cannot do things that afterwards he is not able to control, because that would be a logical impossibility: "creature outside the control of an omnipotent God" is as self-contradictory a notion as "square circle." Human free acts are determined in the same way as other events in the world, but they are determined directly by God.[56]

What does this mean? That, if an action is truly free (assuming the real existence of completely free human acts), this would mean that no other creatures interfere with that act, but God causes the existence of that act because he is the first cause of all the universe. In fact, my action is free in so far as an act of mine is due only to myself and is not due to other causes, *apart* from God's causation, because his causality is unique, he is not an outside cause in the sense that other creatures are.

Causality is similar to spatial presence: created causes compete with each other; usually an activity is due in part to me and in part to other causes that make a difference to my activity: my activity is like this, say, though it would have been like that but for the interference of some other causes. Thus, the more other causes operate the less responsible I am, the

---

53. McCabe, *God and Evil*, 3–4.
54. McCabe, "On Evil," 68.
55. McCabe, *God and Evil*, 10.
56. McCabe, "On Evil," 71, 73.

less free, "but the activity of God does not make any difference to my activity. It makes it what it is in the first place."[57]

McCabe therefore maintains that he cannot use the freewill defence, because all human acts, free or not free, are due to God. Moreover, if God were less than omnipotent (able to do something but not everything) he would be the most wicked creature of all,[58] because, then, he would be a cause internal to the world, and he could operate changes in the world in order to lower suffering and injustice, but he does not, unlike, say, comic-book heroes such as Superman, who save the victims of criminals (as I have already said).

This way, McCabe escapes that criticism that White received from Jung, that is that *privatio boni* doctrine gives too much importance to human agency.[59] Whereas McCabe—while underlining God's omnipotence, refusing the "freewill defence" (by contrast with White), and maintaining *privatio boni* doctrine (in keeping with White and in opposition to Jung)— focuses on the problem of God's goodness, an issue that White had not treated.

HOW EVIL IS CAUSED

What kind of cause produces evil? Aquinas answers this way:

> Only good can be a cause; because nothing can be a cause except inasmuch as it is a being, and every being, as such, is good. . . . But evil has no formal cause, rather is it a privation of form; likewise, neither has it a final cause, but rather is it a privation of order to the proper end; since not only the end has the nature of good, but also the useful, which is ordered to the end. Evil, however, has a cause by way of an agent, not directly, but accidentally.[60]

While saying that evil does stem from good, but not by either formal cause (quality) or final cause (purpose), Aquinas refuses Manichaeism; while saying that good is evil's material cause in particular, Aquinas does not admit an autonomous existence of evil; while saying that good is efficient cause of evil only *per accidens,* he escapes pantheistic emanationism, which used to be Neoplatonic in his times and Hegelian in ours.

57. McCabe, "On Evil," 73–74.

58. McCabe, "On Evil," 78.

59. Jung (reported in Figueiredo, *C. G. Jung, Father Victor White and Privatio Boni*).

60. Aquinas, *ST*, I, qu. 49, art. 1.

On the first three causes McCabe repeats Aquinas' ideas:

> two of these questions (concerning formal and final causality) do not arise in the case of evil, which is a privation of form and of due finality. Evil is, so to say, precisely recognised by the inapplicability of these questions. Evil as we have already seen, must necessarily be subjected in good. Nothing can be sheerly evil, since a privation must be a privation of and in something. This suffices to answer our question about the material cause of evil.[61]

Regarding efficient cause, he wants to provide a linguistic interpretation, in order to suggest that evil does not have any real (efficient) cause:

> when we say that evil has a cause *per accidens* we do not mean that it partly has a cause, or that it has an indirect cause; we mean that as such it has no cause but that we speak as though it had one.[62]

PRIVATIO BONI

McCabe specifies that "evil" does not mean "wickedness," but "badness," like in the sentence "this washing-machine does not work well, it is a bad one." "Badness" is not a thing, such as milk or plastic, something that a cow or man or God can make, it is a characteristic of things. So God is not accused of having made badness (which does not exist) but of having made bad things just as he made red things. However, badness is not like redness because it varies from thing to thing.

> [I]f you know what is like for an apple to be red then you more or less know what is like for a pencil or a nose to be red. But this doesn't work with badness; if you know what is it is like for a deckchair to be a bad deckchair you do not for that reason know what it is like for a grape to be a bad grape. A bad deckchair collapses when you sit down, but the fact that a grape collapses when you sit on it is not what would show it to be a bad grape.[63]

---

61. McCabe, *God and Evil*, 113.

62. McCabe, *God and Evil*, 114; on the same page: "To ask why someone is in the unnatural state of blindness, is to ask what natural effects of other things (germs or other causes) have produced this state in that person. When we ask for the cause of an evil, we reply by giving the cause of some good things that happen to be evil for this other thing."

63. McCabe, *God Matters*, 28.

Let us observe that badness is less specific than goodness, that is, there is just one kind of good washing-machine, whereas there are many kinds of bad ones (those that leak water, those which do not start the cycle, those that give electric shocks). Moreover, badness is negative and parasitic of goodness: you cannot have badness if there is not at least a little bit of goodness left.[64]

That evil/badness is an absence and failure does not mean that evil is not real: it means that *in itself* it does not exist, but as an absence in what exists it is a *real absence*.[65] This definition by McCabe could seem only a verbal expedient, as well as his going back to those two different meanings of *esse* distinguished by Aquinas (which I analyzed in my previous chapter on the "Knowability of God"):

> a proposition which consists in a composition that we indicate by using the word "is"; this is the sense of "being" which corresponds to the question "Is it the case that . . . ?" It is in this sense that we say that blindness is in the eye, or that any other deprivation is wherever it is. And it is in this sense that evil is said to be.[66]

However, McCabe, as usual, provides examples: the omnipotence of God means that everything that happens is due to God; however, we cannot say that, when something is not happening, its not happening is brought about by God; for example, that the reality of a non-existing giraffe in this room is brought about by God.[67] More interesting is when an absence concerns what we expect to be but is not: if I say that a tree has no branches this adds to our knowledge, whereas if I say this fountain pen has no branches, this does not add anything that we do not know already. Where is God in the spoiled tree? In the trunk and in the roots, in the air that occupies the space where the branches would be: but we cannot say that he is where there is the absence of the branches, he is not there because the absence is nowhere.[68] As for the human beings, I will present McCabe's ideas about free will and sin in the chapters on anthropology and Christology respectively.

Since creation is not a change, it is not possible to create well or badly:

> "Before" creation there was not only no chair, but there was no possibility of a chair (except in the sense that God eternally

---

64. McCabe, "Evil," 28, 30.

65. McCabe, "On Evil," 85.

66. Aquinas, *ST*, I, qu. 48, art 2, reported by McCabe, *God and Evil*, 62.

67. McCabe, "On Evil," 73.

68. McCabe, "On Evil," 86–87.

intended to create the chair and its possibility also) and so nothing can be made of the question "Does this created thing conform to the requirements for this kind of thing?" . . . It is not
because God is kindly and loving that he cannot create a defective thing formally speaking (though of course he can and did
create a world containing defective things). It is because defect
and lack of defect are expressions that can only have application
after creation.[69]

No thing is defective in relation to God, not because defect is an illusion, in the same way that although things are temporally related to one
another but not to God, this fact does not make time be an illusion:[70]

To say that things are not defective in their relation to God is not
to say that they are perfect or undefective, so that it would be a
mistake to regard them as "really" defective. Rather, it is to say
that "defective" and "non-defective" are not appropriate words
for speaking of the relation of a thing to its creator. This does not
make these words inappropriate in their own created sphere.[71]

Just as we cannot accuse God of not having created well, so we cannot
accuse him of being negligent because he does not prevent evils that happen
in this world. In fact, neglect is a lack (*privatio*) that prevents every nature
from passing from potency to act. However, God is pure act, he does not
become anything and, therefore, he cannot interrupt the actuation of his
nature because of a neglect.[72]

How can we evaluate McCabe's renewal of the *privatio boni* traditional
doctrine?

Jung warned White: this doctrine diminishes the importance of evil
and, for example, it prevents us from taking seriously important psychological realities such as the so-called "Shadow."[73] This interest for human psychology was not McCabe's concern. Here we see McCabe using this *privatio
boni* doctrine in order to underline the "uniqueness" of the Creator God's
causality, a uniqueness that implies a similarly unique concept of divine
"goodness," as we will see soon.

Nevertheless, I think that in his thought on the problem of evil an
important element is missing or, at least, not sufficiently explicit: an ecologi-
cal and communitarian perspective. A child slaughtered by a totalitarian

69. McCabe, *God and Evil*, 104.

70. McCabe, *God and Evil*, 105.

71. McCabe, *God and Evil*, 105.

72. McCabe, "On Evil," 89–90.

73. Jung, reported in Titus, "The Jung-White letters," 356.

government is not a *privatio* explicable by the means of his theory of a zero-sum dynamics of a natural material world like the lamb/wolf example, because that murder is not "natural." Moreover, it is not explainable thanks to the alleged redemptive force of pain which draws human lives towards a moral growth, because that individual dies before any possible growth. Furthermore, it is not explicable by saying that human actions belong to a special sphere separated from the general worldly causality and from God (in fact, as we have seen, McCabe refuses the freewill defence).

GOD'S GOODNESS

Now Epicurus' three-horned dilemma gets to the point, because McCabe has already stated both a belief in the full omnipotence of God and a full tragic presence of evil in this world: now he has to face the problem of God's goodness.

What is good? Good things do not share common qualities, whereas they share a Creator. If they shared goodness as they share redness, this would mean that we can comprehend the nature of God.[74]

In particular, human beings are not good because they share "goodness," but because, in particular, they possess the cardinal virtues, the intellectual virtues and the theological virtues;[75] if we analyze that, we understand that rational beings, by means of reason, can attain any reality *sub specie universalis* and so get their own perfection in obtaining the universal good, that is God. Therefore, it is logical that God himself cannot be virtuous and tend toward the universal good.[76]

McCabe's main concern is to highlight what is different between God and man, for example by saying that God is unchangeable and therefore human sin does not change God's attitude to us, but our attitude to him: "sin matters enormously to us if we are sinners; it does not matter at all to God."[77] There is a failure in me if I act in a less-than-human way, "but the fact that God has not made me act in a human way is not a failure on his part because this is not what he is for."[78] God, unlike us, is not guilty by neglect, because he does not have obligations to do something; it is not his job to

74. McCabe, *God and Evil*, 59.
75. McCabe, *God and Evil*, 60.
76. McCabe, *God and Evil*, 106; McCabe, "On Evil," 90.
77. McCabe, "Forgiveness," 157.
78. McCabe, "On Evil," 91.

prevent me from sinning; if he had obligations, there would be a greater god that obliged him.[79]

However, an analogy (in this case the attribute of goodness given to both creatures and Creator) is not empty of meaningful contents, but it contains something shared by both the analogical terms.[80] For instance, McCabe suggests when we were small we thought that God was good in the same way that our parents were, nice and cosy and comforting, just as they were; we begin to understand God when we realize that his goodness is different from any other goodness of which we have experience. However, just as a child finds it difficult to understand that his parents are not wicked when they correct him in order to help him, similarly we fail to understand the same about God.

In any case, we must acknowledge that—even after so much reasoning—we remain stuck to the idea that, if we were God, we would behave unlike him; perhaps, McCabe speculates, God acts this way also to make us *aware* that he is different from us.[81]

So radical a reference to the analogical meaning of God's goodness could seem a worthless solution, even though logical. For example, Philip Yaure writes:

> McCabe's argument relies on a construct of the concept of good as it is applied to God (as in "God is good") that puts the essential meaning of the concept beyond our epistemic grasp. . . . McCabe has thus effectively cut himself off from any defence along the lines of omnipotence; there is no sense open to him in which God must sit idly by because of some (questionable) restriction on omnipotence. He instead must reconcile God's goodness directly with the existence of evil in the world. . . . Once a move like McCabe's is made, to put God's goodness beyond the reach of our understanding, the Problem has nothing more to say, because it relies on a creature-usage of goodness. . . . Perhaps McCabe has won the battle and lost the war.[82]

However, I would reply to Yaure: analogy does not mean *absolute* otherness. McCabe specifies that the meaning of the goodness of God or of the word "God" itself derives not from what we know of the nature of God but from what we know of creatures: "it is as though we only had a few

79. McCabe, "Evil," 37.

80. Another way of access is to demonstrate that God is the source of all being (and, so, of all goodness) and that he is always acting.

81. McCabe, "On Evil," 93.

82. Yaure, "The Problem of Evil," 103–4, 108.

fragments of a map of God." Everything we can see on this map points to his goodness, but there are many bits missing in the map: the holes in the map (evil and sin) are spots of it where God is not shown to be good, whereas they are not places where he is shown not to be good. The world is a bad map of God, but it is not the map of a bad God.[83]

83. McCabe, "On Evil," 92.

Philosophy of Human Beings

11

Anthropology

BROAD CONTEXT

Aquinas, in his *ST,* after having treated God as Creator, follows the biblical pattern of the seven days of creation and analyzes creatures, both spiritual ones—that is, the angels—and the physical world, focusing mainly and at length on human beings. One part of this treatise relies mostly on Aristotle's *De anima*[1] and can be called "philosophical anthropology," a philosophical sub-field that, we could note, never lacks a place within twentieth-century neo-Thomistic handbooks. It comes before the exposition of ethics, of which it is a sort of preamble. This, not the theological anthropology, is the part that inspired McCabe and was so cleverly improved by him. Theological anthropology in those decades was improved by some Jesuit theologians: first of all Henri de Lubac in his *Le Mystere du surnaturel* (1965),[2] then Juan Alfaro Jimenez in his *Cristología y antropología* (1973), and then Luis Ladaria in his *Antropología teológica* (1983).[3] The main point of this theological anthropology is to trace the supernatural action of grace since the very beginning of the natural action of

---

1. In questions from 75 to 89, while the following ones rely mostly on the book of Genesis.

2. ET, *The Mystery of the Supernatural,* trans. Rosemary Sheed (1967).

3. Translated into Italian as *Antropologia Teologica* (1986).

creation, and so it conceives human nature as always called to divinization since its very beginning. But McCabe was not interested in it.

Although McCabe dealt with almost all philosophical disciplines, he never wrote a systematic handbook of philosophy. However, he many times and at length wrote about anthropology, beginning in the 1960s with his book *Law, Love and Language*[4] and afterwards adding ideas or repeating himself and providing more or less detailed summaries, thereby showing how much this theme was important to him. Although no commentators have yet published any specific study on McCabe's ideas about philosophical anthropology, and even in the recently published anthology *The McCabe's Reader*[5] only a few pages are dedicated to it, nonetheless McCabe himself had a lot of reasons for dealing with this subject.

As a Thomist, from Victor White he had learnt and realized how it was possible to present Aquinas to contemporary readers in an appealing way: to deliver a persuading exposition of what human nature is, one that convincingly discusses Marxism, existentialism, and positivism, is an important task for a Christian philosopher. As for the *pars destruens*, twentieth-century neo-Thomistic handbooks had indeed started doing it, but, according to McCabe, to an insufficient extent. In particular, against Descartes, the neo-Thomists had been successful in maintaining a sheer refusal of anthropological dualism, so that they could anticipate, McCabe observes, Gilbert Ryle's "ghost in the machine" criticism;[6] however, as for the *pars construens*, they were stuck to both the mindsets and the terminology of thirteenth-century writers.

In the late 1960s, when McCabe became aware that non-Thomist scholars, such as Anthony Kenny and Alasdair MacIntyre, were interested in Aristotelian-Thomistic anthropology, he felt encouraged that he too could escape the neo-Thomistic "ghetto." As an English postwar intellectual, following the example of Elizabeth Anscombe and Peter Geach, McCabe found his main resource in philosophy of language, which, in the Anglophone world especially, acknowledged Wittgenstein as its founder father, at least because of his "second" and "analytical" period works. Probably, as we will see later on in the sections of this chapter that deal with the relationship between thought and speech, McCabe implemented this "analytical" philosophy in the light of European "structuralism," inspired by de Saussure, which was spreading quickly throughout Anglophone countries too.

4. Most times it is not possible to give McCabe's works a date, because in those ones that were published posthumously (the majority) the editor Brian Davies rarely mentions the original sources.

5. Edited by Brian Davies and Paul Kucharski (2016).

6. See McCabe, *God Matters*, 202.

SOUL AND BODY

First of all, he wants to get rid of some widespread misunderstandings. Many think that Christians believe in the existence of the soul as children believe in Father Christmas, that is, something magical: that within the human being there is something invisible—namely the "soul"—that is not subject to decay, and that the body dies while the soul remains unaffected. It is true that *some* Christians, when they do not reflect on their faith, think that the gospel is about saving our souls, because the soul's counterpart, the body, deals with the public world and the realm of Caesar, which passes away. In order not to fuel these mistakes, perhaps we should play down the word "soul," McCabe suggests. Indeed, he says that he himself never used this word while writing a short Catholic catechism.[7]

According to the philosophical vision that best suits Christian faith, however, the "soul" is what distinguishes plants and animals from objects such as stones: *a living thing is something that has the power to move itself;* that is the proper meaning of having a soul.[8] In fact, for a living being having a soul means acting "as a whole and not simply as a set of smaller things that are in contact with each other (as with a machine)," and, therefore, being self-moving and self-controlled. As for us human beings, moreover, this self-control is enhanced by our capacity for expressing our experience of the world by means of language.[9]

It is true that some philosophers maintained that the soul is immortal and thus can exist without a body. However, be that as it may, we must take notice that "I am not my soul" (*mea anima non est ego*): it is not true that at a funeral we bury only the body of our dear one, whereas his "real self" is elsewhere.[10] The immortality of the soul is a completely secondary issue.[11]

More in particular, for a Christian, if a person is identified with his or her immortal soul, as dualist thinkers maintain (Plato, Descartes), then, although it remains true that Jesus is still alive, in this perspective there will be nothing special about that: the mystery of Easter would lose all its dramatic intensity and there will be no reasons for "wonder and rejoicing."[12]

The human body is not a tool; if it was, we should imagine another body using it (dualism arguably implies, despite its protests to the contrary,

---

7. McCabe, "Soul, Life, Machines and Language," in *Faith within Reason*, 123.

8. McCabe, "Soul, Life, Machines and Language," in *Faith within Reason*, 125–26.

9. McCabe, *On Aquinas*, 31.

10. McCabe, *On Aquinas*, 65.

11. McCabe, *Law, Love and Language*, 137.

12. McCabe, "A Sermon for Easter," in *God Still Matters*, 228.

that the soul is an invisible body living inside the visible one). Whereas we must maintain that the human body is communicative in itself.[13] It is different from pens and phones: in fact, we need a body to use them. A telephone for most of the time is an object you can lift, touch, and clean; but when you make a phone call it ceases to be an object in front of you and becomes a means of communication: as it does that, in itself it disappears and becomes a way by which you are with another person. Whereas in the human body it happens in reverse: your human body just occasionally becomes an object you can touch, see and wash, but normally it is a means of communication: "The ordinary way in which you are conscious of being bodily, conscious of 'having a body,' is being conscious of it as your way of being present to the world."[14]

A human body is, moreover, the source of all the other means of communication, which are such because human bodies use them; whereas, nobody uses his or her human body, except in the sense that we may speak of one part used by the whole (for instance, when I use my right hand to comb my hair).[15]

Therefore, the soul is the life of the body, and the body is not the tool of the soul.

MACHINES AND LIVING BEINGS

What is an animated body, i.e., what is a living being? Living beings are organic structures where the parts exist at two levels of language: we can talk of a leg regardless of the rest of the body, we can consider it as muscles, nerves and how they operate, or we can talk of it as an organ, something that has a function towards the whole body, by which an animal walks.[16] We can find these two levels in machines also, and there the second level is the function that a part of the machine accomplishes towards the whole.

However, there is a difference. Let us compare a leopard and a car: since a leopard is a living being, the whole comes first and the parts are just secondary, whereas a car is not living "because we assemble a car from bits which already exist as what they are." Even though "we can dismember a leopard by taking the bits apart, we cannot assemble a leopard simply by adding the bits together." Moreover, when we cut a leg off a leopard it

---

13. McCabe, *Law, Love* and Language, 91.

14 McCabe, *God Still Matters*, 110–11.

15. McCabe, "Easter Vigil," in *God Still Matters*, 110–11.

16. McCabe, "Soul, Life," 131.

becomes a different thing, not a leg any more (whereas, when we disassemble a machine, each of its parts remains the same).[17]

Within a living being, one part can move another part, but we still speak of the way in which the whole moves itself: for instance, although it is true that the brain moves the leg, it is also true that it is the *leopard* that walks, not the brain or the leg.[18]

A living being is a *unity* (a "substance"), whereas machines, since they are imitation-animals, are quasi-unities. Quasi-unities are beings composed by other beings that are not clearly integral parts of the former and could be separated from each other. Also, a constellation of stars, an audience, and a postman are quasi-unites, even though not all of them for the same reasons. For instance, a postman is an *ens per accidens* and not a substance, because the real substance is the individual man, who would continue being a man even if he stopped being a postman.[19]

McCabe, therefore, follows Aristotle's biology-oriented philosophical framework, which is also shared by other Thomists,[20] according to which we can be certain of the existence of very few substances, and almost all of them are living beings. (Consider: in stars, rocks, rivers, clouds, and fires it is hard to find a persuasive rationale of unity.)

THE MEANINGS OF MEANING

Even within machines we find the "function" of one part towards the whole, and McCabe calls the function of a part its "meaning." However, it is within living beings that we more clearly find meaning or significance[21] (perhaps because in living beings any function comes from the whole itself and not from external agents): "a meaning is always the role or function of some part in an organised structure."[22] So, the meaning of the operation of an organ (say the heart or the leg) is "the part it plays in the operation of the whole structure."[23]

There is also another meaning of what a "meaning" is: among the animal's organs there are the senses (sight, hearing, etc.), and these ones, when

---

17. McCabe, "Soul, Life," 127–28.

18. McCabe, "Soul, Life," 126.

19. McCabe, *On Aquinas*, 27–28; 'McCabe, "Soul, Life," 129.

20. For instance, by Sofia Vanni Rovighi: see *Elementi*, vol. 2, 26.

21. McCabe, "Soul, Life," 131.

22. McCabe, "The Logic of Mysticism," in *God Still Matters*, 25.

23. McCabe, *On Aquinas*, 14.

affected by stimuli coming from the external world, make some pieces of the world "meaningful" for the animal.

What is the content of this second meaning of the word "meaning"? It is the "relevance" of that part of the world that is the object of a sensation towards the *active* behavior of the whole animal, which "responds in appropriate ways to its environment, now recognized as significant for it."[24] For example, both the force of gravity and an odor are pieces of the world, but if a cat can indeed behave like an inanimate thing insofar as it is subject to the force of gravity (like a stone), however, when it pounces at a mouse, it moves because it smells and sees, it has sensations, it moves because of what the world *means* to it.[25]

What is the relation between the two meanings of "meaning," that is, between the meaningful organ and the meaningful piece of the world? McCabe argues: "It is because the organs are themselves significant parts of the whole body that what affects them is taken up into the structure of the whole body and is thus meaningful."[26]

There is, also, a third meaning of "meaning," which concerns human beings, as we will see more in detail below: it is the meaning of words. To ask for the meaning of a word is to ask about its relationships to other words, to ask for a definition: just as you do not describe seeing as what goes in the eye itself (the light, that is, some kind of electromagnetic waves), so you do not get a linguistic meaning just from the single word itself, as a mere bunch of sounds; "sensations have to do with the complex behaviour of animals; meanings have to do with complex uses of language."[27] This sentence is not very clear, taken alone: elsewhere, in fact, he writes that words/concepts "interpret" those sensations that, in turn, interpret pieces of the world; he also writes that such intellectual interpretations made by human beings have a "meaning" for their behavior. Whereas, in the sentence quoted above, with its "structuralist" flavor, as if he were a reductionist, he apparently seems to present a "meaning" (a function of a part towards the whole), that relates only to other words, that it, to other parts of the language system.

In any case, we can find a shared feature within all three meanings of "meaning": they are "second-order realities." The meaning of a kidney is not its existence as a bunch of specialised cells, the meaning of a sensation of cold is not the decrease of speed of the air particles around the animal, the meaning of a word is not a bunch of sound vibrations; the meaning of these

24. McCabe, *On Aquinas*, 14.

25. McCabe, "Soul, Life," 134.

26. McCabe, "Soul, Life," 134.

27. McCabe, *The Good Life*, 64.

three things is a "relevance," that is, a particular kind of relationship: an *active* relationship, actually, where A (organ, sensation from the world, word) causes an active reaction in B (organism, sentient animal, linguistic animal).

SENTIENT ANIMALS

Sensation is not in itself a physical reality: if we shine a red light onto a cat's body the redness would be in the cat's fur physically as it would be on any material surface; whereas, the red light shone into the cat's eyes would be in the cat, "as Aquinas would say, 'intentionally,' as a factor in the cat's interpretation of its world." The presence of redness in the visual sensation of the cat now is not "physical" but is "intentional." We have reached the first level of knowledge, because the cat is not simply red but "is aware of redness."[28] In fact, we can say that an animal can see not because we detect its eyes as one among other physical parts of its body, but because we experience that it behaves differently when there is dark from when there is light.[29] All the senses make the world meaningful for the animal because through them the animal reacts to its environment in appropriate ways, the environment has become significant.[30]

A sensation is a peculiar relation of one physical thing (in this case, the cat) to others:

> Aquinas does not hesitate to say that the perceptions of brute animals are "spiritual," meaning that an animal acts in terms of such relations of relevance and not simply as, say, a billiard ball is pushed physically by another.[31]

In this passage it is worth noticing that, both for Aquinas and McCabe, the word "spiritual" is given a non-modern meaning, which has nothing to do with religion or supernatural features, but means rather "non-material." Let us observe a sheep that, seeing a wolf, tries to escape. The sheep acts because this piece of its environment (the wolf) has a certain meaning for its life: the threat of the wolf, which is a physical entity itself (made of claws, teeth, and muscles), becomes a meaning in the nervous system of the sheep, a motive for its action, because what happens in a part (the sheep's nose and eyes) is relevant for other parts and for the whole. Following Aristotle, we can ponder just how different from each other beings are: a rock is a being

28. McCabe, *On Aquinas*, 14–15.

29. McCabe, "The Logic of Mysticism," in *God Still Matters*, 25.

30. McCabe, "Soul, Life," 133.

31. McCabe, *On Aquinas*, 35–36.

and a relevance is a being. Both of them are non-nothing, but they are so in very different ways. The threat embodied by the wolf is made of bones and fangs, as a sensation is made of "relevance."[32] So, it is non-material, i.e. spiritual.

On the one hand, by the means of their senses, the animals are "open" to the world: an animal sees things as dangerous or exciting or repulsive, it is not surrounded by neutral facts, but by things that matter to it; it has a world that is "an environment organised in terms of significance." However, on the other hand, we can also say that the animal is "closed" within a world organized by its sensory system, that is, in terms of attraction and repulsion, which are more the point of view of the animal, than characteristics of the things in themselves. When we are speaking of a world "in itself" behind or beyond the animal's perception, a world where different things exist on their own right, bestowed with "objective" characteristics, we are just speaking of our (human) world, where ideas/thoughts can catch something of the world in itself and not just its meaning for us as it happens by means of the senses.[33]

To the animals and to us *qua* animals to be alive means to be struc- tured in particular ways—actually the first two meanings of "meaning" we mentioned in the previous section—that are fixed and inherited from the species (whereas "the human animal not only shares in much of this but it operates in structures that are of its own making").[34] Animals are born already equipped with a lot of behavioral tendencies (sexual and others) and all these tendencies are supplied by the species, animals "do not have to learn to be sexually attracted to each other or to make preparations for rearing their young."[35]

These "closed" roles are given by the species: just as we can see claws and teeth as means by which the individual animal survives, so we can see the individual animal as a means by which the species survives.[36] The indi- vidual dog is an organ of the dog species because, just as the dog organism is prior to the dog organs, so the dog species is prior to the individual dog.[37] Since a species is an historical entity (because a dog has ancestry and progeny), all dogs are genetically and not just logically related, unlike the

---

32. McCabe, "Soul, Life," 138–39.

33. McCabe, *Law, Love and Language,* 71–72.

34. McCabe, *On Aquinas,* 45.

35. McCabe, *On Aquinas,* 33.

36. McCabe, "Soul, Life," 137.

37. McCabe, "Soul, Life," 136.

classification of all red things, for instance.[38] Therefore, even if all the members of its species were dead, an individual dog still "is a fragment of a larger whole."[39]

LINGUISTIC ANIMALS
AND THEIR MENTAL FACULTIES

We human beings are animals, and, like many other mammals, we have five external and four interior senses. Every sense belongs to a bodily organism and therefore is itself bodily. Every sense can relate to external world bodies: for instance, by the sense of sight, *a* sheep can see *a* wolf. Every bodily (material) entity is an individual, that is, unique: two identical wolves do not exist, neither do two identical sheep or two identical grains of sand. Therefore, every sensation is something unique.

The five external sense are on the surface of the animal's body, whereas the interior ones are inside, in the brain. The first of the latter set is *sensus communis*, which receives sense-images (the sensations "in act," that is, in the very moment they are produced) and put sight, hearing, smell, and taste in relation with the most fundamental sense, that is, touch. Without *sensus communis* we could not attribute the redness, the smell, and the smoothness of a rose to the same substance. The second interior sense is "imagination" because we humans, like other animals, also seek what is not currently present and affecting us through the external senses; this is the reason why imagination "stores" and preserves images:[40] for instance, into my nervous system I have stored the visual image of the face of this morning's security guard when he was starting an answer to the first question from a group of visitors, and, similar to this one, many billions of other images.

The third interior sense is *sensus aestimativus*, an evaluation of the world that makes us feel both attraction and repulsion for the various sense experiences of our life. The fourth one is "sense-memory": just as imagination stores sense-images, so sense-memory stores the tendencies evoked by evaluation of the world, that is, attraction and repulsion. This memory allows sentient animals to have a sense of the past, and, therefore, an awareness of themselves as individuals. In fact, the images themselves are not connected to autobiography: you can imagine a scene without your presence in

---

38. McCabe, "Soul, Life," 136.

39. McCabe, *Law, Love and Language,* 44.

40. McCabe, *On Aquinas,* 111, 116, 129.

it, whereas to claim to *remember* a scene is related to having been present to it and having reacted to what was around as attractive or repulsive.[41]

However, in certain animals—that is, human beings—there is also another memory, which is not a sense, that is, which is not related to an evaluation of evils and goods as perceived by our senses. In order to distinguish it from sense-memory, we can call it "intellectual memory," because it does not store sensations, but "thoughts." In fact, for instance, I always remember that 2+2=4, regardless of the experiences of my past life; whereas, by means of sense-memory, I can remember the attraction and repulsion I experienced during *that* particular situation of my past life when I learnt that 2+2=4.[42] Therefore, there must be a human mental faculty that is not a sense, and which we can call "intellect" or "thinking."

As we will see better later on, according to McCabe thought and language are just one thing and not two. It is for this reason that McCabe, while describing the mental faculties of "linguistic animals," that is human beings, both follows and modifies that famous and debated distinction between "passive intellect" and "active intellect" that we find in Aristotle's *De Anima*. According to McCabe, the former can be called "receptive mind" and the latter "creative intellect": to have a receptive mind means to be able to have a language and therefore a thought; to have a creative intellect means to make an actual language and understand it with its rules that set certain sounds as symbols of accepted meanings.[43] The coexistence of both faculties allows us to explain two facts: (1) we are not born with a language, and the several natural languages develop separately; (2) however, all languages "are potentially one—in that all are, in principle, inter-translatable."[44]

Another human faculty is "will." By contrast with the prevailing tradition of modern philosophy that describes will as something mysteriously independent from thought, McCabe, in accordance with Aristotelian-Thomistic intellectualism, wants to underline that

> [t]his position is not open to Aquinas, for whom the will is simply our being attracted by the good as it appears to our minds. The will is the "being-attracted" component of practical knowledge. Nonetheless he does not take up a Socratic line. He does agree with Socrates that bad actions in one sense stem

41. McCabe, *On Aquinas*, 135. To the extent that an animal can have something of the virtues of courage and temperance, it can remember better, because these virtues govern how we remember: "what we hide from ourselves and what we are prepared to admit," ibid., 138.

42. McCabe, *On Aquinas*, 138.

43. McCabe, *On Aquinas*, 140.

44. McCabe, *The Good Life*, 83.

from ignorance, but for him it is not only true that will depends on understanding; it is also true that understanding depends on will. We come to know what we try to, or are willing to, find out; and when we have found things out, we consider (put in the forefront of our minds) what we want to consider. We may, instead of considering what we rationally know to be the case, find it pleasanter to be doing something else.[45]

We could summarize saying that "We think of what we are attracted to thinking of, and we are attracted to what we think of."[46] However, in order to speak of "thinking" in relation to will, we should find out what thinking is, and, to start with, we have to distinguish it from the senses.

UNIVERSALS

Even though McCabe never explicitly calls thoughts "universals," he always maintains this stand as an implicit assumption throughout all his arguments about language seen as something substantially different from sense experience.

This stand starts with Plato and was debated and refined by medieval philosophers. A thought (idea, concept) is a "universal," that is, a class, a set, a group, a non-individual entity. The concept of "spoon" is the set or group of some individual entities that exist *qua* individuals (unique, unrepeatable) within the extramental world, but which, within our mental world, we group into the same set because of certain characteristics that we think are present within these individuals. As for this example: "spoon" = "stiff, indented, manual tool meant to bring edible liquids and quasi-liquids towards the mouth during meals."

A concept (idea, thought, "universal") can be predicated of (attributed to) an indefinite number of individuals; that is to say, we can "think" or describe an indefinite number of individuals in the same way; that is to say, we can answer in the same way when, as for each one of these individuals, someone asks the question "What is this?"; that is to say, we can group an indefinite number of individuals into the same set, which is defined and circumscribed by the above listed characteristics. *Universale est quod potest predicari de pluribus.*[47]

---

45. McCabe, *On Aquinas*, 94.
46. McCabe, *On Aquinas*, 94.
47. Aristotle, *De Interpretatione*, 7, 17a39–40.

THE BRAIN AND ITS MIND

I am not aware of any direct influences on McCabe of Karl Popper and John Eccles' book,[48] where the authors refuse the reductionist theory that argues that brain and mind are the same thing, and where, more in particular, Popper defends the existence of what he calls "World Three," which is the interpersonally shared world of all ideas/thoughts in their objective contents. McCabe, instead, explicitly refers to Aquinas and Wittgenstein and, I would argue, implicitly to de Saussure.

McCabe thinks that the brain is an organ meant for many tasks among which are also the enactment of the interior senses, but it is not the organ of thinking: "*Imaginatio* is a sense power, and an operation of the brain. It is a myth that the brain is somehow the 'organ' of thought."[49] Linguistic communication, in fact, is the evidence that proves how an interpersonal sharing of thoughts is possible, whereas, it is impossible to share sensations (and feelings) unless we describe them linguistically, by the means of *universalia*, that is to say, while we think them:

> no configuration or activity of my brain cells could be an idea or concept or meaning; any such configuration would be my private property distinct from yours, just as my toenails.[50]

It is not the brain, but it is language that is

> [t]he nervous system of the human community, . . . the non-inherited but home-made nervous system for interpreting deliveries of the inherited nervous system; . . . a nervous system is a bodily structure we inherit, language is another structure which makes possible the interpretation of our sensations.[51]

If you object that my thinking can be hindered by physical damage my brain can suffer, Aquinas would reply that it happens because thoughts are always related to something bodily, namely the images and the evaluations of the *virtus aestimativa*.[52]

Out in the external world everything is individual, as we have already noticed, and there we can find both a "factor of intelligibility," called "form," and a "factor of unintelligibility" called "matter" that we can reach out to

---

48. Popper and Eccles, *The Self and Its Brain*.

49. McCabe, *On Aquinas*, 131–32.

50. McCabe, *On Aquinas*, 122.

51. McCabe, *On Aquinas*, 67, 143.

52. McCabe, *On Aquinas*, 122.

just with our body.[53] If the latter makes every being an individual, the former is what makes it thought, that is to say, connected to other individuals within a universal. However, the former cannot exist without the latter: no thoughts can exist without being "in some way a return to the interior sense he calls *imaginatio*: the interior bodily sense of what it is like to be sensually aware of the world."[54] For instance, when a person thinks the concept of "mother," he might see the image of his mother's face, or the word "mother" childishly handwritten on a white paper sheet, or whatever other image, but he could never help thinking this concept without conceiving an image at the very same time. This happens always, also with abstract concepts such as "justice" and "logarithm."

McCabe observes that "what Aquinas and Wittgenstein have in common in this matter is that both are concerned to criticize a doctrine which assimilates meanings or concepts to sensations," and repeatedly says that Aquinas "thought that one of Aristotle's greatest achievements was to make a clear division between the two"; and also that, still following Aristotle, Aquinas argues that "understanding a meaning could not be a bodily operation—however much it needs the concurrence of bodily events (*phantasmata*)."[55] Understanding is impossible without the use of material things, however, McCabe adds, understanding is not a function of the material properties of things.[56]

What McCabe does, and both Wittgenstein and de Saussure do not do, is to try to connect with the long-lasting debate about spirituality, separateness, and interpersonality of intellect, which started with Aristotle and continued throughout the subsequent centuries by pagan, Muslim, Jewish, and Christian commentators. Here McCabe is original, despite the fact that what he says might be neither true nor clear.

He argues that according to Aristotle, Aquinas, and others, thoughts have to be related to images. But these thinkers take it just as an empirical fact; whereas, thanks to the philosophy of language, we can improve the theory and explain something about the cause, because the modern interpreters of Aquinas (analytical Thomists) "in explaining the essential connection of thought and language, start from the language end instead of, as Aquinas does, starting from the thought end."[57]

53. McCabe, *On Aquinas*, 40.

54. The so-called *conversio ad phantasmata*.

55. McCabe, *On Aquinas*, 60–61.

56. McCabe, "Soul, Life," 147.

57 McCabe, *On Aquinas*, 132–33.

We analyze understanding in terms of human communication whereas Aquinas analyses communication in terms of understanding, and McCabe thinks that, although this is not a big difference, nevertheless twentieth-century analysis is an improvement on that of the thirteenth century, because now we can better understand why what Aquinas thought is true is in fact true.[58]

What is true? Quite bravely McCabe says:

> to have a concept in the understanding (to have learnt and not forgotten what, say, "hallucinatory" or "custard" means) is not to undergo some modification of your nervous system or any part of your body. It is true that if you have forgotten, this may be due to some malfunctioning of the interior senses which would ordinarily accompany recall, but understanding the concept is not itself an affair of the interior senses but of the mind, the capacity for linguistic meaning.[59]

Here McCabe does not say that *to learn* the meaning of a word does not imply bodily changes: in fact, what Popper too maintains while speaking of his "World Two"—that is, the subjective psychological process of apprehending a concept—is not mentioned; McCabe only says that "to *have learnt* and not forgotten" does not imply material changes.

Therefore, that non-material and separate intellect about which, after Aristotle, many thinkers have written, is neither God nor an angelic intelligence, because it is nothing but the non-material part of human language, or, at least, of the several historical languages that, even though different from one another, can be inter-translated.

Moreover, if such an intellect is nothing but this, it is, like every human thing, limited and dependent. In particular, it absolutely needs the human body and its senses:

> for Aquinas, to know about, to try to understand, an individual we need more than a mind, we need a body and its sensual awareness. If we had no bodies, we might know a great deal of rather beautiful theoretical physics, but it would be indistinguishable from pure mathematics, we would not be able to lay hold on what it was about. Put it another way. The only way to be quite sure a cat is the same cat is to keep your eye on it; it is a matter not of your mind but of your bodily senses.

---

58. McCabe, *On Aquinas*, 132–33.
59. McCabe, *On Aquinas*, 62–63.

We must not forget, however, that, without any intellect, we never could know that this "same" cat is a "cat." Concepts are produced by language and not by external material things: "catness itself does not exist as an item in nature. Catness is, if you like, the intelligibility of the cat."[60]

Anyway, several questions are still open. How is the "inter-personality" of language (which McCabe holds as compatible with Aquinas' thought) different from the "oneness" of active intellect, which was maintained by Averroes and refused by Aquinas? In fact, McCabe, while contrasting these two thinkers, does not clarify the point. Moreover, how does an individual human being relate, by his or her brain (as a bodily organ), to language as something distinguished from him- or herself (and from any other individual)? McCabe says that to acquire a concept an individual has "to be sensually engaged with the world," and also that to interpret the world linguistically he has to interpret it sensually, by "involving the nervous system." However, when a concept has been already learnt, that involvement is not needed any more.

Furthermore, from what we reported previously, the reader probably would think that the individual human being has language/thought in order to communicate with others. How can this communication start and work?

Let us try to answer these questions, while following McCabe in his investigation of particular aspects of a linguistic animal's nature.

WORDS

According both to philosophical tradition and to common sense, concepts seem to be non-material entities. Although McCabe agrees with this, he tries to show how they can be non-material and how much they are related to matter. He quotes Wittgenstein: a concept is "a skill in using a word which has its meaning from its part in the structure of the language."[61] Therefore, if a concept is a part of language, it plays a role within something, a system or structure that, as such, is not material. This role within the structure is indeed related to material signs, but in a free way: our concept of apples is the meaning expressed by the word "apple" or by synonyms; although it is impossible to have a concept before we have words to express it, however, "it is plain that many different words or signs may express the same concept."[62]

McCabe says that, according to Aquinas and Wittgenstein, words are tools. Every tool exists at two levels (as we have already seen speaking

60. McCabe, *On Aquinas*, 139–40.

61. McCabe, *The Good Life*, 84.

62. McCabe, "Aquinas on Trinity," in *God Still Matters*, 47.

about organs); for example, a gun exists in two worlds: considered in isolation as a physical object (the world of percussions, explosions, trajectories)
and considered as a human object (the world of combat, marksmanship,
criminality). However, words are meant to achieve "communication" and
not, at least directly, to modify the physical facts of the world. (Of course,
by my messages to other people, I can indirectly obtain remarkable changes
in physical reality, because these people and their behavior are affected by
my messages.) It is true that by those tools that are my words I can make a
person go out of a room, but not in the same way a tool like a screwdriver
can mend a radio. Words are special tools: in fact, the "second level" of a gun
exists when Fred uses it and shoots, whereas the second level of a word cannot be achieved only by Fred's speech. There is potentially something, i.e.,
communication, that does not depend on Fred only, but needs the potential
understanding of at least one interlocutor.

It might even be said that words are very special tools, unlike, say,
guns. A gun can exist at just the first level (physical) without ever existing at
the second level (meaning). But a word cannot. A word can exist only if it
exists at the second level: "words exist *qua* words because they work at two
levels."[63]

To communicate, on the one hand, means to *share* something with
someone else; on the other hand, it means to share *something*. McCabe calls
it an "interpretation of the world," namely, the intellectual interpretation,
as distinguishable from the sensitive one. Such an interpretation—which
tells us something about how the world is—leans onto bodily entities, but it
does this in a different way from, say, a microscope: it is one thing to use a
microscope to see something more clearly, and a completely other thing to
use language to articulate the world more clearly; in fact, microscopes function because of their material features, whereas words do not work because
of them; "they function as signs because of how we use them, their physical
properties do not really matter."[64]

In fact, we have sensations because our nervous system is affected
by some items from the external world; however, we conceive intellectual
meanings not because of the physical shape of the words but because of the
use we make of the words in the human activity of communication with one
another, which is the heart of human society.[65] The meaning of the words

63. McCabe, "Sacramental Language," in *God Matters*, 166–68. McCabe's remark
does not seem so clear to me, because also a gun *qua gun* (as such, not as a bunch of
metal pieces) exists only because of a purpose—shooting—in the same way a word
exists only because of the purpose of communication.

64. McCabe, "Soul, Life," 146.

65. McCabe, "Soul, Life," 147–48.

is "conventionally" (that is to say, by a sort of agreement) decided by us;[66] symbols are material objects that are not used for their material features but for the meaning (let us remember that for McCabe a meaning is "the role or function of some part in an organised structure") we have given to them conventionally *within a structure*.[67]

What does this mean? In linguistic communication, while we are engaged in a sense experience, by sounds or graphic signs: (1) we "share" with other human beings some "concepts" (*universalia*), that is, groupings of individuals that we perceive by our senses, according to characteristics that we identify as "general," and, in order to achieve this, we have (2) to find an agreement on sounds or other signs, (3) to relate a grouping—for example, "apples"—to larger groupings, for example "fruits," (4) to relate this grouping to less large groupings, such as "red apples," and (5) to separate it from other groupings, for example, from "pears."

McCabe says that language, moreover, is *objective*, by language we flee from the subjectivity of our experience.[68] Perhaps—if we go back to what McCabe says about the meaning/role played by a wolf within the sense experience of a sheep—words are more "objective" than sensations because their first purpose is to connect the sensed objects to one another; that is, to put real individuals into a same group, by identifying some characteristics they have in common with one another; whereas, the first purpose of a sensation is to make me perceive what such an individual experience means *to me*, as a sentient animal.

Another reason why language is "objective" is that it needs an agreement (convention) with many other people, and this plurality of persons makes a word/thought public; whereas, a sensation is private, that is, non-shareable (as we will see better later on).

Within words/thoughts there are some *non-material* relational beings: relations among the individual objects grouped into a concept; relations between different concepts (including, included, and excluded); relations among the human beings who communicate to one another. Yet, as McCabe notices, the use of language implies *material* beings in two ways, because it comes from an interpretation of bodily sensations, and, also, it is expressed by bodily entities, the material sounds and graphic signs of the words.[69]

---

66. I write "a sort of," because it is largely unconscious, as de Saussure noticed.

67. McCabe, "Sense and Sensibility," 146.

68. McCabe, "Sense and Sensibility," 149.

69. McCabe, "Sense and Sensibility," 150.

SPEAKING AND THINKING

In 1921 Wittgenstein in his *Tractatus* still held the commonsense view according to which "language disguises thought." However, already in 1930 in his *Philosophical Grammar* he argued: "when we think of language, there are not meanings going through my mind in addition to verbal expressions." This "new" idea, on the one hand, is certainly remarkably later than de Saussure's *Cours*, published in 1916, where the identity of language and thought was already cleared stated, and, on the other hand, Wittgenstein is never as resolute as de Saussure in denying the existence of thought without language; in fact, still in 1951 in his *Philosophical Investigations* he admits that perhaps some non-linguistic animals are able to think.

McCabe, who never quotes de Saussure in his writings, all the same just like him sharply identifies thought and language. He says that we are "tempted" to think that there are meanings apart from signs, and that they exist at first as "concepts" in our minds, and then are attached to words. However, this description does not clarify anything and, like all temptations, only appears to make things easier (in fact, it saves time and trouble to imagine that there is a separate mental world where there are ideas and meanings), but we must not take this image seriously, because there is not any idea or mind or meaning similar to a material thing only thinner:

> there are no ideas, whether in a Platonic heaven, nor in the human mind . . . , there are just people, things and the ways people are present to each other, and the signs by which they establish this presence, and the meaning *of* this sign, that is the role each sign has in establishing a form of presence. So, roughly speaking, "concept" has to be translated "how this sign plays a part in the language"; "having a mind" has to be translated "being able to be present to others in language," not just by proximity.[70]

McCabe follows Aquinas who maintains that thought never begins "in secret"; it is true that we learn how to think, but we learn it only when we use the non-secret means of communication provided by our society, and, afterwards, we can speak both silently and loudly.[71]

According to McCabe, in human thought there is always communication, therefore even an intra-personal one: when a human being, say, hunts, that means that he hunts because he has some reasons to do that, and to have reasons means that it is as he was *saying* to himself certain things, in this case: hunt! According to McCabe (in keeping with Aquinas), a dog

70. McCabe, "Sacramental Language," 169.
71. McCabe, *Law, Love and Language*, 87.

cannot do that; whereas, a human being can propose reasons to himself, which is identical with talking. When we propose reasons to ourselves, we also could have not proposed them: "it is just this 'is but might not have been' that language exists to express." There is a reason why water flows downhill, but water does not have a reason for doing that, whereas an intention seems to be "a reason for an action that is my own reason, something I propose to myself."[72]

Moreover, it would be anthropomorphic to say that a dog is saying to itself "this is the best thing to do"; in fact, we know that it is impossible because it never happens that a dog says to us that sentence. In dogs as well in us human beings it is impossible to have an invisible interior monologue without any exterior use of language: "it is true in our case that we sometimes have thoughts that we do not express, but this is only because we have thoughts we do express. Music consists partly of silences, but it could not consist entirely of silences."[73]

I think that each of us should try to test this statement ("when it seems that we are thinking without speaking it is just because we are speaking silently") personally and empirically, if we wanted to maintain its truth; in any case, McCabe's opinion about it is clear and sharp.

PRIVATE AND PUBLIC

Language is always what is common and not private, regardless of speaking silently or aloud. Although Aquinas borrows from Augustine the metaphor of interior and exterior, he never says that thoughts are subjective or private, apart from the trivial meaning that I do not always read or talk aloud; for him the spiritual is the communal and is immaterial; this view is the contrary of Descartes', who thinks that the spiritual is the private whereas the material (the body) is the public.[74]

Both Aquinas and Wittgenstein think that there cannot be such a thing as a private language,[75] there is a sharp distinction between individual material sensation and non-individual understanding. It is true that, since all of us human beings belong to the same biological species, "our bodies are similar and our sensations, given a situation, are similar"; nevertheless, you cannot have my sensations but only your own private ones. Thoughts, on the other hand, are different because they are not the private property of

72. McCabe, "Souls, Life," 142.

73. McCabe, *The Good Life*, 70.

74. McCabe, *The Good Life*, 36–37.

75. McCabe, *On Aquinas*, 60

individuals but belong to the language.[76] For example, you cannot feel the same emotions I feel while I drink a glass of Guinness, but everybody means precisely the same by the sentence "drinking a glass of Guinness" because the meaning is part of the language and is not owned by any individual in particular.[77] Even though, given the historicity of language, it could be very difficult to think the same thoughts of Homer or Moses (because we cannot discuss it with them), that would be just failing a task, whereas it is impossible in principle to feel the sensations of Moses or even of the person next door.[78]

Aquinas maintains that what is bodily and material about me constitutes my privacy, my individuality: whereas my intellectual capacities liberate me from the prison of my subjectivity. This fact makes us see how thoughts are distinguishable from other acts of the individual sentient animal and that, therefore, they are a sort of "transcendence" of materiality. Summing up: (1) a single dog exists and acts by itself ; (2) I can sense (see) it by the means of my individual body, but my sensations are just mine; (3) I can share some aspects of my sensations with other human beings and therefore exit my "privacy" only if I raise them up into thoughts/words (universals).

From the first part of his *Discourse on the Method*, we know how much Descartes had been annoyed by his teachers, books, and discussions with other people, and that this experience could have persuaded him that thinking is mainly a private activity. However, his stand is controversial, as McCabe notices: for a Cartesian consciousness is something private, but for an Aristotelian it is the most shared and public thing of all, "no one can have my sensations; everyone can have my thoughts." There is an evidence for this second stand: discussions among people. In fact, a discussion is the test by which we know "whether what I take to be my thoughts really are thoughts—they are not unless they can be shared by others."[79] Of course, we

76. McCabe, *On Aquinas*, 121.

77. McCabe, *On Aquinas*, 59–60.

78. McCabe, *On Aquinas*, 25. "What Aquinas and Wittgenstein have in common in this matter is that both are concerned to criticize a doctrine which assimilates meanings or concepts to sensations. Aquinas thought that one of Aristotle's greatest achievements was to make a clear division between the two and to conclude that understanding a meaning could not be a bodily operation—however much it needs the concurrence of bodily events (*phantasmata*), as is shown by the fact that linguistic intellectual life is impeded by some bodily conditions such as being drunk." McCabe, *On Aquinas*, 60–61.

79. McCabe, *The Good Life*, 72–73, 84. This point reminds me of the main thesis of Karl Popper's book *The Myth of the Framework: In Defence of Science and Rationality*: (1) human discussion is possible (against relativism); (2) human discussion is difficult (against essentialism).

do not always understand each other immediately, and, at the beginning of a discussion, we can have different ideas/terms and be at cross-purposes, but, if we are well disposed, we can correct them while in discussion and reach common ground. It is worth observing that McCabe does not hold that while discussing we can always or most times agree on the same statements, but only that we can understand what they mean, what they are about, and, therefore, decide whether we agree or disagree.

This "transcendence of materiality" (said in a medieval way) and this "flight from the prison of privatness towards the public sphere" (said in a neo-Marxist way from the 1960s) are language characteristics that produce "objective knowledge." Therefore, let us consider again the meaning of "objectivity." It has two aspects: (1) it is objective in that it does not vary in accordance with different individual minds; (2) it is objective in that it belongs more to the object than to the mind.

As for the first aspect, McCabe argues that, if we deny that meanings are some secret thoughts in my head, then we must say that they are independent from our will: meanings are as objective as physical objects. For example, since by words I cannot mean whatever I fancy, I cannot assent to a racial legislation and at the same time say that I believe in an equal society. Another example is the word "transmigration": its meaning is its role in the English language. Even if I thought that "transmigration" means "transfiguration," it does not: "its meaning is there, it resists me" (perhaps it is this fact that produced the "reification" of meaning, the idea that there are meanings somehow and somewhere apart from the uses of language).[80]

As for the second aspect of objectivity, McCabe observes:

> To speak of the world is not merely to express how it makes us feel but how it is and is not. It is our linguistic capacity that makes us able to ask and answer questions and thus (with luck) to grasp truth, to escape from the subjectivity and privacy of feeling into objectivity. And this is because linguistic meanings do not belong to anyone in the way that feelings do; meanings are in the language, which is of its nature both public and common.[81]

Therefore, here is a very philosophical point: language/thought does not have two purposes—escaping from individuality by communicating (finding something in common) with other people and transcending the subjectivity of needs by understanding how objects are in themselves—because,

---

80. McCabe, *Law, Love and Language*, 88–89; McCabe, "Sacramental Language," 169–70.

81. McCabe, *On Aquinas*, 59.

rather, it has only one purpose with two indivisible sides. According to this view, we are able to find something in common (communicate) among us human animals just by understanding something of the world in itself; or, the other way around, we cannot understand something of the world without communicating it to one another.

If this is true, that intra-personal silent dialogue of which we were speaking in the previous section has to be interpreted as both a persistence and a development of many other interpersonal dialogues we already undertook throughout our lives, given that the individual human being is immersed within a linguistic community since his or her birth.[82]

THE MYSTERY OF ORIGINS

How did the linguistic community start? According to Darwin, a new animal population stems from the spreading of an individual variation that proves to be an advantage for living in a local environment. However, linguistic variation does not seem to be similar to biological ones, and this makes the problem of the origin of language difficult to be solved. In 1866 the Linguistic Society of Paris banned future discussions of this topic, "the hardest problem in science."

McCabe holds that such origins are not biological, and to prove this he uses three arguments, one empirical and two logical.

From experience we know that there is a huge difference in behavior between non-linguistic animals and us; moreover, the geneticists say that we differ by less than 2 percent in our genes from chimpanzees; therefore "our genes have very little to do directly with our having a language" (and therefore Richard Dawkins is wrong).[83]

As for his first logical argument, McCabe borrows from Anthony Kenny who thinks it nonsensical that an individual was born with the linguistic "mutation," if there were not already other individuals with the same skill: "meanings exist because of the agreed conventions amongst people."[84] It is not possible that an individual using language had an evolutionary advantage over those without language, because it is hard to understand how a language user could exist before there was a linguistic community.[85]

---

82. So confirming the psychonalytical theory of the "internal objects" (by Freud, Fairbain, Klein, and Winnicott).

83. McCabe, "Sense and Sensibility," 140.

84. McCabe, *On Aquinas*, 139.

85. McCabe, *On Aquinas*, 119.

The second logical argument is the following: to invent a tool for a purpose (e.g., a knife to cut material) you need to conceive the purpose in advance; however, it is impossible that an individual person without a language could conceive a purpose of which language could be the instrument and then "devise language as a tool to achieve that purpose."[86]

Therefore, after having said that the Darwinian pattern of a biologically inheritable non-acquired individual mutation does not suit the origins of language, McCabe suggests another pattern that concerns human groups and suits better another kind of change, history, where also we can find inheritance, even if of a different kind, because it is not biological and does concern acquired characteristics. He says that since homo sapiens did not spring out from the evolution of talented individuals, they must have emerged because of the evolution of "new forms of animal grouping." We should postulate new animal groupings whose ties are due to conventional signs rather than to genetically inherited skills. Language means rationality, which both is a special way of being in a group and makes us persons.[87] In another passage, even more radically he suggests that language is a product of a community, not of an individual.[88]

KNOWLEDGE AND TRUTH

What do we know, anyway? For McCabe, a Cartesian—who dislikes both empiricism and Aristotelianism—would say that we immediately know our own consciousness (that is, our individual mind):

> Descartes thought that our own minds are the thing we know best and are most certain about; getting to know about the material world was much trickier. Aquinas thought the opposite: that the natures of material things were what we knew best and it was very difficult to talk about our mental life (and even more difficult to talk about God).[89]

In fact, an Aristotelian holds a view that is different from both empiricists and Cartesians, who think that the mind is passive and that our ideas are just entities that come directly from the external world (empiricists) or from an innate inheritance (Cartesians). Whereas the Aristotelian thinks that the ideas are "made"; for him or her (similarly to the Kantian thinker)

---

86. McCabe, *On Aquinas*, 120.

87. McCabe, *The Good Life*, 26.

88. McCabe, *Law, Love and Language*, 83

89. McCabe, *On Aquinas*, 19.

the mind is active. "He thinks of understanding not on the model of a sensation, sight, but on the model of an activity, talking," in fact, language is always interpersonal and so-called lonely thinking is nothing but a "kind of talking to yourself." Although Aquinas had understood both the activity and the inter-personality of thought, today we should seek for help from philosophers of language and be explicit that this active and interpersonal thought is nothing but language. McCabe says: "we shall often try to explain what Thomas is getting at by starting from the linguistic end. This is because I think this is more intelligible and less misleading for people in our present age."[90]

In order to acquire knowledge, our language must not be "gibberish" (without grammar, e.g.: "Why how shall the be much?") and nonsensical (without respecting the system of other ideas/words, e.g., "the telephone was hungry"). Furthermore, it must make a statement (and not an exclamation or a question), because only a statement can be either true or false. What activities do we have to accomplish to make true statements and, so, to increase our knowledge? "By living in our world and talking with others, arguing and so on." We could call these activities "experience," had not the empiricists spoiled this word while maintaining that experience is "simply being hit by sense-data."[91]

Since to speak about the world is to describe how it is, in our linguistic activity there are several steps: at first we identify bits of the world to understand their impact on us, but, when in the events of our life together with other people we want to argue or disagree with some of them, it is then we have to pass from mere "descriptions" to "definitions," we have to know *what* we are speaking about, so as not to be at cross purposes.[92] The third step is to look for substances beyond *entia per accidens*, for instance, "what is a man?" and not just "what is a postman?"[93] In fact,

> [i]n ordinary language we have very few words whose meaning is simply what something is, words which simply signify an essence; they are nearly always, as it were, adulterated by some additional accidental information. And this is for the very good reason that we name things not in order to celebrate their essential nature but to indicate our interest in them.[94]

90. McCabe, *On Aquinas*, 20.
91. McCabe, *On Aquinas*, 21–22.
92. McCabe, *On Aquinas*, 17.
93. McCabe, *On Aquinas*, 28.
94. McCabe, *On Aquinas*, 26.

A fourth step in the process of thinking is to correct those mistakes that stem from anthropomorphic projections. Even though we are thinking (and not just sensing), and we provide definitions (and not mere descriptions), and also definitions of substances (and not only of *entia per accidens*), nevertheless, we could all the same project ourselves into the object, that is, project qualities concerning human nature onto non-human entities. The sciences, however, have to correct this tendency so that we can find an arboreal meaning in a tree and not a human one: "it is the business of the scientist to see things for what they are in themselves, not for what they are to man."[95]

According to the Aristotelian tradition, there are three acts of thought: conceiving (concepts), stating (affirmations or negations), and reasoning. McCabe argues that the concept of "elephant" is not anything we can see or paint; that is, it is not the image of an individual "elephant," because, as we have already seen, no individual can be the meaning of a word, "we do not understand concrete objects; we can only experience them as meaningful sensually" and the meanings of a word are "the rules governing its position in a structure."[96] Moreover: "words can address an individual thing as a hammer hits an individual nail, but what they refer to is not what they mean, the meaning of a word is how it refers, not what it points to."[97] Furthermore: "the concept, remember, is not *what* is understood but *how* something is understood."[98] This last sentence recalls closely a passage by Aquinas.[99]

The second act of thought is to connect (affirmation) or to disconnect (negation) two concepts to or from each other. It is here that we can properly find truth; in fact, according to Aristotle's logics, a concept is neither true nor false, and the same applies to reasoning; only a statement can be true or false. McCabe, accordingly, maintains that by language we can always make statements about reality and, moreover, we can always deny them.[100] He argues that the empiricists confuse sense images with concepts, but it is impossible to confuse a sensation or a feeling with a statement: in fact, opposite feelings or sensations cannot coexist, whereas to understand

---

95. McCabe, *The New Creation*, 35–36. In this passage McCabe says, even though not so clearly, that we cannot get rid of human meaning; it finds its refuge in dreams, in so-called "irrational" behavior; there is an unconscious mind and religious sacraments, primitive rituals, and psychiatrists can heal the human psyche because they address that unconscious mind.

96. McCabe, "Sense and Sensibility," 142.

97. McCabe, *On Aquinas*, 110.

98. McCabe, "Aquinas on Trinity," in *God Still Matters*, 47.

99. Aquinas, *ST*, I, qu. 84, rt. 1.

100. McCabe, *The Good Life*, 68.

"the cat is on the mat" is identical to understanding the meaning of "the cat is *not* on the mat" for "to understand a sentence is also to understand its negation." There is not any equivalent of this in sensual experience: you never can feel opposite feelings in the same act of sensation, whereas you always understand opposite meanings by the same act of thought. Negation is "wonderful" because it enables us to receive two opposite possibilities, and therefore it enables us to ask questions and try to find their answers.[101]

The third act of thought is reasoning; that is, to connect statements with one another in order to get a new one, the so-called conclusion. McCabe (like both Kant and Popper) does not think it is the most important act of the mind. It is, however, a widespread commonplace that human intelligence consists in making syllogisms. This popular idea can be called "rationalism" and is dangerous only for the reaction that it provoked, that is, romanticism, because the latter, rightly convinced that human intelligence cannot be reduced to calculation, recommended to leave reason in favor of feelings, emotions, and the "reasons of the heart." But the cause of romantic confusion is the rationalist confusion, which does not recognize that reason at its peak is imaginative. The value of logic (reasoning, making syllogisms, calculating) is only to check the validity of our insights.[102]

However, McCabe cares to specify that our statements about the world are not only and even mostly an operation undertaken by the individual person who, as it were, decides on his or her own to examine the reality around them, but, instead, stem from questions and answers within an interpersonal dialogue:

> It is our linguistic capacity that makes us able to ask and answer questions and thus (with luck) to grasp truth, to escape from the subjectivity and privacy of feeling into objectivity. And this is because linguistic meanings do not belong to anyone in the way that feelings do; meanings are in the language, which is of its nature public and common;[103] . . . we do not grasp truth by having a language but by using it in a particular way: to ask questions and look for answers.[104]

101. McCabe, "Sense and Sensibility," 151.

102. McCabe, *On Aquinas*, 131.

103. McCabe, *On Aquinas*, 59.

104. McCabe, "Sense and Sensibility," 151.

FREEDOM

While treating the theme of freedom, a quality of human nature analyzed for millennia both in philosophy and in theology, McCabe shows his awareness of this history. Even though he does not quote the authors, nevertheless he mentions determinism, Aristotle's theory of habits, Aquinas' doctrine of *non voluntarium*, the debate on the relationship between intellect and will (Buridan), psychoanalytical theories on unconscious drives, and Isaiah Berlin's distinction between negative and positive freedom. On his part, he draws inspirations from these discussions and gives two original contributions that stem from his philosophical theology and his analysis of human beings as linguistic animals.

The starting point is the definition of freedom as "being the cause of one's own acts": an action of Fred is free to the extent it is caused by *Fred himself* and not by somebody or something else.[105]

McCabe takes for granted that in the real world the human person is never endowed with two equally weighed possible choices (the Buridan's ass paradox) and he also takes notice both of what Aquinas says about human will—that it is compatible with several kinds of necessity but is not compatible with constraint[106]—and of Berlin's definition of "negative freedom" (i.e., freedom from interference from other agents). Indeed, someone can, to some extent, cause my actions, thereby diminishing my freedom, and, for example, this is the reason why the first public speech of Jesus was about freedom for the oppressed and the enslaved.[107] Furthermore, not only a person but a thing also can diminish my freedom: if I was under the effect of drugs, to this extent my action would not be free.[108] In this world complete "negative freedom" does not exist: "I doubt whether there are any completely free human actions: we are all to a great extent determined by factors outside our control and in ways that we are not conscious of."[109]

Nevertheless, McCabe maintains that to some extent a human person is spontaneous and "negatively" free. However, even though a part of my actions is not caused by causes other than me, this does not imply that I behave randomly or arbitrarily (without any cause); in fact, to some extent I can be the cause of myself. Therefore, McCabe analyses what Berlin called "positive" freedom: free actions are actions motivated and done for reasons

---

105. McCabe, "Freedom," *God Matters*, 11.

106. Aquinas, *ST*, pars I, qu. 82, art. 1.

107. McCabe, "Freedom," in *Faith within Reason*, 163.

108. McCabe, "Freedom," in *God Matters*, 11.

109. McCabe, "Freedom," in *God Matters*, 12.

I have, these reasons stem from both my moral habits (and therefore from my personality) and the present circumstances of reality and are essential to freedom. Internal causes (reasons, motivations) build up freedom and do not hinder it.[110]

Analyzing the causes of this "positive freedom," that is, of that force or power to act (physical capacities, intellectual skills, psychological strengths, moral purposes), McCabe maintains that this "force" does not come from nothing, but, in reality, comes from others. He dislikes a certain kind of liberalism that holds that we need only negative freedom—freedom from control by other people, freedom from social constraints. Negative freedom is necessary but not sufficient: for instance, the Bible says that just to the extent you follow the Torah, you are freed from the enslavement to the "gods" and, so, to other people; it is the Torah that permits the existence of love.[111] By ourselves, namely, without the ideal and interpersonal aid provided by the "law," we are not able to be free.

Certainly, because in his mind he holds to the Christian "new law" and also some psychoanalytical theories on the development of the personality, McCabe wonders how freedom and love are related to each other. Let us follow his argument: around myself I need some "room" where others do not interfere, but it does not exist by itself; in the real world it is given by other people as a gift and among these gifts there is my personality itself; in this space or room a person "can be" without being urged to behave this way or that other way. In fact, people who do not receive love always try to justify themselves in order to be loved, by possessing wealth or other goods. The root of evil lies in not having been loved or in not recognizing having been loved.[112]

Therefore, it is the "others" who give us this gift of positive freedom, which is the power to act. How is it possible, however, to describe it more closely? Here McCabe links Augustine's idea that an action is free only if it refers to knowledge, with some ideas coming from the philosophy of language: the use of any word—new or old—is "creative" in a sense that having a sensation is not creative; what we *see* is determined by the world around us, whereas what we *say* is not so determined. In fact, we can choose to speak of the world in an indefinite number of ways and in this "indefinite number" is the root of human freedom.[113] Other animals act willingly or unwillingly because their behavior is mediated by knowledge, even though

110. McCabe, "Freedom," in *God Matters*, 13–14.

111. McCabe, "Freedom," in *Faith within Reason*, 164–65.

112. McCabe, "Freedom," in *Faith within Reason*, 165–67.

113. McCabe, "Soul, Life, Machines and Language," in *Faith within Reason*, 149.

sensual, but they cannot behave differently, their system of sensed meanings does not include any negation.[114]

We are attracted by the world as we interpret it; sensual interpretation is shared with our non-linguistic fellow animals, but we have also intellectual interpretation and in both cases the cause of attraction is not only in what we are but also in what we *know*: it is different from what a pen does when we drop it and it falls because of its mass and the force of gravity. Like a dog, we are attracted by a steak because we *see* it, but, unlike the dog, we are, say, also un-attracted by it because of what we *say* of it: it belongs to someone else, it is full of cholesterol, it is made of the flesh of poor animals, it is expensive.[115]

It could be observed that this description of freedom tells us that these many interpretations of a piece of reality, if they are true, are as many links of that piece with other pieces (property, health, compassion, economics), and this multiplicity of links can produce innovations: for example, I do not eat the steak, I do not kill animals anymore, and develop a technology for producing vegetable proteins. The more concepts I am able to use to interpret a piece of reality, the freer I am. "Positive freedom" is knowledge.

The theme of human freedom is traditionally also related to the theological problem of freedom "from" God, as if this was part of Berlin's negative freedom (freedom "from" interference). Many debates throughout the centuries presented God's actions and human actions as if they played a zero-sum game: to the extent that God acts the human being does not, and the other way around. In the chapter on the problem of evil we have already seen how McCabe dismisses this idea. He holds that we need a new view of God, since the "biblical theology" movement[116] mistakenly did not care for "hard thinking" and presented the many biblical "images" of God as literally meaning an individual powerful person who acts within the universe, as if such images were actual ideas about God's nature.

Whereas, for McCabe, humans are not less caused by God than the stones or a dog; to think that we are free because God does not act upon us implies an idolatrous idea of God as an inhabitant of the universe. On the contrary, I am freer than a dog because God more directly acts upon me. God causes the causes that cause the dog to act, and he causes me this way too, but God also causes me "directly." If each creature is itself, free human

114. McCabe, *The Good Life*, 69.

115. McCabe, *The Good Life*, 85.

116. Here McCabe is criticizing a fashion of theology widespread in the second half of twentieth century, which was contrasted with systematic theology and used to be suspicious of "Greek metaphysics."

actions are like a "window on creation," because they are actions of creatures who act by themselves more than other creatures.[117]

According to McCabe, what is really new in the biblical idea of God is that God himself takes the initiative to speak to us and, by faith, we believe that he speaks and that his people answer to him. It is true that in this dialogue we could also think that this God who speaks is an individual person, but this is not so important, whereas, the immediate important result of this faith is the refusal of the "gods" and that human beings take their own responsibility for action.[118] Even though many biblical images or metaphors can make us conceive the idea of God reduced to the level of human beings in order to speak with them as an individual, since God is "not an individual nor a set of individuals," we should conceive the opposite idea of human beings raised up to the level of God.[119]

In conclusion, human beings are free to the extent that they have multiple interpretations of the world, by the means of their intellect. Also, they are free to the extent they have enough "room" to be themselves, room that is a gift from other humans and from God: in fact, you love a person when you realize that she is important for the very reason she is there, for her own sake, not because she is a mere means to satisfy your needs.[120] This gift comes from the "others" as far as they "love" each other, and it comes from "God" in a more mysterious way, which is due to be analyzed when we treat McCabe's ideas on grace.

HUMAN LIFE

To be alive for a human being, McCabe says, means, negatively, not to be three things: a machine, a brute animal, and just a creature. To speak about human life, therefore, we need to deal with organisms, language, and grace: "there is a meaning which belongs to organic structure, the meaning which belongs to a life-story, an enacted narrative, and the meaning which belongs to having the life-story of God."[121] In the third section of this chapter we have already seen the difference between living beings and machines, later on in subsequent chapters we will see how McCabe describes human life as transformed by grace; here we want to analyze his views about the "linguistic animal."

117. McCabe, "Freedom," in *God Matters*, 15, 11, 14.

118. McCabe, "Freedom," in *God Matters*, 15.

119. McCabe, "Freedom," in *God Matters*, 16.

120. McCabe, "Freedom," in *God Matters*, 16.

121. McCabe, *The Good Life*, 58.

A wolf hunts for reasons (e.g., to feed itself and its offspring) that, however, it does not articulate to itself, because its actions are essentially based on its bodily structure. A human being, on the other hand, even though he accomplishes the same actions of the wolf and for the same reasons, does not do this only because of his bodily structure, but because of something he *says* to himself.[122] Although all the rest is material (when I meet a wolf: the wolf's body, my body, my sensations, and the sounds of the words by which I think about the wolf's threat), nevertheless, something else exists that is not material, and namely is my *active* way of using these sounds in order to be able to think; in comparison to this, my sensibility is *passive*.[123]

Human life is more active than the life of other animals also because the latter are somehow bound by biological inheritance to serve the next generation; human beings, in addition to this biological inheritance, have also history and tradition, that is, the inheritance of acquired characteristics: in my own lifetime I can adapt myself to the environment and give new arts and wisdom to the next generation, in a way much faster than is possible in evolution.[124]

Moreover, human life valorizes the individual: although an intertranslatable vocabulary allows an interpersonal communication and an objective knowledge, this is not sufficient because, to interpret the world by thoughts, individual questions are also needed, since we seek answers for our individual lives.[125]

Such characteristics (activity, objective knowledge, and individuality enriched by interpersonality) do not "add" to animal characteristics of hunting, eating, and mating, but *transform* them in depth from inside, and this happens because in every animal act we human beings use symbols.[126] Our animal relationships, such as sexual ones (which have an interpersonal meaning and so are relevant for a community),[127] are transformed so that we not only "produce" the next generation, but our own generation and ourselves as well.[128]

Therefore, we human beings not only live, but also want to understand the importance of our life, by giving it a sense for us and for the others, as if

122. McCabe, *On Aquinas*, 46.

123. McCabe, *On Aquinas*, 4.

124. McCabe, *The Good Life*, 108.

125. McCabe, "Sense and Sensibility," 148–50; McCabe, "The Role of Tradition," in *God Still Matters*, 203–4.

126. McCabe, *On Aquinas,* 45

127. McCabe, *The New Creation*, 99.

128. McCabe, *The Good Life*, 32. See a clear explanation of this point in Turner, *Thomas Aquinas*, Kindle loc. 842–47.

it was a "story." McCabe says, "I shall suggest that living a human life, having a human soul, is being a character in a story, or rather in many stories, and that this belongs to being in a history or rather in many histories."[129]

Since each of us shares this storytelling with other humans, we are related to them within a larger story throughout many generations. To discover my identity I need to tell myself the story that reports my life and also the larger stories within which my life is

> this history [that] is more than a succession of teachings, it is a living succession of people who are not logically connected but biologically and psychologically and sociologically associated and in conflict in a huge diversity of ways.[130]

This story can also be called "tradition." From tradition an individual draws her "identity"; if she lost contact with it, she would forget what she is. This bond of tradition does not imply being conservative or traditionalist, on the contrary: a tradition is something that always changes, much more quickly than biological evolution does, and requires an active engagement from the individual, who is asked to give his or her own contribution to these changes.[131]

For instance, in order to teach moral theology we cannot do that by just repeating what the church has always taught, because it is important to present and discuss agreements and disagreements, and make the students understand "that neither agreement nor disagreement is valuable for its own sake, but only in so far as it is part of arriving a little nearer to the truth."[132]

Moreover, a tradition is indeed a "story," that is to say it is not only a set of acts and habits, but also a comprehension of them and a narration addressed both to the storytellers themselves and to others. In each person the narrative voice develops throughout his life and, therefore, an individual continuously re-writes his autobiography as a community re-writes its history, even though "[t]his is not precisely because the previous autobiography or history was mistaken (though of course it may well have been . . . , but because we find new questions to new answers."[133]

129. McCabe, *On Aquinas*, 51.

130. McCabe, "The Role of Tradition," 210.

131. McCabe, *God Matters*, 138.

132. McCabe, "The Role of Tradition," 199.

133. McCabe, "The Role of Tradition," 201. Therefore, McCabe says that George Orwell caricatures a truth when he says that the rulers of his dystopic fictional world are re-writing past history in order to support the current regime; he was an empiricist for whom the facts are unchangeable (*Law, Love and Language*, 25–26).

Although, usually, the word "tradition" recalls what is "local," that is, different identities of groups where the differences are underlined more than the similarities, as happens to historical languages, McCabe highlights that there exists a "dictionary" that makes all the languages inter-translatable. Why? Because each language (each tradition) has to be "learnt." We are able to learn other languages because we have learnt our own native languages. How? "Living (really or imaginatively) together with those who speak them."[134]

Therefore, within a human being's life there is a polarity between two aspects of language/thought: a shared life of a community according to its tradition, and a movement that goes beyond such a community and renews such a tradition. Because of this polarity McCabe presented the "lion" of a famous sentence by Wittgenstein ("if a lion could talk, we could not understand it") in two different ways. While giving his open lectures in Cambridge in 1968, he underlined the importance of a shared life and argued that, since our empathy is limited and so we cannot share the life of a lion, if it could talk, we could not understand it (because words/universals are based on sensations/feelings, which in this case we would not share).[135] Whereas, in an article published in the same year of his death, McCabe underlined the overcoming of our belonging to a community: our language arises from a particular form of life, but it transcends it, it is not determined by it; so Wittgenstein was wrong, because if a lion could talk that means that he also could transcend his life.[136]

To learn how to think/speak is not like to learn other things, such as breathing, eating, or running: in human beings the media of communication (universals) do not exist in nature, but are created by the animal itself. Children learn the language as personal, a matter of their biography. Although words are rooted within our bodily structure and sensual life, their production stems from the history of a community and enables us to narrate biographies.[137] It is as if McCabe, while underlining how human society produces "media" and how individuals personalize them, was proposing a three-fold structure where one element—the media, that is the "cultural heritage"—both could be distinguishable from the other two (society and individuals) and could make them exist. In other words, McCabe envisages a structure of three parts: (1) the community that hands language on, (2) the individual who uses it selectively for particular purposes, and (3) the

---

134. McCabe, "Sense and Sensibility," 148.
135. McCabe, *Law, Love and Language*, 81.
136. McCabe, "Sense and Sensibility," 149.
137. McCabe, *Law, Love and Language*, 76–77, 79–80, 90.

language itself, which is a "cultural heritage" in the sense that it changes historically and preserves the achievements of human culture. In this structure, language can be distinguished from both community and individuals, and, also, we can say that language is a pre-condition of the existence of both: of a human community qua human, and of human individuals qua human.

However, even though McCabe is well aware of the ancient and medieval debates about agent intellect and possible intellect, he refuses the overvaluation of them by Alexander, Avicenna, and Averroes. Aristotelian tradition distinguishes the "force" of creating universal concepts (agent intellect) from the "storing" of those universal concepts (possible intellect), and most of these thinkers maintain that both intellects are not merely mine or merely yours, but are one in their fundamental interpersonal agency. As we have already seen, for McCabe the interpersonal intellect (in both its functions of creating and storing) is just a human artefact, with all its limits. In particular, it does not guarantee any completeness and any stability of human knowledge. By the interpersonal intellect we are just *in search of* knowledge:

> It is just this "is-but-might-not-have-been" that language exists to express. Whenever I act intentionally it is always possible for you to ask me, "What did you do that for?," "What was the meaning of your action?," "What was it that your act was an act of?," "What story is it a part of?" And whatever answer I give will be informative precisely because there might have been other answers.[138]

However, such a search grants neither security for the already achieved results nor a prediction of future ones:

> the thing that education, maturing, growing up is supposed to be for is to develop your humanity. Of course, children already possess humanity. But it is also something they are reaching towards, something unknown. They must live in their childhood as in a tent, as in a temporary dwelling. They must not cling to it as a permanent possession. If they do, it becomes a hiding place, a way of avoiding the call to set out and grow up. But obeying that call means not only venturing into the unknown. It means venturing into the unexpected.[139]

Within our human life there is always a "development," both in the individual and in the community where he or she lives, and in the cultural

138. McCabe, *On Aquinas*, 47.
139. McCabe, *God, Christ and Us*, 3–4.

heritage that the individuals and their community give to the next generations. This development is not predictable, unlike what positivists think, but
it is not similar to the existentialists' "throwness" because there is an important difference between prediction and hindsight: the former is not possible,
whereas the latter is. For instance, in the growth of our understanding of
the word "love," even though that development was unpredictable, "it must
subsequently be seen as in continuity with what has gone before." In this
continuity the old is both contained and transcended.[140]

Summarizing the several aspects presented above, how does McCabe
describe human life? In life the human person is active (i.e., overcomes pas-
sivity) and, as an individual, interrogates both tradition and community,
without which the person does not have an identity. However, the person
innovates tradition and opens him- or herself to other communities, without being able to predict the actual direction of this future development,
but, also, without forgetting his or her past.

HUMAN COMMUNITY

Human life implies accomplishing "roles" because to be human is to be part
of a society: at one level an individual is more similar to a gear-lever than to
a "red blob."[141] Each of us has our own particular skills: I am good at sing-
ing, she is good at dealing with computers. "But what would make her quite
simply good, what would make her a good person, would be a matter of
how she lives with others."[142] We could even say that society is not a product
of individuals, but, on the contrary, beginning with family, to be raised as
humans we need a society.[143]

To some extent the same happens for other animals, in fact *qua* animals we also are related to and depend on a group, that is, the biological
species. Our species unifies humankind through interfertility; but humankind is also a linguistic community.[144] We could say that to have genes and
to have words are two ways of being part of a community.[145] Usually a wolf
does not kill another wolf, because an automatic inhibition prevents it
from doing this, whereas from his society a human receives prohibitions,

140. McCabe, *Law, Love and Language*, 23.

141. McCabe, *The Good Life*, 26.

142. McCabe, *God, Christ and Us*, 47.

143. McCabe, *The Good Life*, 26.

144. McCabe, *Law, Love and Language*, 37.

145. McCabe, *On Aquinas*, 33.

which—in part—replace inhibitions.[146] Both inhibitions and prohibitions are meant for the welfare of the group, but the former are unconscious (because evolution does not have any detectable purposes), whereas the latter are conscious and historical:[147]

> It seems to me quite plain that a human society is a structure in which the bits are related to the whole in ways quite unlike the ways the bits of a typewriter are related to the machine, or the ways the organs of a body are related to the whole animal, or the ways that individual animals are related to the whole species. It seems to me plain that we historically create the ways in which we relate to each other.[148]

However, even though McCabe underlines the importance of community, he does not want to exaggerate. He is aware both of Avicenna's and Averroes' old theories about the unicity of the intellect and of the more recent doctrines from Marxism and structuralism. He follows Aristotle while maintaining that understanding has no corporeal organ. Nevertheless, he does not think that there is any one and separate intellect, unlike Avicenna and Averroes—the latter being too "impressed by the non-privacy of meanings"—and, interestingly, describes this idea as a Neoplatonic relic.[149] There is here a similarity with structuralism, which mistakenly says that the works of Shakespeare are merely the products of the language and culture of his time.[150] However, this is indeed a mistake similar to the Platonic one that considers the soul as a substance. According to McCabe, the soul is not another organ alongside the eye or the ear. Similarly—against structuralism—we should not say that the operation of speech, a string of words, is made by language itself (as if language was another entity); rather, it is made by an individual speaker acting as an "organ" of the language (of the linguistic community) *qua* organ.[151]

Throughout McCabe's reflections, it surfaces that language is not a "substance" (a separate being that exists by itself); it is not a "person,"[152] but, rather, an "interpersonal" (relational) entity. Perhaps it could be said that the ancient and medieval world were not able to "de-substantialize"

---

146. On this point see also Heron, "McCabe and Aquinas on Love and Natural Law," 12.

147. McCabe, *Law, Love and Language*, 42, 48.

148. McCabe, *On Aquinas*, 50.

149. See the profound comment of Denys Turner, *Thomas Aquinas,* 93–94.

150. McCabe, *On Aquinas*, 63, 140.

151. McCabe, *On Aquinas*, 33.

152. That is, *Naturæ rationalis individua substantia*, according to Boethius.

the intellect and, so, they were obliged to attribute it either only to human individuals (Aquinas) or only to a unified hegemonic mind (Alexander, Avicenna, Averroes), either angelic or divine. Similar to this was Marx's and the structuralists' view. Following their path, however, an essential quality of communitarian life is lost, that is the reciprocity of any relationship between individuals and between an individual and a group.

Every "structure," McCabe observes, be it the family, the church, or whatever other, is "used" by individuals throughout their path towards the ultimate end, because all structures are just "tents, shacks." If we consider them as permanent shelters

> then they become hiding places, ways of evading the summons to receive the real city from the terrible hands of God, ways of refusing to be taken down into Egypt and remade, ways of refusing death and, therefore, of refusing resurrection. For faith is about the way we get to the promised land in the most unexpected and least likely way. Not the prudent and reasonable way, but the very opposite.[153]

Every structure, every collective institution, is unable on its own to account for the essence of human community. It is a task better accomplished by the flourishing of friendship: in it personal stories are unexpected, in it the sharing of life is a reciprocally active behavior and not the unilateral effect of a "form," unlike the development brought about by genetically programming a plant or animal. Friendship is not a unity but a continual unpredictable "quest" for unity.[154]

Friendship does not aim to create a stable community, which is neither possible nor desirable, but to gain a priority over an individual life's purposes: the relationship with my friend is more important than my own life.[155] A (provisional) community and language are the necessary means that allow individuals to achieve this purpose of friendship and therefore fulfil their human nature. Moreover, such a fulfilment is not a state but is a journey: complete humanity is not a thing we receive, it is something we are asked to *achieve*. The human achievement is to arrive to an adequate media of communication with others, therefore is not an individual achievement but is a kind of society among humans, a question of history more than of biography.[156]

---

153. McCabe, *God, Christ and Us*, 4.

154. McCabe, *God, Christ and Us*, 47–48.

155. McCabe, *God, Christ and Us*, 48–49.

156. McCabe, "Transubstantiation," in *God Matters*, 121.

We could summarize this section saying that for McCabe—against any scientistic, ecologistic, or "new age" view—human community is not only biological but is also linguistic, cultural, and political. Against religious devotional individualism—widespread in previous centuries—and against a certain kind of nineteenth-century liberalism, he states that human community is essential to the individual; even though any concrete community is nothing ideal and ultimate; and this is stated against any theocratic clerical ecclesiology, Marxist communism, and nationalist communitarian myths of romanticism.

HARDSHIPS AND TRAGEDIES

Christianity's main symbol is a man, Jesus, hanged on an instrument of torture and death, and this religion states that the core of its faith lies in the mystery of Jesus' passion, death, and resurrection.

Jesus dies as all humans do, but only a few of them die so wickedly killed because of their ideals, and, unlike all others, he rises again. Why the second aspect (which is bound to the third)? Why was the founder of Christianity crucified? McCabe answers that in some way or another we all are crucified.[157] It is characteristic of all humans to struggle for their own ideals, to be unjustly persecuted, and to die. Moreover, somehow these aspects of human life are more important than others, i.e., than achievements and fulfillments in affects, society, and culture.

For example, he considers Florence Nightingale's life and observes that she died many years after her great achievements within human society and in the last years she was not able to speak any more and her mind failed. According to "humanism" her death was not an important event, whereas for a Christian it was the most important moment of her life, much more than those she spent with the British army in the hospitals in Crimea: "for the Christian a man's eternal fate depends not on the balance of good and evil in his life but on whether or not he has in him the power of divine love at his death."[158]

Thus, there are two issues: (1) we are afraid to acknowledge that the deep things in life are suffering and death; (2) since there are indeed other things in human life—"achievements"—we have the task of "making value out of suffering and death amongst other things."[159]

157. McCabe, God Still Matters, 95.

158. McCabe, A New Creation, 123.

159. McCabe, God Still Matters, 95.

On its part, Manichaean dualism's solution puts it simply: affective, political, and cultural achievements are worthless and all the real goods lie within an afterlife subsequent to death, so that: (1) we are told not to fear the loss of those (worthless) achievements, and (2) we can find a meaning in our death because it is the threshold to those real goods. McCabe, in fact, acknowledges that philosophical dualism attracts Christians, because, as humans, they feel themselves "as torn between conflicting poles,"[160] however, he does not think that it is a right solution to handling those two problems (fear of loss, lack of meaning).

To distance ourselves from dualism is not easy at all. For instance, we cannot rely on Darwin's monistic framework, because, in McCabe's opinion, we humans are a "non-adapted" species, for two reasons. The first one is our attitude to death, which is different from that of other animals. McCabe thinks that death is natural to them but not to us:

> because we do not just have a life-time fitting into the rhythms of nature. Rather, we each have a life-story. . . . Every human life is not just a cycle but an unfinished story which we have been telling . . . when we die at the hands of nature, nature is a usurer taking away more than we received from her. Hence our sense of injustice and outrage. . . . We do not just belong to the natural world. We reach beyond it. This is what first of all makes human life mysterious and human death a mystery. And this is why human death is something that needs to be made sense of.[161]

The second reason for our "non-adaptation" is the wickedness of the species towards its own members. Jesus, for example, was a good member of the human species, and he was killed, precisely *because* he was good.[162]

McCabe underlines that Jesus did not belong to a sort of "Cathar" selected group of "clean," "pure" people detached from the world and the shared condition of human life: "He belonged to a family of murderers, cheats, cowards, adulterers and liars. He belonged to us and came to help us."[163]

These two reasons for humans "non-adaptation," however, could find a reciprocal link and, possibly, a solution in Christianity. For McCabe, baptism tells us that we are born to belong to the condemned Christ who is also

160. McCabe, *Law, Love and Language,* 85.

161. McCabe, *God Christ and Us,* 146–47.

162. McCabe, *God Still Matters,* 96: Jesus died of being human. More than that, all humans die, but he was *so* human he *had* to be killed.

163. McCabe, *God Matters,* 249.

the risen Christ.[164] That is to say, if we humans, like Jesus, try to be fully human, we will be "condemned," that is, persecuted and killed by the "world" (i.e., a wicked system or alliance of other humans), but, also, we will "rise again," that is, we will find that final "meaning" of our "human death" that, otherwise, would be meaningless and "unjust":

> It is good news because we believe that precisely by taking on death, by submitting to death out of loving obedience to the demands of that love he called his "Father," he took on death and conquered it. In itself, human death is senseless.[165]

A sacrifice for the sake of the others is meant to respect the very ontological essence of the human person, who does not subsist within past achievements and the expected future ones, but, instead, within the tension between the two: "the self I look at is no longer me, I am not to be found in what is looked at, but in the looking"; to be both alive and myself is to go beyond the self I possess; when Jesus said that only he who loses his life will save it, he was "talking about what it is to be a human being: always to be going beyond a self which has become a possession, a property, something to be proud of."[166]

Such a "looking" concerns both the achievements and the joy that stems from them, because humans naturally seek pleasure and "more real harm is done by not having enough delight and enjoyment in your life than by having unpleasant things happening to you."[167] However, such a look at achievements and joy is not a "possession" of them, but, rather is a "hope" that the "cross" (a sacrificial death) will not destroy them, but, somehow, give them a meaning, which is impossible to get from their own transience and from any deceitful and fragile feeling of pride:[168]

> To believe in the cross, as distinct from knowing it happened or expecting it in the circumstances, is to believe that this challenge to the world at the cost of destruction is not only right but the key to what human life is about.[169]

Such a "belief" has to be justified through a comprehensive ethical survey of "super-natural" virtues (faith, hope, charity), preceded by a treatise on "natural" virtues, which, in turn, stems from an analysis of "natural

164. McCabe, *Law, Love and Language,* 148.
165. McCabe, *God, Christ and Us,* 145.
166. McCabe, *God, Christ and Us,* 75.
167. McCabe, *On Aquinas,* 76.
168. McCabe, *God Still Matters,* 95.
169. McCabe, *God Still Matters,* 97.

law." We will deal with the latter in the next chapter about McCabe's ethics and with the former at the end, while speaking about divine grace.

CONCLUSIONS

Philosophical anthropology can be defined as "a discipline within philosophy that seeks to unify the several empirical investigations of human nature."[170] Brian Davies, while introducing a new anthology of McCabe's writings, concisely says:

> As interested as he was in God, however, McCabe was equally interested in people, in what they are and how they behave. So, his writings contain a lot of material on philosophy of the human person and on ethics. Or perhaps I should say that a lot of them contain material bringing these two subjects together since, for McCabe, our thinking about ethics will significantly depend on what we take people to be.[171]

It is a typical habit of Thomists to treat human nature and ethics in two distinct sections, as Aquinas has done in his *Summa*.[172] McCabe, on his part, sometimes "brings together" the two topics, like in *Law, Love and Language*; at other times he treats anthropology separately, like in his writings collectively published by Brian Davies in *On Aquinas* and in the long article "Sense and Sensibility."

Although, as we noticed at the beginning of this chapter, this part of McCabe's thought has not been investigated yet by the critics, it is well articulated and very original. The short words written by a few commentators rightly underline how in it McCabe intends to link Aquinas to a philosophy of language, namely Wittgenstein's.[173] However, these brief observations do not do justice, by themselves, to the abundance of ideas we have identified. Stephen McKinny says:

> Scholars and students of the other Thomist schools may contest McCabe's approach and thinking, but, given McCabe's mastery of the material, they will find much to admire in this work

---

170. *Encyclopaedia Britannica* online.

171. Davies, "Introduction" to *The McCabe's Reader*.

172. A massive study on it can be found in Pasnau, *Thomas Aquinas on Human Nature*, 75–89.

173. See O'Grady, "McCabe on Aquinas and Wittgenstein," 636, and McKinney, "Aquinas and Philosophical Anthropology," 514.

which, like all authentic philosophical writing, provides great intellectual stimulation and excitement.[174]

Alas, in his short review of *On Aquinas*, McKinny does not find space to develop this correct observation.

McCabe's anthropology provides many structured doctrines. Some of these could prevent philosophers from repeating deadlocks inherited from the past: confusion between images and thoughts; "spirit" seen as a separate substance; a view of freedom where human will is independent from human intellect; statements of human life as an autonomous individual story. Moreover, these doctrines could be effectively received because of the style of McCabe's prose, which is clear, wisely learned, rich in examples and wit and, sometimes, even beautiful.

---

174. McKinny, "Aquinas and Philosophical Anthropology," 514.

12

A System of Ethics

From his anthropology McCabe takes some substantial ideas: human nature is both sensitive and linguistic; humans need to live within a community; both individual and collective life is historical; a sort of tragic non-adaptation is ubiquitous in human life. However, while treating explicitly moral matters, he develops those ideas keeping in mind the "practical" (aimed to action) nature of ethics and of its necessary counterpart, politics. Moreover, he explicitly discusses the classical ethical theories from the philosophical and theological tradition, such as: natural law, the moral relevance of feelings, virtues, the relationship between intellect and will, the incapability of Nature for happiness, and the need of grace, and, therefore, the necessity of a Christian ethics to integrate philosophical arguments.

Was McCabe's effort influential? Stanley Hauerwas wrote: "the change in MacIntyre's views of Aquinas' significance from *After Virtue* to *Whose Justice? Which Rationality?* no doubt is due to many factors, but surely Alasdair's regard for Herbert's reading of Aquinas had some effect."[175]

McCabe deals with ethics incidentally in many writings, for instance in his sermons, but to it he dedicated his book *Law, Love and Language* in the 1960s and he was planning another book, which remained unfinished and was published posthumously under the title *The Good Life.*[176]

---

175. Hauerwas, "An Unpublished Foreword," 292.
176. Davies, "Foreword," in McCabe, *The Good Life*, viii.

There were three reasons why McCabe wanted to write an ethics: his will to oppose both the ethical relativism typically widespread in British culture and an ossified traditionalism present in Catholics handbooks; also, his commitment to replacing the "conscience and free will" theory with Aristotelian virtue ethics. Moreover, his interest in revolutionary politics leaned onto a "tragic" version of ethics, because human good cannot be delivered by a pacific reformist evolution but needs a painful struggle for radical changes.

Brian Davies observed that, although McCabe intended to provide an ethics suitable to both believers and non-believers, all the same, "McCabe, like Aquinas, was not just a secular moral philosopher like Aristotle but was a Christian thinker ultimately concerned about ethics with uniquely Christian notions in mind."[177]

This integration of these two points of view—secular and Christian—by the key concept of "communication" seemed original and powerful to Hauerwas, as we have seen.[178] He writes:

> I think he is right to insist that human morality is about doing what we want, and ethics at its best is but an attempt to assemble reminders to aid us to be what we were created to be, that is, to enjoy life. Not to be missed, however, is Herbert's equal insistence that . . . any theory of ethics that attempts to avoid moral tragedy cannot help but mislead us. Accordingly, Herbert rightly insists that the crucifixion of Christ transforms the problem of ethics—that is, the problem of the significance of human behaviour—into the problem of sin and holiness.[179]

L. Roger Owens, for his part, acknowledges the efficacy of McCabe's criticism of some ethical theories that were widespread in those times ("situation ethics," "proportionalism," "new natural law theory"); however, in his opinion, "McCabe's most important contribution lies in how his theological ethics cannot be separated from his sacramental theology."[180] We shall accordingly return to the sacraments in a later chapter.

177. Davies, "Introduction" to *The McCabe's Reader*, 22.
178. Hauerwas, "An Unpublished Foreword," 291.
179. Hauerwas, "An Unpublished Foreword," 294.
180. Owens, "The Theological Ethics," 572.

WHAT IS ETHICS ALL ABOUT?
A HISTORICAL OVERVIEW

McCabe while discussing all the basic concepts of ethics, addresses all the principal positions held during the history of philosophy. He follows mainly Aristotle and Aquinas, and criticizes other philosophies, such as Platonism,[181] ancient and modern relativism,[182] Stoicism,[183] Kantian legalism,[184] positivism,[185] and pragmatism.[186]

He holds that human reason is historical and not timeless, and we should acknowledge that historically embedded Christianity has played a large part in the making of human decency.

It is true, however, that at times Christians have made methodological mistakes and have confused two distinct sets of issues: "manuals" for ethical life improvement and "rule books." In his comment to *Veritatis Splendor* by John Paul II, McCabe presents a metaphor derived from the game of football:

> If you want to play football well, you will, let us suppose, make use of two books. The first is written by an experienced coach and tells you what the good and bad moves are in the game and how to practise the former and avoid the latter. It aims to help you acquire certain football skills. . . . In fact, as you become more skilled you will refer less and less to the manual. . . . Thus, the book provides for the learner a reliable but not infallible guide to playing good football.
>
> Besides the training manual, however, you will also need another book: you will need the rule book. This will tell you, amongst other things, what moves count as fouls. A foul is a bad or forbidden move, but it is not playing football badly: it is not playing football at all, but pretending to. . . . The rule book defines the context within which we may become skilled players: it in no way helps us to do so.[187]

According to McCabe, it seems that many texts of ethics are written by people who think that their "manual," that is, their thoughts about the

---

181. McCabe, *God Still Matters,* 104.

182. McCabe, *The Good Life,* 3.

183. McCabe, *Law, Love and Language,* 45

184. McCabe, *Law, Love* and Language, 95.

185. McCabe, *On Aquinas,* 52.

186. McCabe, *God and Evil,* 89–90.

187. McCabe, "Manuals and Rule Books," 62.

best ways for living a good life, right or wrong as they may be, are the "rule book," that is, the very few basic requirements (actually, prohibitions) that allow a good life to exist at all. As a result, they put forward too much non-essential advice, pretending that it is essential, and in so doing they crystal-lize mere debatable cultural traditions and hinder both a healthy criticism of them and research into new "really excellent moves."[188]

Moreover, when, back in the 1960s, McCabe was preparing his series of lectures on ethics, he was taking account—even though only to some extent—of the pervasive influence that in those years was coming from the "all-you-need-is-love" ideology. Also, he was maintaining the traditional doctrine of "natural law," even though giving it a minimalistic interpreta-tion (that is, defining it as a rule book, and not as a manual). Furthermore, he underlined how much the good life of the linguistic animal is based on interpersonal communication.

These three points of view (love, law, and language) are not exclusive to one another and McCabe thinks we can accommodate the good of one into the others.[189]

ETHICS AS LOVE?

In the 1960s in Western societies there was a flourishing of so-called "reli-gion of love," to use the words of French intellectual Edgar Morin, who lived in San Diego and Los Angeles in 1969. Some elements were the liberation of sexual behaviors from their previous repression,[190] equality of genders, opposition to war's violence, a general non-judgemental attitude towards youths, homosexuals, communists, drug-users, and so on.

Within Christianity, a versatile idea by Saint Augustine—"love and do whatever you want"—was adopted by the teachers of so-called "situation ethics," which spread quickly, and in 1956 was condemned by the Vatican.[191] For the moralists who followed this theory, good ethical behavior has to be decided time after time on the basis of real circumstances, without be-ing necessarily bound by either a natural law or church rules, but, rather,

---

188. McCabe, "Manuals and Rule Books," 62.

189. McCabe, *Law, Love and Language*, 1–2.

190. Most influential was Herbert Marcuse's book *Eros and Civilization* (1955).

191. *Acta Apostolicae Sedis*, annus XXXXVIII—Series II—Vol. XXIII, 144. In 1966 the Anglican priest Joseph F. Fletcher published his *Situation Ethics: The New Moral-ity*, which was translated into five languages and made this theory popular among the learned public.

being driven by the much more reliable advice that comes from love as one considers a specific and nuanced situation.

McCabe criticizes a fundamental point of this stand, namely "do *whatever*": for the sake of love it is logically impossible to hold that "whatever" behavior can be "loving," because the very phrase "loving behavior" itself is meaningless if there is not at least one non-loving behavior, if there are not any "absolute" prohibitions, even though they may be few.[192] It is, therefore, the job of ancient natural law theory to find out what these non-loving behaviors are.

However, having said that, we see McCabe mainly in favor of this new sensibility so characteristic of his times. He quotes Aquinas who says love is the "form" (soul, life) of the other virtues and without it they are "dead" like the corpse of a dead dog; it is indeed the life of every human behavior qua human:

> Sexual desire in man is a matter of sexual love and if we are to criticise some forms that the satisfaction of this desire takes, it is by criticising their relevance to love. Love is not added to sex; sex without love, or sex with bogus or imitation love, is distorted in itself, one of its essentials is missing.[193]

For McCabe, "love" is a "growing word"; although some words remain still throughout our lives, like "perhaps," others do not and, instead, have a story, which each one of us has to recall. As for "love", it has to be approached from its crudest forms in childhood.[194] Moreover, I cannot predict the further meanings of this word coming into my future life. However, this growth does not imply that there are no paths that cannot be trodden, that there are no actions that are absolutely wicked. It only says that we do not know the future path that will lead us towards a deeper understanding of this word as we grow older.[195]

Mature love, McCabe holds, is not like that between father and son, because this love lacks equality. Taken to extremes, love between non-equals is not actually love.[196] Here, on the one hand, McCabe takes something from Aquinas' idea that charity is a "friendship," that is, a relationship we are used to thinking of as one between equals; on the other hand, he takes something from that "religion of love" of the 1960s, because he says that mature love

192. McCabe, *Law, Love and Language,* 20. Here McCabe is probably exaggerating the tenets of "situation ethics."

193. McCabe, *The New Creation,* 108.

194. McCabe, *Law, Love and Language,* 19.

195. Heron, "McCabe and Aquinas on Love and Natural Law," 4–5.

196. McCabe, *God Still Matters,* 6.

is similar to the erotic feelings of somebody who falls in love.[197] With the outcome of the gospel humans are meant for love: not just caring, but a relationship of equality, recognizing "the otherness and independence of others"; because of this, "all structures of hierarchy, whether overtly benign or exploitative and unjust, become relativized, temporary and irrelevant."[198]

Fundamentally, by love we are freed from fear. Around us there are old "gods" like Astrology and new ones, such as Nationalism, Racism, the Market, the Leader; we should never put our trust in these mundane things, giving them all our heart and worshipping,[199] because in one way or another none of them allows us to be truly ourselves. Nevertheless, we rely on them out of fear, thinking that if we do not worship them we do not matter and are forsaken. Love is the opposite of fear, the more you are deprived of love the more you fall into fear.[200]

In fact, we can understand what means to love ourselves if we focus on the opposite process, that is, not to love ourselves: fear! lack of confidence in oneself, fear that I do not matter, that there is nothing in my innermost self, apart from a role I play or a disguise I wear. So, I become desperate and try to do everything to fill that void and to prevent the others from taking off my masks. We hate those who threaten our self-image and we cannot believe that we are worth living just because we are ourselves.[201]

Now, a human being is not just loved by others, but also loves them. Furthermore, Aristotle famously said (and McCabe agrees) that to love is more characteristic of a human being than to be loved. So, we "need" to love. However, as we have already seen, this act of loving, which is so natural to us, is hindered by others:

> If you don't love you will not be alive, if you love effectively you will be killed.[202] . . . [B]y love . . . you do not rejoice in wrongs but only in what is right. . . . Well, you know what happens to people like that: they are patronised, taken advantage of, used and despised.[203]

---

197. C. S. Lewis had already proposed this point: God's love for humanity is not a senile benevolence, nor an authoritarian father-son relationship, but is more similar to love between man and woman (*The Problem of Pain*, 23–25).

198. McCabe, *God Still Matters*, 5.

199. McCabe, *God Still Matters*, 32, 34.

200. McCabe, *God Still Matters*, 173.

201. McCabe, *God, Christ and Us*, 70.

202. McCabe, *God Still Matters*, 68.

203. McCabe, *God, Christ and Us*, 28.

ETHICS AS LAW

We have already seen that, to give any comprehensible meaning to the word "love," we need to single out at least a few non-loving behaviors. In this way McCabe introduces another point of view, ethics as *law*. When we commit a foul while playing football, we are not just playing badly (and maybe losing the match), we are not playing *at all*! In a similar way, in ethics there must be some behaviors that are always forbidden. For instance, McCabe says that to kill children is absolutely wrong.[204]

What is law? For Aquinas, it is "an ordinance of reason promulgated by competent authority for the sake of common good."[205] Now, the ethical good is not that one of a human being qua football player or doctor, but *qua human*, and God, having created human nature, promulgates a "natural law," which is meant for a human community qua human. It could be defined as a set of innate potentialities belonging to members of humankind since birth; potentialities that, if actualized, bring humans to their fulfilment, but if not, bring them to failure.

How can this natural law be known? *By reason*, holds McCabe, following Aquinas. Although to know the natural law is very difficult, a divine revelation is not necessarily needed.[206] This answer is quite generic, however, because human reason works through different operations, for instance, it knows human laws by consulting documents written by other humans. But what are the "documents" or "sources" of natural law? This knowledge depends on real, existing communities, which are different from one another, and no one of them is that overall community that we could call "humankind." McCabe does not think either that such "humankind" already exists. The weakness of "natural" law theory is to assume too easily that mankind is a community that exists by nature, whereas the unity of humanity is something that we have to move *to*, a *goal* of history.[207] However, although confined to particular communities, moral values are not "relative" and are as objective as meanings of the language; they are, in effect, the meanings of behavior.[208]

In any case, McCabe wants to underline how importantly the "law" adds something to love, mainly an awareness that we are inserted within a community and this necessarily requires rules (human law): to be under a

---

204. McCabe, *Law, Love* and Language, 7–8.

205. Aquinas, *ST*, I-II, qu. 90 art. 4

206. McCabe, *Law, Love* and Language, 59.

207. McCabe, *Law, Love and Language*, 67.

208. McCabe, *Law, Love and Language*, 89.

law means to belong to a community.[209] Why? On the one hand, we realize that, as individuals, we are too weak and not able to decide everything by ourselves because we are not very intelligent, we are too busy and so without enough time to focus on the uncountable problems of life, and also we are too vicious, that is, hindered by warped forces within ourselves that prevent us from undertaking trustworthy paths towards our true good.

On the other hand, even if we were rational, meticulous, and virtuous, still we would need laws because of the problem of predictability. For instance, in a country there are car drivers and the government must issue a law specifying on which side of the road it is mandatory to drive. If such a law was missing, each and every car driver could not "predict" where and in which direction she would encounter traffic and, therefore, to avoid accidents, she should drive very slowly, so that, at least in towns, traffic would be stuck. Absorbed by the work of prediction we would not have time for what we want to do. Therefore, intelligent and virtuous humans still need laws and an authority over the community.[210]

ETHICS AS COMMUNICATION

According to McCabe, communication lies at the foundation of both the individual and society; language/thought has only one purpose with two indivisible sides—escaping from individuality by communicating (finding something in common) with other people and transcending the subjectivity of personal needs by understanding how the objects are in themselves. According to this view, we are able to find something in common (communicate) among us human animals just by understanding something of the world in itself; or, the other way round, we cannot understand something of the world without communicating to one another (see chapter "Anthropology" in this book).

Communication is not only *inter*personal but also *intra*personal. Languages are translatable and thoughts are shareable, even though, while in biological species sexual fertility is in actual fact universal, the moral community is universal only potentially, and in any given moment we are "in the realm of the local."[211]

Because of this paramount feature of human nature, the love model and the law model alone are not sufficient for ethics; we need *a language model* also.

209. McCabe, *Law, Love* and Language, 36.
210. McCabe, *Law, Love and Language,* 50–52.
211. McCabe, *The Good Life,* 32.

Unlike sense-perception, linguistic communication is relevant to ethics because it sets up the moral ideals and the ways to pursue them.[212] Therefore, "[e]thics is just the study of human behaviour insofar as it is a piece of communication, insofar it says something or fails to say something."[213]

Communication can fail when we speak of irrelevant things and waste our and others' time: these are human verbal expressions but do not constitute true communication and therefore are a failure to express oneself, to give and realize oneself; such behavior diminishes life and my existence (in fact, the point of evil is a deprivation of reality).[214] Communication mostly fails while we lie; in fact, to engage in a direct attack on a medium is something sinister. Just as torturing is worse than killing, in the same way, lying is worse than hiding the truth because in the former actions (torture, lying) we attack directly the mediums (body, truth).[215]

More in general, self-expression is different from self-assertion, the latter of which substitutes domination for communication: by fear of becoming vulnerable to others by opening ourselves in communication we seek to control them so that they "fit into our own world." By contrast, real communication "disturbs" our present world because most of the time we prefer to stick to our familiar ways of life.[216]

Communication can succeed, however, when in all ways—words, arts, and sciences—it makes our lifetimes be life stories, so that our lives are in our own hands.[217]

On the one hand, communication successes and failures are the properly *human* good and evil. This is because although other animals, just like humans, can physically kill or protect their peers, *unlike* humans they cannot build a story of good and evil deeds based on communication. On the other hand, there does not exist any privileged communication—distinguishable from other kinds of communication—that we can call "moral" or "ethical":

> [T]here is not such a thing as *the* moral level. Moral judgements do not consist in seeing something at "the moral level" or "in the light of morality"; it consists in the process of trying to see things always at a deeper level . . . Whereas, in some activities a man has not lived in his medium, his action made sense at some

---

212. McCabe, *On Aquinas*, 47

213. McCabe, *Law, Love* and Language, 92.

214. McCabe, *Law, Love* and Language, 101.

215. McCabe, *Law, Love* and Language, 102.

216. McCabe, *Law, Love* and Language, 101.

217. McCabe, *On Aquinas*, 54.

superficial level of meaning but it does not make full human sense.[218]

AFTER VIRTUE

What is this "deeper level"? Since the 1980s both McCabe and MacIntyre maintained a few core ideas in common: that it is worth going back to Aristotelian virtues ethics, because it explains human actions better than the Kantian ethics of rules; that natural moral values are not literally "natural," because they are communitarian and historical; that natural moral values do not provide happiness to the human individuals.

In writings subsequent to *Law, Love and Language*, McCabe extensively treated the virtues ethics coming from the Aristotelian-Thomistic tradition, which is, among other things, an "intellectualist" ethics, that is, based on knowledge, but, also, based on acquisition of "habits" (the virtues), which require educational commitment, steady enforcement of will, a lot of time, and a cooperation with our sentient animal nature. This ethics was forgotten by "modern" authors such as Occam, Descartes and Kant, who underrated both the senses and the intellect, and overrated will:

> The modern campaign in favour of virtue-based ethics, although it began in the 1950s, in Oxford, with the work of a tiny minority of people like Philippa Foot and Elizabeth Anscombe, was given its greatest international boost by Alasdair MacIntyre in *After Virtue*.[219]

Various effects stem from this forgetfulness of virtue ethics. Today, prudence is confused with the pragmatic behavior of the business man who calculate profits and losses.[220] Moreover, moral virtues are confused with techniques and skills, whereas, according to the old doctrine, the former aim at the perfection of the agent (development of the self) and the latter at

---

218. McCabe, *Law, Love and Language*, 97, 100. Unlike the Stoics (who said that virtues and vices are relevant for ethics, while death and life, loneliness and company, pleasure and pain, wealth and poverty, are not relevant for ethics), and the liberal-libertarians (who say that private behaviors that neither affect the public sphere nor harm other individuals are ethically irrelevant), Aquinas (*ST*, Ia-IIae, qu. 18, art. 9)—and after him McCabe too—says that there are no human acts without ethical relevance, since they are always conceived by human reason, which aims towards real goods or false goods (evils).

219. McCabe, *On Aquinas*, 103.

220. McCabe, *On Aquinas*, 104.

the perfection of the product.[221] Furthermore, the very word "virtuous" has been confined to sexual and alcoholic continence, without considering, for instance, other moral issues such as pride and humility. Also, it has been externalized into a sort of social respectability and inserted both into a legalistic framework of blame and praise, and into a hierarchical framework of superiors and inferiors, so that, in any criticism of "philistines" and "bourgeois" it was given a negative meaning. From a modern standpoint perfectly virtuous people seem inhuman, because they allegedly do not have human weaknesses. For McCabe, all this comes from a deep misunderstanding:

> Virtue, whatever else it means, at least means being more human; it would not be virtuous if it did not. Sin, whatever else it means, means being less human, more stiff, cold, proud, selfish, mean, cruel and all the rest of it. It is not in fact our sins that make us attractive. Weakness, of course, is frequently attractive, but just because it is human weakness, that is virtuous weakness. There is a perfectly definite virtue involved in letting yourself be helped by others, and a perfectly definite vice in declining to be helped. What makes us more human is, of course, being more loving.[222]

If we take an overall evaluation of his approach, we see that McCabe recognizes that in the second part of the *Summa*, that is, Aquinas' ethics, there is an "Aristotelian" level where human society is based on friendship (which, on its part, stems from justice and prudence).[223] However, in Aquinas there is also another, Augustinian, level where the "earthly polis is just a shadow of the Kingdom, based not on justice but on agape/caritas"; when he deals with the real depth of human life, he states that its foundation is not ethical (human ideas, aims, initiatives, decisions, commitments, efforts) but is a share in "divine" life.

We have already seen that the human being is a "non adapted animal" for two reasons: the "injustice" of human mortality (unlike that of the other animals) and the contradiction between the expression of the good natural qualities of a human person and the certain opposition undertaken by other humans who want to oppress and destroy such an expression. This is the reason why human virtues are not sufficient and Christians speak about faith, hope, and charity, the *theological* virtues. Following Aquinas, McCabe

---

221. McCabe, *On Aquinas*, 57.

222. McCabe, *God Still Matters*, 96.

223. McCabe, *God Still Matters*, 105, 107.

says that the human moral and intellectual virtues are "transformed" by living together with the theological virtues, and they become "infused."[224]

If Aristotle was right, and together with him the common sense of parents, mentors, teachers, and psychotherapists, his ethics is worth following: we should appreciate and develop through thoughtful decisions and constant practice the good habits of justice, enduring the failures, and aiming at future improvements.

However, this is only one part of the story: our occasional capability to think and decide for the good is not ultimately rooted in us; we are capable because we are inserted into a life-story that is not decided by us, for a purpose we have not set by ourselves and we don't even know. If we are drawn into a deeper level of our lives, what drives our conscious strategies for developing virtues is not practical wisdom but "love," actually "divine love," i.e., something we do not understand. Also, this love that leads the development of virtues is just "the love we have," that is, the love we live in different ways according to the different phases of our life. If this is true, what happens to our laboriously acquired natural virtues?

On this crucial point ("grace does not destroy nature but perfects it") McCabe does not provide an explanation of those difficult texts Aquinas wrote on the relationship between "acquired" and "infused" virtues in *ST*, 2a-2ae,[225] nor even any Socratic understatement of knowing that one does not know.[226] However, I think that it is possible, at least to some extent, to find a solution in McCabe's writings, if we approach this issue from a different point of view. I mean, we should not focus on a timeless moral psychology of the individual, but, rather, we should look at the broader reality of human communities and their history.

When Alasdair MacIntyre was asked whether he was ever influenced by McCabe, he said the only occasion he recalled was when they discussed together the contents of his prospective book *Whose Justice? Which Rationality?*[227] There MacIntyre argues that it is impossible to build up an ethics outside a particular historical community, one among several others. Ethics is indeed based on rationality, but, in reality, we do not have any

---

224. McCabe, *God Still Matters*, 70.

225. Where Aquinas even says that infused cardinal virtues can coexist with contrary acquired vices, for example, infused courage can coexist with acquired cowardice,: *ST*, 2a-2ae, qu. 65, art. 3 ad 2.

226. He just vaguely says that when we receive the infused theological virtues they change the acquired virtues and charity becomes the "form" of all virtues, our life a sharing in divinity (*The Good Life*, 89).

227. MacIntyre's email to me on 28 August 2016.

"universal" rationality. This happens because our communities are local and partial.

HUMANKIND AND OTHER COMMUNITIES

McCabe neatly states that an individual human being can exist, qua human, only within a community, in other words, within a network of interpersonal relationships, bestowed with a certain amount of unity. But in these relationships, there are distortions. Let us pay attention to the super-ego, McCabe says, that voice of conscience that is just an internalized desire to please adults: if I read only because I would feel guilty otherwise, this means that I am unable to enjoy the good of reading for itself and it implies that the educational process has failed.[228] In fact:

> In the early stages of education, a child, with luck, behaves well because she wants to please her parents or teachers or whatever. He or she is "controlled" from outside. Her good acts do not spring immediately from herself, from what she is disposed to do, but for good but extraneous reasons. Her good act is done for a good reason—but it is not her good reason. If she has good parents and/or teachers she will learn to internalize her reasons and become, not just one who does the good thing, but a good person, who simply wants to do what is good and does it by her own decision, of herself. Now it is important to see that an almost exactly similar psychological process can take place with, say, a young Nazi brought up in the Hitler Youth to despise human beings of the "wrong" race.[229]

In this passage McCabe describes the psychology of a human being, regardless of his or her moral commitments. In fact, we see both the aspects by which we evaluate a human being (i.e., the attempt to perform actions in order to please others) and the internalization of the good received from others. However, even the latter is not a guarantee of a truly good life. A young Nazi could live the Nazi ideals out of gratitude and not out of fear of not being accepted, but would nevertheless still acting for a bad reason, even if an internalized, genuine one.[230] In other words, when the young Nazi accomplishes the Nazi ideals out of gratitude he does that because he thinks they are truly good for himself and not just because he fears retaliations if he does not show some actions to the others. However, he can be wrong, that

228. McCabe, *The Good Life*, 47.

229. McCabe, *On Aquinas*, 91–92.

230. McCabe, *On Aquinas*, 98.

is, he can adhere to those ideals, authentically and without a hidden agenda, but, nevertheless, these ideals can be ultimately destructive both for himself and the others. In both the case of the girl and that of the young Nazi the interpersonal bond is mandatory. Both the girl and young Nazi live within their respective communities, identifiable by historical and sociological characteristics. Both of them, however, are human beings, belonging to a larger "community," humankind.

McCabe wants to reshape the traditional universalistic natural law framework, underlining how ethics is both objective (not a matter of individual subjective desire, but of rules in a community) and "relative" because it is related to a particular community or tradition.[231] In fact, although in the biological species sexual fertility is universal, in the moral community we are "in the realm of the local."[232] We do not have a universal brotherhood of the human race and the closest thing we have to such a unity is the solidarity of the poor against their oppression; this solidarity exists but is not enough to establish a universal community.[233] We could even say, together with John's Gospel, that any attempt to state that there is one is a deception.[234]

Although linguistic communities are not as fixed as the biological one and maximise the creativity of their individual members,[235] there are several of them, and each of them is limited, which implies that the individuals within them are limited and imperfect as well. Each particular community nurtures imperfect individuals, supporting their expectations against the "others"; in such communities—which are the norm—love is not sufficient and hatred for "others" is needed as well.[236]

This imperfection, therefore, logically hints at a possible or at least desirable perfection. Roger Owens suitably comments:

> McCabe asks, "How big is my situation? I mean does it mean the people immediately around me, whom I know, or does it extend to everyone who may be affected by my activities?" McCabe

---

231. McCabe, *The Good Life*, 14.

232. McCabe, *The Good Life*, 32.

233. McCabe, *God Matters*, 78–79.

234. McCabe, *God Still Matters*, 170.

235. McCabe, *The Good Life*, 34.

236. McCabe, *Law, Love and Language*, 128. There is not any established awareness that the differences (language, laws, religion, other habits) are only provisional and that the commitment of a particular community should instead be to unite with the others, overriding the differences. Because of the lack of this awareness, the differences are absolutized and the community needs an amount of hostility towards the other communities in order to explain to itself why the other communities are different and make a plurality, why there is not a united humankind yet.

thinks that it belies the bourgeois character of most situation ethics that they draw the situation rather narrowly. They miss that our actions have intelligibility from being situated in the midst of overlapping communities and indeed in the not-yet-fully-achieved community of humanity.[237]

There is not yet any humankind as a structure of meaning, distinguished from the biological species, to which all humans belong:

> In fact, mankind does not form a single linguistic community, and this implies a defect of human communication not only in extension but also in intensity. The fact that mankind is split into fragments which are in imperfect communication with each other means that within these fragments, too, full communication is not achieved. Because I cannot express myself to all men, I cannot fully give myself to any.[238]

Despite the foundation of the United Nations and the so-called globalization of culture and the economy, the manifold differences and conflicts among nations, religions, and other non-geographical communities seem to show the difficulty of achieving the proposed unity.[239]

For McCabe, the relevance of Christianity to human behavior is a matter of politics: we should distance ourselves from an era when the purpose of the Christian was individual salvation, related to "private" virtues. One reason for this is that loving fathers, loyal friends, hardworking and obedient citizens, and chaste spouses can be found also in unjust societies like Hitler's and Stalin's; a second reason is that these types of people are often blind to devastating social injustice and to the agony of those they do not need to include in their societies.[240]

What, then, if any, is the improvement achieved in respect of "legalism" by the virtue-based ethics of *After Virtue,* the writings of McCabe himself, and those of many other later authors? This return to virtue ethics reminds us to consider and value the wonderful capacities of human nature. So, we can explore them and realize how important they are in the pursuit of happiness.

On the one hand, since the moral and intellectual virtues are not widespread and the good communities are often not good enough, many of us to some extent suffer from injustices caused by other people, from mental

---

237. Owens, "The Theological Ethics of Herbert McCabe," 579.

238. McCabe, *Law, Love and Language,* 98–99.

239. McCabe, *Law, Love and Language,* 113.

240. McCabe, *Law, Love and Language,* 162–63.

and physical diseases also, and all of us die. Moreover, to some extent and in different ways, everybody is spoiled by moral vices. Therefore, all of us might need "eschatological" or "post-revolutionary" infused virtues that tend towards "another order" of reality, because, within this order, both our weaknesses and our vices are incurable.

On the other hand, if it is true that, for many and perhaps for everyone, human virtues, although important, are not sufficient for happiness, then it could be said that these virtues, based on prudence and therefore on intellect, are still worth pursuing, at least for one reason. Which one? Because they are necessary to rear better human communities, which, without them, cannot even be born, let alone endure. All of us need a good community around us that supports both us as individuals and others, so that: (a) we can exercise, at least intermittently, the acquired virtues, which always give pleasure to the agent, as opposed to the infused virtues, which often do not[241] (and without a good community it would be impossible to obtain acquired virtues); (b) we do not suffer from too many obstacles that hinder our acceptation of the infused virtues, because the good community wipes out many of those obstacles; (c) we can nurture a hope of further improvement in our lives, because we realize that, since no particular community is yet humankind, perhaps we are actually proceeding towards it.

THE UNIVERSALITY OF PAIN

According to McCabe, there is not such a thing as distinctively Christian ethics, but just ethics;[242] in fact, the so-called teachings of the church in moral matters that seem incompatible with a modern humanist ethic are often just the prejudices of the last generation maintained by conservative and fearful people. To show this, McCabe provides descriptions of human "good life" in those Aristotelian terms that Aquinas assimilated correctly assuming they are universal. A more difficult task is to try to show how Christian ideas such as "the cross," "sin," and the need for "grace" are universal features of human life. Here McCabe explicitly says that the cross is carried by *all* human beings, and not just by Christians, even though only the Christians are articulating this universal truth so explicitly, while pagan religions and secular philosophies are not so aware of it.

McCabe thus tries to show how Christian ethics explains the life of *all* humans, just like Aristotle does, although with important differences. As Aristotle demonstrates, you do not need divine revelation to understand

241. Aquinas, *ST*, Ia-IIae, qu 63, art, 2–4.
242. McCabe, *God Matters*, 19.

that there are many goods and many evils both around you and within you—traditional human wisdom will suffice. Whereas, quite differently, the gospel is not about virtues but about rescue, not about safety but about salvation.[243]

For McCabe, suffering is universally widespread.[244] There are many kinds of pain, physical and psychological: as for the individual, human emotional and imaginative lives are warped and this entails a difficulty in thinking straight.[245] As for the human community, despite the simplistic optimism of some humanists, there is no human community where we are safe and do not suffer from injustices.[246]

Terry Eagleton (a "disciple" of McCabe and a thinker who intensely absorbed the new culture of the 1960s and '70s) from McCabe concludes that at the core of human existence there is this dilemma: if we human beings do not love, we are dead, whereas, if we love enough, we are killed.[247] This very idea suggests that the new universality of ethics cannot be found if we unilaterally focus on acquiring human virtues: whereas, it can be found in this solidarity of sinning, suffering, fighting, journeying, hopeful human communities.

REVOLUTIONS

According to both Aristotelian and Christian ethics, humans struggle to achieve the Ultimate End. However, for all of us, this achievement passes through a "revolutionary" moment or process. McCabe, as a person strongly committed to the public affairs of his times, from the 1960s onward admired many aspects of the political revolutions taking place in Vietnam, Ireland, Cuba, and other Latin American countries. For McCabe, in general, it is important and just to unmask the lie of the powerful and rich that their interests coincide with the interests of the community.[248]

These revolutions, like those of the nineteenth-century in France, Ireland, and Italy, are not just "secular" events, in fact the Christians "belong with them," even though they do not "belong to them" because the Christian revolution extends in greater depth to the "ultimate alienation of

243. McCabe, *God, Christ and Us*, 63–64, 29.

244. McCabe, *God Still Matters*, 95.

245. McCabe, *On Aquinas*, 161.

246. McCabe, *God, Christ and Us*, 143.

247. Eagleton, "Lunging, Flailing, Mispunching" (review of Dawkins' *The God Delusion*).

248. McCabe, *God Matters*, 184.

humans," sin, and the ultimate transformation that is death.[249] The church and the sacraments are not this revolution themselves, but are simply means invented to cope with our lives warped by sin. McCabe thinks that we could agree with Marx who says that religion is a sign of alienation and, when redemption is completed, it will disappear, vision will replace faith, and secular rites, although transformed, will replace the sacred. However, to achieve this, Marx's revolution and Freud's psychoanalysis are not enough, we need to pass through death.[250]

Both the physical end and the ethical end of human life are something future. Therefore, ethics looks into the future; since it is based on hope and is revolutionary, we cannot explain it in terms of the present.[251] While injustice and vice consist in settling for the present and resisting the revolutionary change that beckons us, all the true political and religious prophets have denounced this temptation, which affects everybody.[252]

Taking the political revolutions as a model, McCabe applies their features to our individual lives: in an important moral decision, like in a revolution, we have to ask ourselves "Who am I?" and we must reinterpret our past life. It is a difficult process because it is not enough to act differently in the future: we also need to reshape our past, and until the new order is not seen as consistent with the (reinterpreted) past, my change is not fully accomplished.[253]

However, when McCabe goes back to the proper political revolution, it is only here that he explicitly mentions the "resurrection" aspect of the crisis and also the "after-life" (after-revolution): death and resurrection do not mean leaving this world to go to another world, to substitute another life for the current one, they mean a revolutionary transformation and therefore enhancement of this bodily life. A future revolutionary Britain, for example, can lose some features we think characteristic of Britain and yet, after the revolution happens, we could see that it is more British than before.[254]

I think that the ethical value of these considerations stems from McCabe's persistence and insistence in reminding his listeners how human life cannot be reduced to a corporate career within the "firm of virtues," nor to a wise "governmental plan of reforms." These things can, occasionally, be

249. McCabe, *Law, Love and Language*, 166.

250. McCabe, *On Aquinas*, 163.

251. McCabe, *Law, Love and Language*, 154.

252. McCabe, *God Matters*, 123.

253. McCabe, *Law, Love and Language*, 28–29.

254. McCabe, *God Matters*, 124–25.

included within it, but it goes far beyond them, into a greater depth and a more startling drama.

CONCLUSIONS: AFTER REVOLUTION

From the burning issues of his time, McCabe picked up and advocated what was more suitable both to his personality and to his role as a preacher and educator: equality in love, a critique of the relativism implied by the "religion of love," an uneasiness with traditional legalism and interest in virtues as the major means for a flourishing good life, a focus on communication (open dialogue, social concern, science, and friendship), and, also, a dismissal of a merely descriptive ethic that does not enhance current political commitment. In fact, if the "moralist is doing his job well he is promised he will encounter the hostility of the world, of the established power."[255]

McCabe was a protagonist of a virtue-based ethic, together with Alasdair McIntyre, and, although his contribution is not as widely commented on and celebrated as MacIntyre's, nonetheless it came first and was a partial inspiration for the latter.

Both philosophers consider the naturally acquired intellectual and moral virtues as a way to create enough good communities that proceed towards a further higher good, a way that can be trodden only by some individuals and for a limited time in their life. Whereas, the ethics of suffering and solidarity is for all and in whatever part of their life-stories.

Since all of us live within communities, however, the worse they are the less likely is the persistence of our individual lives, and, therefore, the specialised virtuous contributions by the "limbs of the body" have a meaning for all of us. The Revolution, even though undertaken only by some, affects everybody, in diverse ways.

McCabe's is a system of ethics stemming from the last decades of the twentieth century. In it the different components deeply and vividly represent—either in acceptance or in refusal—the main different voices of those years. Did this ethic leave a legacy for the thinkers of today?

Halden Doerge complains that McCabe is underrated, at least by theologians (since certain philosophers with a theological interest, such as Terry Eagleton, Alasdair MacIntyre, and Anthony Kenny, "acknowledge the significant influence of his thought on their own work").[256]

255. McCabe, *Law, Love and Language*, 164.

256. Doerge, "Herbert McCabe: the Underrated Theologian" (Doerge is the book review editor for *The Other Journal* and a member of the Church of the Servant King in Portland, Oregon).

As for ethics, at least, it would be worth exploring on an educational level how McCabe's position provides an effective alternative to both the relativism of "situation ethics" and the heavy armor of any non-minimalistic traditional legalism. In fact, the quest for a "third way" between legalism and relativism is a long-lasting debate that has become more important today. In the days of McCabe, it was an issue internal to the ethical journey of the individual, a level that is still lively today. However, in our time, the globalized world and the rise of new nationalisms have added a further level—political—to the debate: can the cosmopolitan universalistic attitude of liberalism comply with the national cultural identities?

For this purpose, I think that the distinction between "manuals" and "rule book" made by McCabe is a unique and precious legacy from the debates of those years (1960s to 1980s) and from that individual theologian. In fact, the teachings of both the manual and the rule book are necessary in ethics, even though their nature is quite different. The rule book is short and stable, or, better said, minimal; it sets up the few unavoidable rules required to "play the game" of human morality. Whereas the manuals are long and in progress, and they provide a particular community in a particular time with all the tools (taken from reason and experience) that are suitable to play the game at its best.

Revealed Theology

13

McCabe's Revealed Theology

Since the first encounter between Greek philosophy and Christian faith an important difference manifested itself: in the former it is humans who search for God, whereas in the latter it is God and God alone who establishes a relationship with them.[1] In Christian scholarship, therefore, there is "an important distinction: between theology properly so called and that branch of philosophy which is called 'natural theology,'"[2] in the words of McCabe's mentor Victor White. In the words of McCabe:

> here when I say "theology" I mean what is sometimes called "re-vealed" theology, as opposed to natural theology. There seems to me such a great difference between these two that it is a mistake to use the same word for both. What is called "natural theology" is part of philosophy; it is a certain kind of reflection on the world, it has no immediate connection with faith or dogma.[3]

McCabe was interested in both: addressing the secular culture he wanted to advocate Aquinas' philosophy as something "new" in comparison with other philosophies,[4] and as a Dominican priest wanted to debate all the relevant topics of Christian faith.

1. Benedetto XVI, *Il Dio della fede e il Dio dei filosofi*, Kindle loc. 137–39.
2. White, *God the Unknown*, 9–10.
3. McCabe, *The New Creation*, 1–2.
4. Interestingly both the anthology edited by Brian Davies (*On Aquinas*) and the

213

In his opinion, the first thing to be ruled out is fideism (a refusal of reason): it is a bad thing when people seek an authority who can think on their behalf and do not want to grow up, like "that loathsome Peter Pan." The church is never to be taken as an absolute authority, even the Chalcedonian Definition, for example, can and should be improved, and to do this the theologians should take inspiration from scientists and secular philosophers.[5]

Intelligo ut credam: human need of believing requires a true philosophy (not whatever philosophy), which could provide the proper *preambula fidei*. McCabe rejoices in observing that in Europe the Cartesian era has finished, at least among the philosophers, and this was achieved mostly by Wittgenstein and the Gestalt psychologists.[6] In fact, Descartes was the "enemy" who, by his "poisoned vocabulary," spoiled the comprehension of Aristotelian philosophy.[7]

McCabe criticizes the authors of *The Myth of God Incarnate* (1977, editor John Hick) because their ignorance of philosophical theology is "quite standard in the theological departments of British universities": they do not know that philosophy has already demonstrated that God is not a thing among other things, and so, as for revealed theology, they make mistakes when speaking about Incarnation.[8] As Turner says, following McCabe, theologians today

> seem to prefer to talk about Christ, as if you could theologise with Christological adequacy without standing on secure doctrinal ground concerning God. This seems perverse, being somewhat akin to an English person's attempting to describe to an American the conduct of a cricket match while suppressing any indications that cricket is a sport.[9]

Andrew Gleeson, speaking of McCabe's philosophical theology, says that

> little familiarity with specifically religious phenomena is necessary to follow the arguments, only intelligence, intellectual honesty and perhaps philosophical training. An atheist could

---

essay "A Very Short Introduction to Aquinas" (in *Faith within Reason*, 94–111), deal only with philosophy.

5. McCabe, *God Matters*, 67.

6. McCabe, *God Still Matters*, 142.

7. McCabe, *The Good Life*, 59.

8. McCabe, *The Good Life*, 59.

9. Turner, *Thomas Aquinas,* 100.

follow the arguments as well as a convinced believer. If the arguments succeed, they validate faith from outside it by showing that practices like prayer and confession are not in vain since their putative object, God, exists.[10]

As for McCabe, to state that God exists is not at all to claim to know what God is in Godself. Revelation does not make us know him either.[11] Here McCabe is suggesting (a legacy from White's teaching of Aquinas) that *revelation is no less apophatic than philosophical theology.*

However, elsewhere he says that faith in the gospel adds something: *credo ut intelligam.* We "take up religious faith" when we are frightened by thinking that there is not a God in charge of the universe who can protect us, and, then, faith allows us to recognize "certain historical events as part of God's plan of redemption, and to interpret them correctly in terms of our salvation."[12] Moreover, revealed theology changes radically the meaning of philosophical words, as we see of Aristotelian "substance" in the dogma of "trans-substantiation."[13]

We could say, then, that, for a Christian, truth relies on both *fides* et *ratio*, within a bidirectional dynamic. On the one hand, in the words of Aquinas, "[t]he existence of God and other like truths about God, which can be known by natural reason, are not articles of faith, but are preambles to the articles; for faith presupposes natural knowledge."[14] But, on the other hand, in the words of Joseph Ratzinger, "faith harbours within itself philosophical theology and perfects it": Aristotle's God is the one and same God of Jesus, but we, by faith, can comprehend him more deeply and purely.[15]

---

10. Gleeson, "God and Evil: A View from Swansea," 333.

11. McCabe, "Coming to the Father," 321.

12. McCabe, *Faith within Reason*, 1,7.

13. McCabe, *God Matters*, 146.

14. Aquinas, *ST*, I, qu 2, a2, ad 1.

15. Ratzinger, *Il Dio della fede*, Kindle loc. 108–11.

14

Christology

INCARNATION

MccCabe does not speak frequently of Incarnation, even though he talks extensively about Jesus Christ. For McCabe, the Chalcedonian dogma, while warning us against blind alleys, must help us in our quest for Jesus, so that we can approach the mystery of God; but we should not worship the formula itself, which, instead, has to be deeply modified.[1] Therefore, McCabe is not interested in filling, say, the eight gaps that Sarah Coakley noticed in the Chalcedonian definition,[2] but had his own agenda, which was more related to the events of his times than to the history of the dogma.

The Transcendence of God

One key event, at least on the cultural level, was the publication of the collective book *The Myth of God Incarnate*, edited by John Hick and published in 1977. McCabe reviewed the book and then in *New Blackfriars* publicly debated the topic with one of the authors, Maurice Wiles, who had responded to the review.

1. McCabe, *God Matters*, 74.
2. Coakley, "What Does Chalcedon Solve and What Does It Not?"

Firstly, McCabe is keen to adjust the distances between him and his fellow theologians. On the one hand, he wants to tell them that he supports them, since he is a man of his century who is attentive to the results of contemporary culture and who also agrees that the dogma of Chalcedon should be greatly improved, using the resources of contemporary culture. Furthermore, he applauds the authors of *The Myth of God Incarnate* for wanting to show that Jesus was fully human, for this is to oppose Docetism, and that is good. But, on the other hand, he disagrees with them because their anti-Docetism comes *solely* from twentieth-century culture and mentality, not drawing from tradition. Moreover, he finds it peculiar that these authors oppose Docetism but also its contrary, that is, Incarnation: according to them Incarnation is nothing but a myth.[3]

Secondly and above all, McCabe wants to set up his treatment of this dogma of revealed theology using the concepts of his philosophical theology on the transcendence of God (God is Creator and therefore is not part of the universe). Robert Ombres, a long-time friend of McCabe at Blackfriars, recalls that one of the fixed points of McCabe's teaching and conversation was exactly this one, and how, according to McCabe, it could help in the *intellectus fidei* of the mystery of Incarnation.[4]

How can the two natures of Jesus, divine and human, be united without contradicting and limiting each other? At first, McCabe notices that many Christians do not understand that God and man do not occupy the same space, different from, say, a man and a sheep, which make two animals. What do a man and God make? Part of the meaning of "man" is that it is not another creature (e.g., not a dog or a fish), not that man is not God. God is not part of the universe, so he is not something you have to disregard if we want to know what a man is. We do not understand, of course, what it means for a man to be God, but it is not as contradictory as to say that a man is a sheep. It is very mysterious, but "it is not flatly contradictory" because the human and the divine do not occupy the "same universe" (in fact, "the divine does not occupy any universe").[5]

From this generic observation of "negative" theology we can argue, more specifically, against the so-called "pre-existence of Christ," a doctrine that seems to want to safeguard the transcendence of God (the Son), but which in reality risks putting on the same worldly and temporal plane man and God: "there is no such thing as the pre-existent Christ." This doctrine, McCabe argues, was invented in nineteenth century to distinguish the

3. McCabe, *God Matters*, 54.
4. Ombres, my interview.
5. McCabe, *God Matters*, 57–58, 47–48.

eternal procession of the Son from the incarnation of the Son, by those who wanted to say that Jesus did not become the Son of God because of incarnation, since he was already the Son of God before it. But, if we speak of pre-existent Christ, we imply that God has a story other than incarnation: we imagine God living for ages before incarnation, like a man or another creature, and at some point of his "career" he "becomes" man. But this is incompatible with the traditional doctrine about God as unchangeable. Eternity is timeless, but not like an instant, which is a border between two times; it is *beyond* time. "To be eternal is to be God." God is not before or after or simultaneous with any event or history. The depiction of God *becoming* man is a powerful metaphor but is not literally true.[6]

Therefore, there is not any "moment at which the eternal Son was not Jesus of Nazareth," because in God's life there are not moments. The eternal life of the Son does not precede nor is it simultaneous with his human life: "there is not a story of God 'before the story of Jesus.'"[7]

Moreover, there is certainly a time when Jesus was not born. Moses could have said truly that Jesus does not exist (because the future does not exist), but Moses could also have said with truth that "The Son of God exists": that the two propositions are both true might be called the pre-existence of the Son, suggesting that before Jesus' birth we were allowed to make an apparent distinction between the Son of God and Jesus. But we were not: in fact, the phrase "pre-existent Christ" seems to imply that, at the times of Moses, the proposition "the Son of God exists now" is true as well. Whereas it is not true, because the "now" is temporal and the temporal existence of the Son of God became true only when Jesus was conceived in the Virgin Mary. McCabe maintains that, *apart from the historical existence of Jesus,* there is not any *time* when is true that the Son of God exists.[8]

McCabe says that those who think that God exists at the same level of reality as creatures and has temporal existence, albeit an everlasting one without beginning and end, will not be able to make sense of the notion that God does not pre-exist the universe nor that the Son of God does not pre-exist Jesus. But in the tradition this is precisely the mystery we must articulate when we speak of God.[9]

Now we will move on to explore what McCabe has to say about the two natures and the hypostatic union.

6. McCabe, *God Matters*, 49.

7. McCabe, *God Matters*, 50.

8. McCabe, *God Matters*, 50.

9. McCabe, *God Matters*, 50.

Chalcedon Revisited

Although McCabe would have liked to change the terms of Chalcedon "a lot," he actually continues using them (human and divine nature, personal union). However, he strongly emphasizes that even faith in revelation does not allow us to know the divine nature of Christ. Following his mentor Victor White, McCabe maintains that the only knowledge we can have of Christ is of his human nature. When we think to know what God is in himself because we know what (the fundamental qualities of) Jesus Christ is, we are wrong, since what we know and understand is just his *human* nature and *not* his divine one, as we will see below. "The revelation of God in Jesus in no way, for Aquinas, changes the situation. By the revelation of grace, he says, we are joined to God as an unknown, *ei quasi ignoto coniugamur.*"[10] For example, we do not know what the intratrinitarian relationship is between the Father and the Son; however, both by faith and reason we know Jesus' attitude of obedience to the will of God, and by faith we hold that this "is just what the eternal procession of the Son from the Father appears as in history."[11] McCabe thinks that a better understanding of the humanity of Jesus will help us to go towards the mystery of God: that is, we can improve our "understanding of" Jesus' humanity, but his divinity is a "mystery."[12] For instance, unlike his forebears, McCabe thinks that Jesus was a lot less self-consciously messianic; also, unlike scholars living before the twentieth century, he thinks that Jesus was quite involved in the political turmoil of his times.[13] But—if what McCabe thinks is true—this improvement of our knowledge of Jesus' humanity does not involve a better knowledge of his divinity.

Thirty-seven years after the debate with Wiles and twenty-seven after its re-publication in *God Matters*, a contemporary theologian, Ian McFarland, resumes this observation of McCabe's and provides us with historical examples of alleged "divine" qualities of Jesus: perfect God-consciousness (Schleiermacher), Jesus' intention to found the kingdom of God (Ritschl), refusal to claim any goodness for himself (Baillie), absolute subordination to the will of the Father (Pannenberg). These Christologies share the same basic claim: Jesus' humanity is seen in what is average and everyday, while the divinity abides in his extraordinary qualities. But this temptation has to be resisted because we can only point to what is created, and those aspects

---

10. McCabe, "A Sermon for St Thomas," 195; McCabe, *God Matters*, 41.

11. McCabe, *God Matters*, 23.

12. McCabe, *God Matters*, 74.

13. McCabe, *God Matters*, 73.

are just human, not divine. If we take the humanity of Jesus seriously, then "no aspects of it can be treated as a proof or manifestation of his divinity." "None of them, taken singly or in combination, establishes that this person is the second Person of the Trinity," and whatever miracle Jesus performs, they can be performed by other humans also.[14]

This point had been made clear already by McCabe: there are topics where historical research overlaps with the definition of faith and potentially could contradict it (e.g., if the archaeologists found the body of Jesus). But there are others where it does not: e.g., the doctrine of the Incarnation is not vulnerable because it does not make statements about the human behavior of Jesus or even "his inmost psychology."[15]

What does the Incarnation tell us about the divine nature? It is most important to observe that to be divine is not to be a kind of thing (just as to be a creature is not to be a kind of thing), whereas to be a man means to be a kind of thing, actually that kind that Jesus was.[16] God is not part of the universe so God is not something to disregard if you want to know what a man is.[17]

Thus, the two natures are not like an engine and a sail to provide movement to a boat but are two levels of speaking of Jesus. They are also a way to say that Jesus exists on two levels.[18] And McFarland follows McCabe on this point as well: Chalcedon says that Jesus is fully divine but, since the divine nature is invisible and ineffable, it cannot be shown and so treated as an observable property of Jesus; in fact, any observable property of Jesus can be exhibited also by other human beings. The divine nature in the mind of the fathers of Chalcedon has qualities such as omnipotence, eternity, and the like, but, for the very reason that they are super-human, Jesus cannot *exhibit* any of them in his *human* life. An impressive example, McFarland quips with his tongue in his cheek, is divine impassibility and how Jesus "exhibited" it on the cross.[19]

The divine nature is not something that can be known by us, neither by reason, nor by faith. The divine nature of Jesus for us is not a series of qualities or ideas, but is a relationship with us. When we study Jesus historically, we understand he was a man and not an angel or a supernatural visitor; but we do not only study Jesus historically: we also *listen* to him, and this

14. McFarland, "Spirit and Incarnation," 49, 57.

15. McCabe, *God Matters*, 69.

16. McCabe, *God Matters*, 71.

17. McCabe, *God Matters*, 57.

18. McCabe, *God Still Matters*, 110.

19. McFarland, "Spirit and Incarnation," 56.

communication of his to our faith and his friendship with us points to his divinity. "The insight that Jesus was uncreated is available only to those in whom this rapport is established, to those 'who have faith in his name.'"[20]

So, the hypostatic union appears only in the transformative relationship with the believer:

> It is in the contact with the person who is Jesus, in this personal communication between who he is and who I am, that his divinity is revealed in his humanity, not in any, as it were, clinical, objective examination of him. Any such examination will simply reveal correctly that he is splendidly and vulnerably human.[21]

The so called *communicatio idiomatum*, also, matters only for the believer who hopes for salvation and eternal life from Jesus; whereas for the non-believer it is completely useless, as McCabe summarizes: Aquinas says that it is one thing is to say that God was nailed to the cross, and another thing to say that God "as such" was nailed onto the cross. When we say that God died on the cross, we do not mean the divine nature but the person who had that nature, "in this case the man Jesus of Nazareth." Jesus was human and so we can say he was hungry, and we cannot apply such predicates to, say, a chair. That he was divine allows us to say he is Creator, Eternal Son of God, omnipotent, etc. The traditional doctrine says that the two series of predicates apply to the same person referred by the name "Jesus."[22] Since this person has two natures, we can qualify him either with human or with divine terms, it makes no difference whether we call him Son of Mary or Son of God. Actually, it makes no difference in the subject part of the sentence. We may say that the friend of Peter sat down by the well, or that the Son of God born before all ages sat down by the well: the two "are exactly the same proposition."[23]

The Purpose of the Incarnation

In the traditional textbooks about the Incarnation one section was titled "On Christ's Predestination," treating the purpose of Incarnation, and

---

20. McCabe, *God Matters*, 71.

21. McCabe, *God Matters*, 71.

22. McCabe, *God Matters*, 47. Here McCabe makes a mistake because, according to Chalcedon, the "person," the "who" (hypostasis), is not an individual man but is the Word of God, even though that person is also referred to by the term "Jesus."

23. McCabe, *God Still Matters*, 108.

providing many different solutions throughout the centuries.[24] On this point, the Thomist McCabe takes sides with Scotists in favor of the "absolute" predestination of Christ: the purpose of Incarnation is independent from our original sin; Incarnation aims to deify us and free us from mere creature-hood:

> Every student in a seminary is taught that to say that God spoke to the prophets is not to assert a change in God but in the prophets and that the incarnation is not an event in the history of God but of man. The coming of the Spirit does not mean that God moves towards the world of man; it means that man is enabled to enter deeply into himself to know and love the divine reality which has been there all along.[25]

How, in particular? Jesus' life has its final meaning in the cross, showing how a human life reaches its purpose and finds its meaning in suffering for love, "and that therefore God's love is expressed and enacted for us in the suffering of God."[26] As McCabe repeats many times in his works throughout the decades, Jesus wanted to be fully human, and, given the fallen world where we live, this was the reason of both his death and his resurrection, that is, of the particular shaping of his human nature, and of his belonging to the divine nature, which he wants to share with us.

Which Demythologization?

From the above we can see that McCabe's Christology is situated within a progressive demythologizing theology. For example, Dietrich Bonhoeffer wrote that in humiliation Jesus is not more man and less God, nor in exaltation he is more God and less man. Always he is fully God and fully man.[27] Henri de Lubac maintained the fundamental idea that there are not two parallel realities, that is, the "natural" and the "supernatural":

> Neither the Fathers nor the great scholastics had ever envisioned the possibility of a purely natural end for human persons attainable by their own intrinsic powers of cognition and volition, some natural beatitude of an order inferior to the intuitive vision of God. For these earlier thinkers, there was only one

---

24. You can read an articulate historical report of them in Carol, "The Absolute Predestination of the Blessed Virgin Mary."

25. McCabe, "Dr Robinson's Book."

26. McCabe, God Matters, 87.

27. Bonhoeffer, Christology, 110.

concrete order of history, that in which God had made humanity for himself, and in which human nature had thus been created only for a single destiny, which was supernatural.[28]

A Christian can say that *everything is natural* (grace consists entirely in
the external and internal events of the historical world), and she or he can
say also that *everything is supernatural* (every temporal space element of the
world is created, that is, supported in existence by God).[29] And Nicholas
Lash held that in God we can see only Jesus Christ: if not, what other "aspects" of God could we see in God? In Jesus there is nothing missing, there
is nothing more to see.[30]

In fact, McCabe also holds that a human person just is a person with
a human nature and it makes absolutely no difference to the logic of this
whether this same person does (as in Jesus) or does not (as in us) exist from
eternity as divine.[31]

However, McCabe is not demythologizing Jesus (and God) quite like
Bultmann or the authors of *The Myth of the God Incarnate*. On the one hand,
it is true that from Bultmann and the like he took the fundamental idea that
there are "traditions of men" to be distinguished from the commandments
of God: specifically, the cultural habits of the first century CE to resort to
magic and marvels. On the other, unlike Bultmann, McCabe still relies on
Chalcedon, on the God Man, and, therefore, on the relevance of Trinity for
Christianity, since the theology of the Trinity started from the problem of
the God Man.[32]

JESUS' LIFE AND DEEDS

Between Myth and Mystery

Like Bultmann and many other contemporaries, McCabe accepts the invita-
tion to demythologize, and never mentions a literal interpretation of the
miracles of Jesus. In fact, to use the words of Bonhoeffer, the miracles do not
provide an inner conversion; "nothing happens in me if I assert my belief

28. Schindler, "Introduction." In de Lubac, *The Mystery of the Supernatural*, xvii.

29. De Lubac, *The Mystery of the Supernatural*.

30. Lash, *Believing Three Ways in One God*, 80.

31. McCabe, *God Matters*, 72.

32. Whereas "there is no role for Trinity in Bultmann's theology": Powell, *The Trinity in German Thought*, 177.

in miracles." Rather, contrary to the myth that seeks to decipher what is not comprehensible, McCabe adopts a "negative way," which, to quote Bonhoeffer again, states what we cannot say of Jesus.[33] Jesus is a mystery, not a myth.

Reviewing *Honest to God* (1963), the popular work of Bishop John A. T. Robinson, McCabe fully agrees with the author that we need to demythologize expressions such as "the descent of the Holy Spirit" or Christ "ascending into heaven and sitting at the hand of God the Father." However, he blames Robinson's iconoclasm, which rejected a straw-man notion of God never held in the tradition, and, in this case also, we see his characteristic concern for an innovation that does not forget the continuity with tradition.[34]

The Life of Jesus

A good short definition of what the Gospels are is provided by Nicholas Lash: they are good news about the resurrection of Christ, narrated as a sort of biography of Jesus.[35] So, the purpose of the Gospels is the believer's transformation by grace, but the actual content is Jesus' human life.

As for McCabe, he had already presented Jesus' life without any privileged features: there is no formula that summarizes both Jesus and his mission. For example, Luke tells us about a boy who leaves his parents and that this is the beginning of his public life (a display of intelligence). Moreover, in John's Gospel we see that although Jesus was not interested in politics, politicians and other people of power were very interested in him.[36] Another example: the fact that Jesus was without sin does not imply that he was "cold and inhuman, but rather just the opposite": he was free and spontaneously able to love, not afraid of others.[37]

Jesus was indeed a rabbi, who started preaching the coming of the kingdom of God, continued teaching an original and profound set of ethics, and in his criticism of the religious habits of his times was also a prophet who, as McCabe says, was persecuted for the sake of what is right, tortured and killed. They killed him because he taught the people to live for each other and that they should set aside certain rules and laws (the tradition of men).[38]

33. Bonhoeffer, *Christology*, 114, 77.
34. McCabe, "Dr Robinson's Book," 30–31.
35. Lash, *Believing*, 65.
36. McCabe, *God Still Matters*, 85.
37. McCabe, *God Still Matters*, 96.
38. McCabe, *The Teaching of the Catholic Church*, 8, 12.

As for Jesus himself, he was not afraid to be human because he saw his humanity simply as a gift from the one whom he called the "Father." He lived gradually exploring himself and asking the question "Who do I say I am? He found nothing but the Father's love. This is what gave all the meaning to his life."[39] In fact, if we humans are fortunate, sometimes we are aware that we are loved. As Jesus grew up his awareness of being loved increased, and this is surely what shaped his idea of the Father.[40]

In his writings about ethics McCabe thinks that human life, by its very nature, is full of deadly anxieties, which are contained and overcome when we feel a "security that comes from the certainty of being loved and accepted." The central fact about Jesus' "personality" is his capacity for love, whereas the central fact of his "person" is his being loved, that "he rose from the dead—that the love which sustains his personality brings him through death into life."[41]

This love is shared with us. How? Christians actually say that they do not know God. They know that they will be defeated by the powers of this world. But their faith is not in themselves, that is, in their understanding, and in their success; their faith is in the power of God "and they know it is by accepting this darkness and defeat that they will get light and victory," as in actual Jesus' life.[42]

The "defeat," among other things, is death itself. Columba Ryan, McCabe's former teacher and fellow Dominican, recollected some of his sentences about death in the speech he gave at McCabe's funeral:

> Herbert took the matter of death very seriously. "Death, which is the punishment of fallen man, has become, because of the Cross, the way to resurrection and new life." "The whole of life is a preparation for death because it is only from death that eternal life can spring."[43]

The Resurrection of Christ

With this "eternal life" springing from death, we approach the theme of the ties between death and resurrection. McCabe reminds us that according to Chalcedon we can say literally that God suffered hunger and death: the

39. McCabe, *God Matters*, 95.

40. McCabe, *God Matters*, 95.

41. McCabe, *God Still Matters*, 174.

42. McCabe, *God, Christ and Us*, 141.

43. Ryan, "Homily at Herbert McCabe's Funeral," 312.

doctrine, while affirming that God is incapable of suffering, also states that
God suffered in the same sense I suffer. One consequence is that we can
say God was nailed to the cross.[44] Because of the cross, whatever pain and
evil we have to endure, we can always say that Jesus not only understands
these ills but has also experienced them.[45] He was fully human and so we
have complete solidarity with him, beginning with the origins; if we look
at the ancestors of Jesus in the genealogy provided by Matthew, we see that
he does not belong to a clean and comfortable world and not even to an
honest, reasonable, and sincere world: he belonged to a family of murderers,
cheats, adulterers, and liars; he was one of us and came to save us and give
us hope.[46]

However, "God was nailed on the cross and died," and his divine nature appears to the faithful by "God resurrecting him from this death." What
is the resurrection? Lash conveniently observes that the accounts of Jesus'
resurrection are so different from one another that you cannot say: this is
the meaning of the resurrection! We know that the resurrection and, for
that matter, the ascension are not meant to be two separate events, but just
two aspects of the same destiny shared by Jesus and humankind.[47] What
destiny?

McCabe recalls Jesus' words, "whoever believes in me will never die."[48]
He denies that the resurrection is the last step of a series: passion, death,
burial, and then resurrection. It is, instead, something on its own, the celebration of *the meaning of the whole series:* there is a passion-play that re-
enacts the events of the passion and another passion-play that re-enacts the
meaning of it.[49] Could we say then that, for McCabe, Jesus' resurrection is
"outside" Jesus' life? Also, given the New Testament accounts and the tradition of faith, is the resurrection "spiritual" or "bodily" or both? To the first
question he responds *yes;*[50] to the second he says that resurrection is the
"meaning" (therefore, as such, something "spiritual") of Jesus' life; but this
meaning is *embodied:* Jesus is "'with us" bodily.[51]

44. McCabe, *God Matters*, 46.

45. McCabe, *God Matters*, 107.

46. McCabe, *God Matters*, 249.

47. Lash, *Believing*, 61.

48. McCabe, *God Matters*, 109.

49. McCabe, *God Matters*, 106.

50. McCabe, *God, Christ and Us*, 90.

51. McCabe, *God Matters*, 110.

Jesus Christ and Us

What is the presence "with us" of the resurrected Jesus Christ, before our death, after it, and after our resurrection? McCabe shares the sensibility and appreciation of his times about the body: we form part of the human species because our bodies are linked to those of our ancestors; we belong to future humanity because our bodies are linked with "the risen body of Christ."[52] When we feed the hungry, "we encounter Christ, not in a metaphorical way, but literally."[53]

Not just feeding the hungry, but, also, in a broader sense, maintaining good interpersonal relationships. In fact, with regard to the ontology of the Eucharistic gathering, McCabe takes sides: the Eucharist exists qua sign of our unity: this is the reason why the body of Christ is here, he is present because of this, not the other way round, as though the "great thing" was (and it is not) the consecrated wafer in the tabernacle.[54]

However, Christ now, after *his* resurrection, is present, but *ambiguously present*: the presence we directly experience is the presence of each other; but after *our* resurrection, Christ will be present without ambiguity. In the meantime his presence is also an absence: "we proclaim your death, until you come again."[55] It seems to me that here McCabe is saying that our presence in the company of one other can be largely disappointing and we may experience solitude, suffering, and helplessness, even though we are provided with hope: a hope in the second coming of Jesus and his presence without "ambiguity," after "our resurrection," and, therefore, our death.

In the meantime, the risen Christ is seen only when he shows himself: we cannot imagine him being seen unawares. Moreover, even when he shows himself, he is recognized just by faith, we need faith to recognize Jesus.[56]

Characterization and Conclusions

McCabe's depiction of Jesus' life and deeds on the positive side tends to stress the *necessity* of Jesus' story: he felt that he was the beloved of the "Father," and, because he wanted to spread this love trying to live a full humanity, therefore, he necessarily had to fight against the wicked opposition of

---

52. McCabe, *The New Creation*, 57.

53. McCabe, *God, Christ and Us*, 40.

54. McCabe, *God Matters*, 84.

55. McCabe, *God Matters*, 112.

56. McCabe, *God Still Matters*, 220.

a fallen humanity. This positive side wants to understate any exceptional characteristic of Jesus, and underline a destiny shared with all of us: if you do not love, you cannot live, but if you love enough, you will be killed.

On the negative side, McCabe, by means of his philosophy, intends to criticize certain theological "absurdities," such as: God being within time (Moses cannot say "The Son of God exists now"); resurrection as a distinct chronological further step within a series; the risen Christ's presence without a living community; interpersonal presence without an intentional act of communication.

REDEMPTION

Introductory Concepts

What is redemption? If we focus on the concept of the "atonement" of Jesus, as reformed Christians generally do, we could say that redemption is a metaphor (a "second purchase") for what is achieved through that atonement, and, therefore, that there is a metaphorical sense in which the expiatory death of Jesus pays the price of a ransom, releasing Christians from bondage to sin and death.

As for McCabe, who was Catholic and not particularly interested in the idea of "atonement," the function of redemption is to make us "holy," that is, saints. The way or mode of this process is, however, "painful."[57] The scope of the matter is vast because such realities as famine, pestilence, natural catastrophe, illness, physical and mental suffering, and death itself reveal that evil is by no means exhausted by what is termed *malum culpae* (moral evil), but covers also *malum poenae* (suffering), whether this be evil in itself or arise from the limitations of nature.[58] The human attitude towards redemption should be humble gratitude; in fact, the Christian God is scandalous because he loves the sinners more than the righteous, so that we also have to love sinners and so that we realize that the gospel is not about being *safe* but being *saved*.[59]

In addition to the aforementioned characteristics, redemption has two purposes, or, better said, two "levels": (a) liberation from sin and (b)

57. McCabe, *God Matters*, 99.

58. International Theological Commission, 13th point. See chapter "The Problem of Evil" in this book.

59. McCabe, *God, Christ and Us*, 29.

liberation from creaturehood, that is, divinization.[60] For McCabe, we do not need God in the first instance because we are sinners, but in order to be elevatwed to God's nature and to share his self-knowledge. Our good news is not only that we were saved from sin but also that we are taken *beyond creaturehood* into the life of God himself: "this, indeed, is what our doctrine of Trinity tells us."[61]

Ultimately, Jesus' death on the cross unites the two levels. On the cross *both* sin *and* death are defeated. The cross is the manifestation of both the sin of the world and the redeeming God.[62] Let us examine each one of these levels.

Atonement and Forgiveness of Sins

The first and traditionally more obvious level of redemption is a sort of cure from that distortion of human nature called "sin." This cure is two-fold: one side of it is the expiatory reconciliation accomplished by Jesus (atonement), the other side is that we humans are "redeemed" and so freed from our sins. In other words: atonement is about resetting a broken relationship between us and God; redemption is about healing or freeing us from the consequences of this break.

As for the atonement, McCabe lists the traditional theories about it and comments that each theory says something true, but they have one thing in common: they all answer the question, "Why did Jesus decide to be cruci-fied?" But McCabe says that the ordinary Christians who have kept the cross as a sign of their faith never had this problem at all: they were not puzzled by the cross, they took it for granted that man was naturally crucified; "Aren't we all?" They feel that crucifixion expresses what life is about, but it is not easy to acknowledge. In fact, we are afraid of suffering and death. The divine reaches these deep parts of life that we are afraid to look at.[63]

Therefore, Jesus' "mission" is just being in history, being human, noth-ing but being the Son of Man. His life was tragic only because this is what being human implies: most of the time we are not human enough, because, if we are, we will be crucified. His crucifixion was just the manifestation of

---

60. McCabe, *God Still Matters*, 181. A thorough report of the two traditions (East-ern: deification; Western: salvation from sin) is provided by Hart, "Redemption and Fall."

61. McCabe, *God Still Matters*, 233.

62. McCabe, *God Still Matters*, 173.

63. McCabe, *God Still Matters*, 94–95.

the wicked and unjust world we made: we do not need theories to explain why the Father wanted Jesus to die.[64]

This is what McCabe says about atonement. The other side of redemption as a "cure" is forgiveness of sin. Sin, he says, has three meaning. The first meaning is the sin of the world also known as original sin, where the word "original" does not point to the old one of our remote forebears: rather, it is our "origin", because each one of us was "born in" an already distorted world. According to Christian faith, by means of our baptism we are liberated from original sin, even though not completely: it is true that we are not enslaved any more by it as a "master" of ours, but we suffer from it as an "enemy" that we must win by grace; for this reason we must "struggle for a more just society." If we do not, this is the second meaning of sin, "mortal sin," when we betray our baptism and join the enemy, the establishment; this way, we betray the world of future life: it is the collective failure of being fully human. The third meaning is "venial sin," when we fail to grow in love.

Since we are not pure spirits, but are embodied social animals, there is a wide and complex psychology of sin. On the one hand, sin is a deep isolation of people from one another.[65] On the other hand, because of this isolation we fall into fear. The root of sin is the fear that we are nothing; so, we have the compulsion to flatter ourselves, to believe in ourselves: all sins are failures in being realistic. Even the childish sins of flesh have their roots in anxiety about whether we really matter, so that we could say that every sin is to build an "illusory self that we can admire, instead of the real self that we can only love."[66] In fact, the only way to escape the compulsion of flattering and deceiving is the faith that we are loved by God, even if we are sinners.[67]

Therefore, analyzing our psychology, we could say that every sin has two sides: (1) a carelessness of God's love and choosing another thing, as in mortal sin, or not showing our gratitude in our daily life, as in venial sin; (2) it is an attachment and even an addiction to lesser goods. The forgiveness of sins deals with the first side: the miracle of contrition and conversion and the enhancement of love. The aftermath of forgiveness deals with the second side: we can remain attached even when the sin is forgiven, as a wound to be healed remains after the blow.

However, on both sides (forgiving and healing), who is the "Redeemer"? Ignatius of Antioch uses the soteriological title *Christos iatros*, that is, Christ physician, the healing doctor; Justin and the apologists emphasize

---

64. McCabe, *God Matters*, 23.

65. McCabe, *God Matters*, 80.

66. McCabe, *God, Christ and Us*, 17–18.

67. McCabe, *God, Christ and Us*, 60.

the *Christos didaskalos,* i.e., Christ teacher; Irenaeus stresses the notion of "recapitulation," which implies the restoration of God's image in man.[68] But, McCabe would say, all these qualities—doctor, teacher, restorer—are fully human. Even being sinless is a human quality: when we say that Jesus did not have sin, this is because to have sin is to be less than fully human.[69]

McCabe makes much of this point: we are not saved by the intervention of a god "but by the great sanctity of one of ourselves," so that when we encounter Jesus there is a chord that resonates, he shows us the humanity that is hidden in us, he is the human being that we do not dare to be. He is the Son of God, but *it is by his human sanctity,* his obedience to the Father, *that he saves us.* Jesus' mission was to be human: the Father sent him not to suffer and die, but *to be human,* to be loving.[70]

What, then, about his divinity? Given the emphasis McCabe puts on Paul's image of the "body," he would have embraced the following passage by the Vatican Theological Commission, where the divinity of Jesus in not a characteristic of his inner personality, but is his external and objective "position" or "role" in the historical journey of the church:

> Who is the Redeemer? This question can only be answered from within the Church and through the Church. To know the Redeemer is to belong to the Church. Augustine emphasized this in his teaching on the whole Christ, *Christus totus,* Head and Members together. As Gregory the Great put it, "Our Redeemer is seen to be one person with the holy Church that he has made his own." 115 The life of the Church as the Body of Christ is not to be amputated from the life of the Head.[71]

Transformation

The second and traditionally less obvious level of redemption is the transformation of human nature into the divine. The Thomistic tradition states that there is not any real relationship in God as Creator towards his creatures, as we have seen already . However, the redemption brought by Christ

68. International Theological Commission, *Select Questions, Part III—Historical perspectives,* nn.3, 4, 6.

69. McCabe, *Teaching of the Catholic Church,* 7. "Jesus is more human than we are for he is like to us in all things except sin for, because of sin, we are less than human."

70. McCabe, *God Matters,* 99, 93; McCabe, *God, Christ and Us,* 66; McCabe, *God Still Matters,* 92–93.

71. International Theological Commission, *Select Questions, Part IV—Systematic Perspectives, A—The Identity of the Redeemer: Who Is the Redeemer?* n. 4.

makes creatures upgrade to a supernatural status. Love is possible only on a basis of equality, which allows the reciprocal friendship between God and humans.[72] What could this mean? If we said, with McCabe, that when we try to set up a community by "purely *natural* means, whether be it the family or the political community, we fail to reach real unity,"[73]this would be a failed attempt for improving us *qua* humans (social animals) without God's grace. If we received and accepted God's grace for unity, however, this attempt would be successful but will still be only an improvement of human nature.

Jesus himself was misunderstood and opposed by the Jews—something to be expected—but he did not carry on confronting them and, rather, eventually realized that "death is unavoidable."[74] Jesus no longer wanted to seek worldly success and began to accept being guided towards a goal that, in itself, is not really a human purpose, does not respond to a human need; that is to say, death. To use the words of the Vatican Theological Commission, the purpose of redemption is not a known answer to human needs.[75] In the same way, McCabe remains apophatic and does not say what the supernatural (not only human) purpose of redemption should be.[76]

Our life is a journey. Sin or idolatry is settling for the current state of affairs, in resisting the call of faith, the call of revolutionary change.[77] From an ethical point of view:

> [l]ife in Christ . . . is a seeking into the meaning of human behaviour which involves a constant reaching out beyond the values of the world. Sin consists in ceasing to reach out, refusing to respond to the Father's summons, and settling for this present world. . . . Of course, trying to live in the present world a life in accordance with the future is a dangerous business, as Jesus found out. The Christian may expect to be crucified with him.[78]

But the ethical point of view is only a provisional one. Redemption is more mysterious than an ethical struggle: "Christians do not claim to have any secret and private knowledge about God or to have discovered any new

72. Aquinas, *ST*, IIa-IIae, qu. 23, art. 1.

73. McCabe, *The New Creation*, xi

74. McCabe, *God Matters*, 90.

75. International Theological Commission, *Select Questions*, part I, n. 2.

76. As for me, following the "egalitarian" line of McCabe (in creation, anthropology, and ethics), opposed to all hierarchies, including the one between God and humans, the human (not the super-natural!) purpose of redemption could be a non-hierarchical mindset in the individual and a non-hierarchical structure in the society.

77. McCabe, *God Matters*, 123.

78. McCabe, *Law, Love and Language*, 153.

secret way to the Father."[79] We are not allowed to rely on a plan revealed to us:

> It is to say that the picture of the prearranged plan worked out by God up there, to which we must conform, is only a provisional picture, an inadequate one. There is no heaven waiting for us; it is we who will create heaven, but only because of the divine life we already have within us.[80]

Contextualizing

How to place McCabe's soteriology in the context of other soteriologies? In the first place, its strongest emphasis is on redemption as a supernatural transformation: both humanity and individual persons are called to share the mysterious and unpredictable divine nature. In fact, acquiring intellectual and moral virtues is still on this side of the human/divine divide: the outcomes of our transformation are not predictable.

Secondly, as for the side concerning atonement and reconciliation of the sinner with God, McCabe has his preferences among the various theories. There are many such theories and recent theologians have committed themselves to group the minor and classify the main ones. Ted Peters distinguishes six kinds,[81] Joel Green and Mark Baker five,[82] Colin Gunton four,[83] Gustaf Aulèn three.[84] As we have already seen, McCabe is quite far from the Anselmian model of "vicarious satisfaction" and, on this point, he differs also not only from Calvin but also from Aquinas. Instead, he is closer to the thinkers of his own time, such as his fellow Oxford theologian Paul Fiddes, who prefers the moral influence model, just as McCabe says that Jesus saves us by his human sanctity. McCabe is similar also to Joel Green and Mark Baker, who criticize the penal substitutionary atonement theory because it is too anthropomorphic and is implicitly based on the ideology of success in life and, so, an easy way to explain failures.[85] And he is close to J. Denny Weaver who opposes the violent dimensions of satisfaction atonement and proposes a revised version of Christus Victor theory;

---

79. "Coming to the Father," 320.
80. McCabe, *God Still Matters*, 181.
81. Peters, "Six Ways of Salvation," 223.
82. Green and Baker, *Recovering the Scandal of the Cross*, 23.
83. Gunton, *The Actuality of Atonement*.
84. Aulèn, *Christus Victor*.
85. Green and Baker, *Recovering the Scandal*, 24–25.

for Weaver, we do not need to explain why the Father sent Jesus to his death: "In narrative Christus Victor, the cause of Jesus' death is obviously not God. . . . Rather, in narrative Christus Victor the Son is carrying out the Father's will by making the reign of God visible in the world."[86] In Weaver's words we recognize the same points so dear to McCabe, who linked continuously two models of redemption—moral influence and Christus Victor—to provide a Christological hub for the revolutionary struggles for justice which seemed to him so important in the politics of his times. Political revolutions are not just "secular" events: in fact, although Christians take part in them, the Christian revolution goes more deeply.[87]

86. Weaver, *The Nonviolent Atonement*.

87. McCabe, *Law, Love* and Language, 166.

15

Trinity

A LUKEWARM ATTITUDE

A joke on the internet highlights the abstract and brain-teasing nature of one of the foremost Christian dogmas, the Trinity: "Trinity is made of 5 notions, 4 relations, 3 persons, 2 processions, 1 nature, and 0 comprehension."[1] Christian theologians from the 1960s to the 1990s could not sympathize more with this hilarious skepticism, and, at their best, could maintain just a lukewarm attitude towards the traditional systematic analysis of this dogma.

McCabe operated as an intellectual exactly during those decades, a period of change in the Western cultural environment, and also in theology: the old scholastic textbooks were no longer valued, and our contemporary revival of systematic theological treatises had not started yet. The medieval schoolmen and their systems were put aside and biblical, liturgical, and pastoral studies were flourishing and meant to be the "right" decent move of theology.

---

1. In the old Catholic seminaries the students were encouraged to memorise Aquinas' doctrine on Trinity by means of numbers. The five notions are innascibility, paternity, filiation, active spiration, passive spiration. The four relations: paternity, filiation, active spiration, passive spiration. The three persons: Father, Son, Holy Spirit. The two processions: filiation and passive spiration. The one nature: Godhead. To these Bernard Lonergan allegedly added: and 0 comprehension.

It is true, in fact, that McCabe wanted to structure his little catechism with a trinitarian framework,[2] but he meant this only as a symbol of that reverence he wanted to kindle in the pastoral context. Similarly, he found in the liturgy of baptism and in the Bible all that is essential to the "doctrine" of Trinity: "this is my Son in whom I have delight."[3] But pastoral concern, liturgy, and the Bible are not dogmatic theology.

McCabe, on the other hand, was not at all the kind of theologian who despises the tradition of old and "Greek" philosophical concepts of ancient dogmas, because they are allegedly too "abstract." He acknowledges that in theology Trinity is a difficult concept, but also comments that this difficulty should not bring the Christian to think only about the Lady of Fatima and the Eucharist, because if we do not consider the Trinity, Fatima and the Eucharist could yield to confusion also.[4]

Therefore, he occasionally does tackle this theological topic, and pours his intellect into some traditional questions. Although he is uncommitted to that geometry of notions, processions, which the joke hints at, he faces it in any case and deals with it, as we shall see.

TRADITION REVISED

Having already spoken of the only one God and his divine simplicity in the previous *quaestiones* of the *Summa*, Aquinas should have added that for Christians in this God there are three "persons." However, McCabe observes, Aquinas does not say there are really three persons because in our English (and in his Latin) "person" means individual center of understanding and will, whereas Father, Son, and Spirit have the *same mind*, they do *not* have three knowledges or three loves: the Son/Word is just the way God is self-conscious, when he knows what he is, the Spirit is the delight God takes in "what he is when he is knowing it." If we do not say this, then we are tritheists.

In fact, the unity between Father and Son is more than in human beings: the human parent brings about a child like himself, but they are not one; they are two distinct centres of consciousness. Therefore, the word "persons" in the context of talk about God does not mean people. In God there is only *one* understanding and *one* will: like (to some small extent) in

2. "Introduction," *The Teaching* ix.

3. McCabe, *God Still Matters*, 232.

4. McCabe, *Faith within Reason*, 38.

two lovers who seek to have one mind and one heart, in the Trinity Father and Son are one mind and one heart.[5]

It is strange that Aquinas cites Boethius' definition of person as an "individual substance of rational nature," even though—McCabe observes in a witty and clever way—in the case of the Christian God every attribute is negated: "the 'persons' of the Trinity are not individuals, not substances, not rational and do not have natures." So, this is a unique case in which "person" means "relation." Aquinas still speaks of "persons" out of his "pietas" towards the church and her traditional language. Yet even in his times, it was already the case that "person" (*persona*) did not mean "relation." In our times even more: for us, the person is the isolated individual, "the bastion of individuality set over against the collective." Even if we piously criticize individualism and sugarly praise communities, the word "person" "does not become relational enough to use in an account of the Trinity." Aquinas should have made better use of the original sense of the words *prosopon* (Greek) and *persona* (Latin), which is "mask." His doctrine could have been more easily understood today if we spoke of roles "in the strict sense of the three roles in a theatrical cast."[6] Therefore, McCabe, in his account of Trinity, never uses the word "person."[7] Many years later Catholic theologian Karen Kilby agreed with McCabe: while dealing with the Trinity in order to avoid tritheism we should get rid of the word "person."[8]

What kind of "relations" are trinitarian relations? "Subsistent" relations, that is, relations that exist regardless of the existence of the terms that they are relations of. In fact, in a note in the beginning of *God Matters* McCabe writes that he is not happy any more with saying that the Spirit is the love between Father and Son because this suggests that Father and Son are "persons" in the modern sense of the word.[9] However, perhaps to concede something to imagination, when McCabe speaks of Father, Son, and Spirit, he speaks *as though* they were human people, each one of them with his own characteristics and activities. As for the Father, his "mission" (quite an unusual attribute for the first person) is to achieve his purposes out of Jesus' death.[10] As for the Son, the most important thing said and lived by Jesus is that he is loved by the Father: so, the Father "grows up" and is able to love on

5. McCabe, *God, Christ and Us*, 51.

6. McCabe, *God Still Matters*, 52–53.

7. McCabe, *God Still Matters*, 52.

8. Kilby, "Perichoresis and Projection," 434. As for an apophatic interpretation of Aquinas' doctrine of Trinity, see her "Aquinas, the Trinity and the Limits of Understanding."

9. McCabe, *God Matters*, 1.

10. McCabe, *God Matters*, 99.

a plane of equality a Son who is not a creature any longer.[11] The whole teaching of Jesus is: the Father loves him and his followers are invited into their love.[12] His gift to us is two-fold: love itself (which is God) and the revelation that the Father loves him.[13]

The story of Jesus is the story of God. In one sense, God does not change and does not have a story, but in another sense he has a story in Christ. The story of Jesus "is nothing other than the triune life of God projected onto our history."[14] The crucifixion/resurrection is what the procession of Son from Father looks like when projected onto "sinful human history."[15]

As for the Holy Spirit, McCabe was not keen on some sugary representations of him in the post-Vatican II liturgies: where everybody is meant to shake and vibrate their body and arms and sing loudly, hug the others, and constantly smile pretending to be a loving friend of everybody else. Whereas, when Jesus says to the disciples that he is giving them joy, he is not reassuring humans, saying that everything will be well; or, at least, not only this. That joy given to us by Jesus is the Holy Spirit, the joy that God has (or is), his joy for being God.[16] McCabe thought that, rather, the Holy Spirit was an unpredictable force that transforms peoples and individuals, but to achieve his goals he has to dismantle and renovate. In fact, similarly to the mission of the Son, the sending of the Spirit and the existence of the church is what the procession of the Spirit looks like while projected onto a sinful world. This is the reason why the Spirit appears destructive and catastrophic, like a "revolutionary force" for a new society and a new church. And new individuals also, but by "reducing them first to chaos."[17]

The Spirit of God is not the gentle ethereal "spiritual" thing of our delicate "spirituality." The doctrine of the Trinity was born when the church wanted to keep and protect the tremendous truth that the Spirit we have received from the Father through the life, death, and resurrection of Jesus is not a created thing or gift, is not a "perfection of our human life," but is *the life of God himself.*[18] The New Testament has many names for the Holy Spirit: joy, peace, unity, koinonia, the community of disciples, but above all

---

11. McCabe, *God Matters*, 18.

12. McCabe, *God Matters*, 96.

13. McCabe, *God Still Matters*, 4.

14. McCabe, *God Matters*, 48.

15. McCabe, *God Matters*, 23.

16. McCabe, *God, Christ and Us*, 52.

17. McCabe, *God Matters*, 23.

18. McCabe, *God Matters*, 95.

it is love. However, when we receive the Spirit we delight that God is God,[19] and this "love" has another and much more mysterious meaning than the ordinary one.

These three "persons," Father, Son, and Spirit, however, are not persons, that is individuals: God cannot be two individuals any more than he can be one individual.[20] While in a theatre there are people (individuals) who perform the roles, in the Trinity we should think just about the roles, and the system of these roles, which has meaning only in their mutual relations: the role of parenthood, of childhood, of love/delight. This is not, McCabe specifies, a description of the Trinity as if it was just talk about three *aspects* of God, as Sabellius has allegedly taught. Why? Because essential to the doctrine is that the works of the Trinity on the outside are indivisible (*opera ad extra sunt indivisa*). However, while the attributes (such as wisdom, omnipotence, and eternity) are not really distinguished in God's essence, but only in relation to us, the three "persons" are distinguished in God himself: "it is in his immanent activity of self-understanding and self-love/delight that the roles are generated."[21]

The scholastic distinction between "immanent" and "economic" Trinity says that within the Trinity the three persons relate to each other in different ways, but they act always together towards the universe. However, we creatures perceive these acts in different ways, because of "appropriation":[22] for example, the Father creates the universe *through* the Son *by* the Spirit: the Spirit gives us the life *of* the Son *from* the Father; the Son redeems us *thanks to* the Father *by* the Spirit. McCabe usually describes the works *ad extra* in this traditional way, for instance, saying that the mystery of the Trinity is "revealed" to us when we have faith in the "deepest meaning of the life, death, resurrection and ascension of Jesus"; or that the life of God is not first of all in sustaining the being of creatures, but is the life of love between the Father and the Son, and their delight is the Holy Spirit; or that we join Jesus in his sonship with the Father by receiving the Holy Spirit.[23]

19. McCabe, *God Still Matters*, 232.

20. McCabe, *God Matters*, 18.

21. McCabe, *God Still Matters*, 44, 53.

22. According to Augustine and Aquinas an appropriation is a theological procedure whereby we attribute especially to one divine person the common operation *ad extra* of the three persons. It is based on convenience with the properties, according to the way our minds work. Here again we should observe that McCabe, while focusing on the doctrine of creation, had already ruled out a God that was a powerful cause within the universe.

23. McCabe, *Teaching of the Catholic Church*, 9, 8; McCabe, *God Still Matters*, 236.

On the other hand, a couple of times McCabe says something obscure and non-traditional (an "original contribution," in his words): according to the tradition, the missions in time of the Son and Spirit reflect the immanent processions, but McCabe says that they are not only reflections but also "sacraments" that contain what they mean. In other words, Jesus' mission is nothing different from the generation of the Son.[24] The missions of the Son and the Spirit are not only "economic," but also "immanent," that is, unlike creation, redemption is not merely an *opus ad extra*, because it is the act by which we cease to be "extra" to God and "come within his own life."[25]

CONTEXTUALIZING

At some point in the late 1980s more and more theologians started expressing the idea that the study of the Trinity had been wrongly underrated in modern theology. One example among many is that of Nicholas Lash saying that the Trinity is necessary to individuate the Christian faith; it is central because the Trinity is the Christian God.[26] Thirty years afterwards, the Trinity scholar Fred Sanders (who eloquently titles his article "We Actually Do Not Need a Trinitarian Revival") reviews the writings of those theologians and, speaking about the changes of the rate of interest in the Trinity, observes:

> They all agree that there was a golden age, a fall, and a revival in our own time. But there is no agreement about when that fall occurred. Was it in the 19th century? The 17th? Perhaps the 5th or 4th centuries? . . . "Make the Trinity Great Again" turns out to be a pretty unstable slogan as soon as we ask a couple of basic chronological questions: When was it great before? When did it stop? How are you restoring it?[27]

So a certain degree of skepticism is in order about the "revival."

This perceived revival was triggered, in part, by the diffusion of "Rahner's rule," as Barth scholar Darren Sumner notices:

> Karl Rahner's famous "rule" states that the immanent Trinity is the economic Trinity, and vice versa. This was proposed in order

24. McCabe, *God Matters*, 48–49.

25. McCabe, *God Still Matters*, 53.

26. Lash, "Considering the Trinity."

27. Sanders, "We Actually Do Not Need a Trinitarian Revival," *Christianity Today* (online), May 23, 2017, *https://www.christianitytoday.com/ct/2017/may-web-only/we-dont-need-trinity-revival-fred-sanders.html*, accessed on 11/3/2019.

to cut off a number of unsavoury ideas, including the notion that God as God truly is remains hidden from us. No, when we see God acting in the world, we really do know God as God is![28]

The confident kataphaticism of this position was relevant in particular to the era of "social trinitariansim" in theological studies, where the relations between the three persons are seen as both the model and the cause of good interpersonal relationships within good human communities.[29]

The "Augustinian-Hegelian" approach of Lash is also kataphatic: he maintains that the dialectics of experienced life best corresponds to the number 3 and, therefore, is most adequate to symbolize the divine life. Lash maintains that it is quite true that our language is saturated with dualisms: inner and outer, mental and physical, spirit and flesh, public and private. It is to this dualism that "the God of modern theism seems . . . tailor made." Yet the triadic account of human experience that seeks "harmony between feeling, knowledge and desire: between tradition, explanation and choice" insists on the unity of human experience as well. Thus to pursue what has been imprecisely called "psychological" analogies of the experience of God's Trinity is, according to Lash, a legitimate way of working out the elements of the Christian Trinity.[30]

McCabe, by contrast, was apophatic, and was not at all keen on "social trinitarianism." In recent years, social trinitarian has been subject to piercing theological critique from many quarters. One deep criticism has been made by Karen Kilby, who digs into its causes. Relating the Trinity to the world of human relationships and its social issues was seen to be far less "elitist" and abstract than transitional discussions of substantial relations, properties, notions, and processions. She writes:

> [there is] a concern in recent theology to re-establish the vitality and relevance of the doctrine of the Trinity, and in fact I think it is here that the whole thing actually starts to go wrong. Does the Trinity need to be relevant? What kind of relevance does it need to have?[31]

Kilby maintains that these theologians act out of desire for popularity, in fact, "[i]f one is going to make an abstraction, a conceptual formula, relevant, vibrant, exciting, it is natural that one is going to have to project onto it, to fill it out again so that it becomes something the imagination can latch

---

28. Sumner, "What Is the Immanent Trinity?" n.p.

29. As critically reported by Kilby in "Perichoresis and Projection," 432.

30. Lash, "Considering the Trinity," 192.

31. Kilby, "Perichoresis and Projection," 442–43.

onto."[32] Kilby denies that the point of the doctrine about Trinity is providing us with an "insight into God" or a "picture of the divine," and argues that instead it should be "taken as grammatical, . . . as a rule for how to read the Biblical stories."[33] In this she sympathizes with McCabe's apophaticism:

> McCabe in fact argues quite explicitly that although the Trinity is a mystery, it is not as though things get any worse for our understanding with the introduction of the doctrine of the three persons—God is entirely a mystery from the beginning. . . . I have a good deal of sympathy for these lines of thought.[34]

CONCLUSIONS

An overview of McCabe's thoughts about the Trinity shows that it was important for him to relate the Trinity to redemption, where the significance of Jesus' life and death is seen not only as liberation from sin but also as divinization.

In a not-so-clear passage McCabe relates the presence of the Trinity to our painful human condition: the prayer of the Christian faithful is never just the prayer of a creature to her or his Creator, because it shares in the cross and resurrection of Jesus and, so, the dialogue between the Son and the Father. If we look at the cross and we are filled with the Holy Spirit, we see that the Trinity is there. This is "strange," but it is also strange how human beings look in our history, despised and tortured.[35]

Here McCabe seems to say that being divinized in the Trinity is at the same time both a liberation from the painful injustices of our fallen world and (because of the link between cross and resurrection) a liberation from our mortal creaturehood.

For McCabe, Incarnation, redemption, and Trinity can be summarized saying that: (1) God is Creator and cannot love his creatures qua creatures; (2) God loves Jesus, who is equal with God; (3) Jesus is sent by the Father; (4) we can believe this because we are brought from our creaturehood into the Holy Spirit. Therefore, abstract theory about the Trinity is just the message that God is love and is not a "boss" in charge of the world. Our relation to the mystery is to start from love and not from power.[36]

32. Kilby, "Perichoresis and Projection," 443.
33. Kilby, "Perichoresis and Projection," 443.
34. Kilby, "Aquinas, the Trinity and the Limits of Understanding," 425.
35. McCabe, *God Matters*, 100.
36. McCabe, *God Matters*, 22.

Thus, as we have already seen in the chapter about creation, we see here that one consequence of his thought about the Trinity is to disprove the ancient Neoplatonic hierarchical model. A non-trinitarian God leaves us with the idea that God is a "boss" of the universe and our master;[37] but if we take the Trinity seriously we must reject this idea, because for Christianity the deepest truth is that people are loved, and this is only possible because we are taken into the love between Father and Son, because we are allowed to share that love among equals within God.[38] Therefore:

> The picture of the creator God surrounded by his creatures, all dependent on him, is in the end an infantile picture. It does not allow God to experience the mature relationship of love. The announcement of Jesus is that this picture is out of date. In Jesus the Father has one whom he loves as an equal and the gospel is that we are called to share in the exchange of love between them, to share in the Holy Spirit. The doctrine of the Trinity lies at the foundation of the Christian gospel because it announces the most ultimate liberation of people, their liberation from God, or to put it less dramatically, their liberation from mere creaturehood. The gospel announces that we stand before God not simply as creatures before a benign creator. We stand before him as Jesus does, as equals in an exchange of love.[39]

Since Jesus was fully a human being and so are we, McCabe makes the two very theological doctrines of redemption and Trinity merge and flow into a sort of paradoxical humanism.[40]

37. Because in the non-Trinitarian God there are not any missions of the Son (redemption) and of the Spirit (sanctification) which take us up into the life of God and into (as adopted children) a system of relationships between equals.

38. McCabe, *God Matters*, 98.

39. McCabe, *God Still Matters*, 181.

40. McCabe, *God Still Matters*, 181.

16

Church and Sacraments

CONTEXT

First Henri de Lubac and then Karl Rahner developed their theology of the church as the second principal "sacrament of salvation" after the uber-one, that is, Jesus Christ, the God Man. Following their view, the Second Vatican Council highlighted the distinction between the church (penultimate reality, sacrament) and kingdom (ultimate reality). Edward Schilleebeckx reports the long conflictual discussions of the bishops then, when eventually a majority gathered and stated that the "mystery of the church" is *not* the "Roman Catholic Church."[1]

This stand of the Catholic council gets close to the old "Protestant Principle," that is, the relation between visible and invisible church: they must never be separated nor identified but understood as existing in continuous tension with each other.[2]

Along with this image of sacrament, to depict the church Anglican theology took two other typical Vatican II images: the people of God and the body of Christ, and added two more Protestant depictions: the communion of faith, hope, and love and the creation of the Spirit.[3]

---

1. Schilleebeckx, *Church—the Human Story of God*, 190–93.
2. Hodgson and Williams, "The Church," 230.
3. Sykes, "Foundations of an Anglican Ecclesiology," 36.

McCabe, while writing his short catechism and his book about sacraments, stated a few very basic and "impartial" definitions of the church: it is the community that believes in Jesus thanks to the Spirit, and it is recognizable by her handing down (tradition) the word of God and his sacraments throughout time; the church is the community of the people who have been baptized and have not denied their faith; the church is also the community of the people who go to the Mass.[4] I say "impartial" because these definitions do not claim any holiness nor any moral superiority towards other religions and non-believers. They allow us—to some extent!—to *distinguish* Christians from others, but they do not advocate the *superiority* of Christians.

Additionally, McCabe agrees with the Protestants and the Vatican Council's bishops in complicating some previous definitions of "the church" and introducing mystery. A believer cannot recognize all the members of the church: there are, in other words, people united to the church by the means of links that are not visible.[5]

However, there is something more peculiar to him, related to his long-lasting political concerns; when the conservatives prevail, the church can be the "cement" for society, when the liberals prevail it can be the "model," when, instead, a totalitarian government takes power, it can be an "alternative" society. But always it is a "challenge." In the rare moments when the church is morally healthy, she is not interested in political power, but political power, for its part, has had a hostile interest in the church.[6]

So, McCabe somehow proudly advocates the prophetic role of the church, but, at the same time, he humbly wants to understate it ("rare moments"). If any Christian or theologian forgot the second element, he or she could build a sort of theocratical dualism *a la* Innocent the Third. Pride in the church, for instance, is shared by the adherents of today's Radical Orthodoxy movement, but not humility. In the words of McCarraher:

> First, McCabe's conception of the relationships among theology, politics, and culture are grounded in a much more modest ecclesiology. . . . The sacramental life of the Church points beyond itself to the future, where the Church will no longer exist. . . . [N]ot understanding this . . . makes Radical Orthodoxy so prone to ecclesial fetishism and sociological unreality. One of

---

4. McCabe, *The Teaching of Catholic Church*, 21; McCabe, *The New Creation*, 51.

5. McCabe, *The Teaching of Catholic Church*, 61.

6. McCabe, *God Still Matters*, 90. I comment that this "hostile" interest is twofold: (1) infiltrating the ecclesiastic institutions as summarized by the maxim *religio instrumentum regni*; (2) persecuting the church when it resists.

the things I came to like about McCabe's understanding of the Church is that it's so unpretentious and provisional.[7]

A RESPECTFUL CRITICISM

Historically, as Peter Hodgson and Rowan Williams say, the Reformation challenged the unity and holiness of the Roman Catholic church, and, a couple of centuries later, the Enlightenment challenged the supernatural and supra-historical character of any church. The Christian denominations were not destroyed by the massive criticism coming from the deism and the atheism of the "philosophes," but certainly from them took a more realistic and humble awareness. Today it is evident that the church is both united and divided, catholic but also sectarian, traditional but always needing renewal: more fundamentally, her holiness does not rule out her sins.[8]

Herbert McCabe agreed with all these critiques and still he remained loyal to his church. The only time he became "famous" among the general public was during the so-called "McCabe Affair" in 1967. McCabe, as editor of *New Blackfriars,* on the one hand defended Charles Davis, then the most important English Catholic theologian, who had decided to leave the priesthood; on the other, he stated that even though the church is "plainly corrupt" the individual must remain loyal to her. He wrote:

> It is because we believe that the hierarchical institutions of the Roman Catholic Church, with all their decadence, their corruption and their sheer silliness, do in fact link us to areas of Christian truth beyond our own particular experience and ultimately to truths beyond any experience, that we remain, and see our Christian lives in terms of remaining, members of this Church.[9]

In his criticism McCabe was respectful, by words also, but most of all by his actions, because, unlike Davis and many others, he remained loyal.

7. McCarraher and Keller, "Meet the New Boss, Same as the Old Boss," part three, n.p.

8. Hodgson and Williams, "The Church," 232, 235.

9. McCabe, "Comment," *New Blackfriars* 48.561, February 1967, 228–29.

THE STATUS AND ROLE OF THE CHURCH

Any criticism of the church from a progressive point of view, which was McCabe's, implies a constructive commitment towards the "world." In the spirit of the Vatican Council's *Gaudium et Spes* constitution, one of the most progressive Catholic theologians and a personal friend of McCabe, Edward Schillebeeckx, arguing that without secular history the churches are incomprehensible, reshaped Saint Cyprian's classical sentence into a new one: "*extra mundum nulla salus*," outside the *world* there is no salvation, that is, without a salvation of the world a special history of revelation is impossible. The churches are not the aim and the place of salvation, but, more humbly, the place of the explicit recognition of the overall salvific work of God.[10]

McCabe distinguished the world as the tangle of flawed compromises with "secular power" (that the church "sooner or later" must abandon, thanks to the Holy Spirit), from the world as *ecumene* of people and other creatures which has to be saved.[11] Because of the common priesthood that comes from our baptism, our task as Christians is to bring the world to God and God to the world; we are "condemned" to it because baptism is a sort of "sentence to death" whereby we do not want to conquer the world and we accept to share Jesus' priesthood on the cross.[12]

The words chosen by McCabe (condemned, sentence) show that for him the task is not well described by Trent's theology of "cooperation" or by Descartes' philosophy of "free will," but points to transcendence and eschatology, similarly to what Irenaeus said: "service [rendered] to God does indeed profit God nothing, nor has God need of human obedience; but He grants to those who follow and serve Him life and incorruption and eternal glory."[13]

Priesthood is related to sacraments. If we understand that the most fundamental priesthood is not the "ministerial" but the "common or universal" one coming from baptism, then we arrive at describing the "ontological status" of the church in a new way, because *all* members of the church deliver sacramental actions by their lives. As Lutheran theologian Robert W. Jenson says: "This teaching, that the church is herself a sort of sacrament, has become a centre not merely of Catholic ecclesiology but of ecumenical discussion."[14]

---

10. Schillebeeckx, *Church,* 12–14.

11. McCabe, *God, Christ and Us*, 13.

12. McCabe, *God, Christ and Us*, 154.

13. Irenaeus, *Against Heresies*, IV.14.1.

14. Jenson "The Church and the Sacraments," 207.

McCabe uses this concept in order to get rid of any triumphalism: "sacramental reality" means that the church is neither only the visible society nor some sort of invisible community. Both church and sacraments exist at an "intermediate level," in between human and divine reality.[15]

If this is the status of the church, what is the role she plays? It has been noticed by George Lindbeck that the church of today is more similar to the first church of early Christianity than to the church of intermediate periods, because it is small, less powerful, and even less visible.[16] Hauerwas (and many others) argue that this is not just a fact but also a *blessed* fact: the church must be prophetic, small, and alternative to the world's values; it is a bliss that today the church is weaker, less numerous; this is a unique opportunity.[17]

More than ruling and shaping the world according to her own ideals, the church of today would willingly embody the peculiar force of the Christian God, that is, love. Not a paternalistic love, however, in the words of McCabe, because from the model of a non-paternalistic God the church also must understand that hardworking volunteering, kindness, and benevolence are not the deepest levels of love and friendship. True love is between equals and therefore unpredictable. A paternalistic Christian "wants nothing to happen for the first time. But love is strictly connected with things happening for the first time."[18]

SACRAMENTS

In the sacraments God does what he shows and shows what he does, says McCabe quite traditionally, but, also, explaining that "sacrament" is a term that can be interpreted in different ways: in the deepest one it is not just a symbol of God, but also a symbol of God's plan for human destiny.[19]

Questions abound. Are the sacraments *necessary*? What *are* they actually? *How many* of them are there? Lutheran Jenson answers:

> [I]t depends: necessary for whom? . . . [T]here is in fact notable ecumenical agreement: Eucharist and baptism (the latter

15. McCabe, *The New Creation*, xiii.

16. Lindbeck, "The Church," 190.

17. Hauerwas, *Resident Aliens*, 17–18.

18. McCabe, *God Still Matters*, 180.

19. McCabe, *The New Creation*, 23; McCabe, *The Teaching of the Catholic Church*, 27.

including "confirmation") are necessary for all, and the remaining rites on the Tridentine list are surely necessary for some.[20]

However, all of them, even the necessary ones, are not sufficient. McCabe underlines that sacraments are just "intermediate" and "provisional" realities: the sacraments do not belong to the vision of God but to the age of faith in this intermediate period between Christ's resurrection and our resurrection; the sacramental life is "ironic" because we do not have anything to gain; it is not the future kingdom and it points to the future kingdom only insofar as we recognize that the church that gives us the sacraments is not the future. We need sacraments because we live in an alienated world, whereas in the kingdom we do not need them because there will be a direct exchange of love.[21]

As for the single sacraments, McCabe holds the views widespread at the time of the Second Vatican Council, even though with incisive focus. For instance, he says that the meaning of the Eucharist is the very "human stuff" of eating together. Also, it is a "thank you" because gradually humankind is brought together. In fact, it is friendship, but a dramatic friendship, because of the link with the "blood and torture" of Jesus' cross: in the sacrificial meal we show our "solidarity with each other and with all the victims of this world"; we are reunited with the person on the cross through whom humankind "is brought through death and out of death to unity in the eternal life of love."[22]

Using the words of older Catholic theology McCabe says that in the Eucharist is present a "mystery of the church" (the consecration of our offerings) and a "mystery of grace" (the unity of the disciples in the spirit of love). Using words of the Vatican Council's theology, he says that the greatest sacrament is the Eucharist, where the future unity of humankind in the kingdom is anticipated.[23] He discusses transubstantiation at length, also because he thinks that the sacraments are a divine "language."[24] Much of his thought is sacramental, and he uses the sacraments as analogies with which to think through many other things.

20. Jenson, "The Church and the Sacraments," 214.

21. McCabe, *The New Creation*, xiii–xiv, 178; McCabe, *God Matters*, 175.

22. McCabe, *God Matters*, 51, 86–87; McCabe, *God, Christ and Us*, 155.

23. McCabe, *The Teaching of the Catholic Church*, 24–25.

24. McCabe, *God Matters*, 116–79

CONCLUSIONS

The concepts McCabe highlights in his ecclesiology are those that were considered up-to-date around the years of the Council among progressive Catholics. He never distinguishes and compares the Catholic church with the others, Protestant and Orthodox. In his arguments the church is only the church of Christ. Also, there is not any triumphalism towards the "world"; on the contrary, he says that the church is "plainly corrupt." Moreover, there is not any identification between the church and the kingdom of God: the church, being a sacrament, points to God, but is made of vulnerable material.

However, all having been said, to oppose the pre-Council clerical triumphalism, from his philosophical anthropology and from his political commitment, McCabe repeatedly states and prophesies that the church is "the sacrament of the future united humanity."

17

Life in Grace
and the Eschatological Perspective

A TRANSVALUATION OF ALL VALUES

The slogans *sola fide* and *sola gratia* express that teaching of Saint Paul (Eph 2:8) that was variously interpreted in the doctrinal battle between Catholics and Reformers five centuries ago. 482 years later, in 1999, in Augsburg, Catholics and Lutherans signed the *Joint Declaration on the Doctrine of Justification*, subsequently signed by the Methodists (2006), the Anglicans (2016), and the World Communion of Reformed Churches (2017). In it we see a substantial historic theological reconciliation between these two branches of Christianity:

> We confess together that good works—a Christian life lived in faith, hope and love—follow justification and are its fruits. When the justified live in Christ and act in the grace they receive, they bring forth, in biblical terms, good fruit.[1]

However, throughout the last five centuries, for all of the signatories, the very concepts of justification, grace, works, and the like, have changed meaning to such an extent that I find it appropriate to title this section using the Nietzschean phrase "transvaluation of all values." The change in

1. *JDDJ*, 37 [http://www.vatican.va/roman_curia/pontifical_councils/chrstuni/documents/rc_pc_chrstuni_doc_31101999_cath-luth-joint-declaration_en.html .

eschatology, both Catholic and Protestant, is one of the easiest to see: in the sixteenth century all Christians were dealing with grace and works in order to guess something about the afterlife destiny of human beings: heaven or hell? Today few Christians speak (or think, for that matter) about hell. One of the major victories of the much despised and criticized liberal theology is indeed the widespread ecumenical agreement about eschatological universalism, if not explicitly, at least by means of omission.

Still today grace and works (as fruits of grace) are meant to bring us to what both the ancient philosophers and the common sense of the everyday person call "happiness," and, also to what Christians call "holiness" or "sanctity." But how so? Not any longer as a divide between inferior and superior, damned and saved as two definite categories of fellow human beings. No. For many today the Christian message has abolished hierarchies and imaginings about the "afterlife sojourn." Instead, *sola fide/sola gratia* works first of all by maintaining faith (within an increasingly atheistic world); secondly, in finding ethical directions (as was always the case), and, thirdly, in nurturing an eschatological hope (often visualized more as a mysterious dimension of our lives, than as an afterlife sojourn).

McCabe fully embraces this line: we are made children of God by the Holy Spirit. This is the good news. When we depart from grace, we have a false God, and his righteous wrath is only the projection of our guilt. In reality, God does not react to the world, to good or bad people, he loves us even if we are not good. He does not forgive us because we repent, but the other way around: we repent because he has already forgiven us. He does not demand anything from us.[2]

"Jesus comes to us in a complete failure, in one who suffers and is defeated, as a condemned and despised and executed criminal,"[3] therefore he is really a non-demanding model, in terms of success. Likely our parents and many other agencies of society were or are indeed demanding and ask us to perform successful deeds. But God the Father in Jesus shows us that failure is ubiquitous and for everyone, but, also, that in the midst of failure hope may be present. *Sola gratia*, indeed! But while for John Calvin the acceptance of grace was as demanding as Ignatius de Loyola's exercises, for McCabe and many of us grace means mainly God's love and initiative. McCabe's theology of grace follows the mainstream "transvaluation" of the late twentieth century, which gets rid of hell and focuses on God's acceptance much more than on his refusal.

---

2. McCabe, *The Teaching of the Catholic Church,* 10; McCabe, *God Still Matters,* 9; McCabe, *God, Christ and Us,* 61, 27.

3. McCabe, "Coming to the Father," 321.

Contemporary sensibility sees grace mostly as a gift meant for our wellbeing, rather than a challenge and a responsibility. It is true that some gifts are not easy to be discerned. Are riches, security, and health gifts of God? However, life is God's gift in itself and we are to enjoy and to be grateful for it.[4] This life is transformed by the Holy Spirit, which is received while not merited by us.[5]

> [T]he good news is that the Father comes to us. In one way, a negative way, Christians do perhaps understand God better; because they won't have any substitutes, any idols, any gods. They have the sort of clearer, uncluttered, understanding that atheists have.[6]

In fact, most of all, we do not understand. Our theological language is both as imperfect and ambiguous as our sacramental celebrations and our political actions are, because we live in the "pre-revolutionary" era when "the gospel seeks to be at home in a transitional world."[7] But we are all the same allowed to live a good life through our friendship with God and with other people. This good life is really friendship and happiness when to our natural virtues God adds the supernatural or theological virtues, and we can perform acts of happiness, those very ones acted by the poor, the meek, the persecuted and the like, that is, the beatitudes.[8] And how happiness can identify with the beatitudes is something we do not understand.

TRANSFORMATION

Since God's grace provides happiness through the beatitudes, this means that our life paths do not follow our plans. At the beginning of my life I tread the path of mundane goods and human natural virtues. It is true that God at the end will show me, says McCabe, that the thing I want most is God himself; but to get this end there is not any shortcut: we all start as children and need time to grow up; there is no good in faking that we have already arrived. Never treat a child as an adult, otherwise she will not grow up into a real adult. If you treat yourself as a saint you will never become one, nor

---

4. McCabe, *God, Christ and Us*, 65.

5. McCabe, *The Teaching of the Catholic Church*, 11.

6. McCabe, "Coming of the Father," 322.

7. McCabe, *God Matters*, 175.

8. McCabe, *he Teaching of the Catholic Church*, 11, 49. For the relationships between virtues, gifts, and beatitudes according to Aquinas, see Erlenbush, "The Beatitude of Poverty, the Gift of Fear, the Virtue of Hope': the beatitudes are not habits nor stable realities of the soul, unlike virtues and gifts, but are acts, like happiness itself is an act.

you will want to become one.[9] Therefore, the path of seeking the natural (Aristotelian) virtues is something that we should not skip.

However, afterwards, we realize that we are called to a continuous quest, and we have to leave behind our personality, which we used to interpret as complete; now we see that it has to be reshaped in a way we are not able to fully anticipate in advance.[10] Christians cannot give simple advice on how to get a better understanding of God: "there is no straight and settled road towards God. . . . God in man may be anywhere at any time. He is like a thief at night time." You never know when the revelation is offered to you. The gospel does not explain God to you; at best, it makes you ready, open and vulnerable "to the sudden flashing out of divinity at the most unlikely moment."[11] Grace surprises us.

This preparation, in which we detach ourselves from our past personality, in which we become ready and open to the unpredictable, is indeed a transformation of our natural potentialities, personal desires, and the habits we have acquired from society. However, McCabe underlines that the agency of this transformation is not our own: there are ways to become more human (e.g., following commandments, developing virtues), but no means to become divine: this in fact is *God's* business.[12]

One major proof of this transformation is our attitude towards love. If to love (and not just to be loved) is our natural need, when we do love, we are challenged in depth and feel fearful because we see that we have to abandon ourselves. But if love wins over fear, when we love, we indeed overcome that fear of losing ourselves and discover that to love God is similar to loving ourselves. What is fear? A disbelief in myself, because I think that I do not matter, I do not really exist, it is fear to play a false part, wearing a disguise. But, although this is a common experience in loving other people, this does not apply to my love for God, because I know that he loves me unconditionally. All this is transformation.[13]

As we have already seen while speaking of redemption, that is, from the point of view of the Redeemer God, in the same way now, from our point of view, by "grace" we mean that *we are given divinity* (apart from being forgiven and cleansed from our sins).[14] We could have been able to con-

9. McCabe, *God, Christ and Us*, 9.

10. McCabe, *God Matters*, 94.

11. McCabe, *God, Christ and Us*, 144.

12. McCabe, *God Still Matters*, 104, 103.

13. McCabe, *God, Christ and Us*, 71; McCabe, *God Matters*, 174, 93, 95; McCabe, *God, Christ and Us*, 70.

14. McCabe, *God Matters*, 22. Grace is the effect of redemption: what we receive. We receive the theological virtues and the gifts of the Holy Spirit.

ceive the idea of the Creator God just contemplating the world, but without a divine revelation we would never have been able to know that God loves us, not just to make us flourish and be happy, but also to share his friendship and divine life.[15]

In fact, this divine friendship is not a clear and conventional "flourishing" of any sort. The mission of the God Man Jesus was to be fully human, but this goal implies defeat: because of the natural "unjust" death we have already mentioned and because of the wicked structures of human community. Jesus failed, and the Easter Vigil can be interpreted as the celebration of the meaning of Jesus' life, passion, and death, rather than a new step in the series.[16] Death is inevitable for us human beings, but thanks to life in grace we live it as a gift and as divinization.

LIFE IN GRACE: THE THEOLOGICAL VIRTUES

A contemporary Dutch theologian, Pieter H. Vos, maintains that

> [i]t is commonly held that Reformed ethics is basically accomplished as an ethics of divine commandments, creational orders and—to a lesser extent—(human) rights, whereas theological virtue ethics is in particular developed in the Roman Catholic tradition.[17]

Why so? There is a long historical path, which started in the sixteenth century with the Reformers despising the non-biblical (pagan) treatise of the virtues. Catholic theologians, instead, did not idealize the apostolic times and appreciated the long-lasting tradition coming from ancient Greek wisdom up to us. More in particular, as for that particular Catholic that McCabe was, first of all, intellectual and moral virtues including self-control cannot last for long without "divinely inspired self-denial"; in themselves human virtues soon degenerate into "subtler forms of selfishness and pride."[18] McCabe argues that for everybody, and more clearly for Christians, it is the theological virtues (faith, hope, and charity) that "bear on our friendship with God."[19] When we say that we "share" God's life by "sanctifying grace" we mean that we are given the three theological virtues: faith makes us relate

15. McCabe, *God, Christ and Us*, 63.

16. McCabe, *God Matters*, 99, 106.

17. Vos, "Calvinists among the Virtues," 201.

18. McCabe, *The New Creation*, 78.

19. McCabe, *Teaching of the Catholic Church*, 50.

to the Father, hope makes us trust in his justice, and charity allows us to be a friend of God.[20]

Let us now analyze these virtues in turn. Faith is a saving gift because is something positive for us humans. It is a sort of optimism, as it were. In fact, the traditional Augustinian doctrine (*intellige ut credas, crede ut intelligas*)[21] points to a reciprocal reinforcement of two acts of ours that are, in any case, necessary, and to whose flourishing it would be regrettable if they conflicted with each other: the act of believing somebody else and the act of examining and understanding reality by ourselves. Augustine says that in order to understand for ourselves, we need a previous story of believing and trusting in others (faith oriented to reason), and that we then investigate personally and carefully by ourselves, in order to be able to give trust to a person non-blindly (then it is reason oriented to faith).

As for *intellige ut credas* (reason oriented to faith), McCabe says that if we examine the reasons of those who reject faith, while pondering their arguments, we could deepen it, distinguishing our faith from prejudices and purifying our beliefs, finding a better way of formulating them.[22] We see Christians that exercise their reason state

> that they know nothing of God. Christians think that anyone who claims to know God has set up some kind of idol in place of God. Christians say that they are in the dark; it is the special darkness they call faith. Christians are not proud of being in the dark; they just know that they are.[23]

Now, faith is not fideism (a blind faith not sustained by the *praeambula fidei*, that is, reasoning). When McCabe was a child, he was taught that Christians show their "loyalty," their "faith," by believing what is hard to be believed in, thus, to embrace humility; the great enemy was "spiritual pride." But when he grew up, he disliked this interpretation of faith, and leaned towards the teaching of the book of Hebrews, where faith is related entirely to understanding.[24] I observe that only such faith is leaning on a true humility, not on a false one, which comes from laziness and cowardice.

As for *crede ut intelligas* (faith oriented to reason), McCabe says that in faith we interpret both the history of humanity and our life-story as centred on the love of God as revealed in the Son of God Jesus, so that our eventual

20. McCabe, *Teaching of the Catholic Church,* 50, 61.

21. Augustine, *Sermones,* 43:9.

22. McCabe, *Teaching of the Catholic Church,* 53.

23. McCabe, "Coming to the Father," 321.

24. McCabe, *God, Christ and Us,* 1.

understanding of our existential path derives from an initial vitalizing trust that makes us raise our head.[25] On the same line, he says that sinners may think that they cannot be loved if they reveal their sins: however, faith is precisely the conviction—which comes from Jesus—that God loves us *even when we are sinners*. Therefore, faith come first, when still we do not see, and understanding of God's love comes second.[26]

This optimistic experience of integration and reinforcement, as we have seen, is a gift. The giver hands it out to us through the community of the other receivers, that is, the other faithful, the church. To a candidate for baptism we ask: what do you want from the church of God? And one's answer is *faith!* The church gives us our faith and also is the custodian of it.[27] Faith in what? What is central in Jesus' teaching? It is not easy to answer; however, it is the Christian community *as a whole* that is entitled to say what is central, not lone individuals within it.[28]

If faith plays an optimistic role in our lives, paradoxically the second virtue, hope, is not an evidently easy form of optimism. For McCabe, according to Christianity, we just have to accomplish our tasks for justice, for the poor. Because of this struggle for justice, Christian hope goes through suffering and the cross. However, we sacrifice our lives only if we have hope that God will bring life from this defeat.[29]

The principal expression of the virtue of hope is our prayer.[30] Starting from our requests addressed, as children, to our parents, we experience love and gratitude when through prayer we see that we receive good things. However, our parents would have given us those good things in any case, at least most of them. In the same way, but even much more, in the case of God the Father, we do not change his mind, but he changes ours, in order that we can recognize what he has given to us, and so we believe in him and love him.[31]

Because of hope we pray, but hope is God's gift, and so is prayer also. My prayer is the action of God in me, it is God who prays. In fact, prayer, as everything, starts from God. He decides that we pray and he answers our

25. McCabe, *Teaching of the Catholic Church,* 50.

26. McCabe, *God, Christ and Us,* 60.

27. McCabe, *The New Creation,* 44.

28. McCabe, *The New Creation,* 82.

29. McCabe, *God, Christ and Us,* 15.

30. McCabe, *Teaching of the Catholic Church,* 55, 57–58.

31. McCabe, *God, Christ and Us,* 6.

prayer giving us: (1) what we ask, or (2) more than what we ask, but (3) never less than what we ask.[32] This is the divine side of prayer.

Whereas, the human side of it is the embodiment of it within our life-story and concrete desires. Actually, this is Victor White's idea followed and preached by McCabe: the good prayer is the petitionary prayer, too often despised in favor of "spiritual" ones. We should ask God for the "little" or "material" things that we really desire and treat God as a father or a friend; in fact, more than them, he accomplishes our good desire.[33]

Apart from prayer, we exercise the virtue of hope through contrition, that is, that pain that comes out of repentance. In fact, we allow ourselves to feel contrition only because we hope that God will forgive us and transform this sinful world. Since prayer and contrition are the actions of hope, they cannot thrive when we fall into the vices opposed to hope: presumption and despair. Despair says it is useless to pray for God's grace and to work for the kingdom. Presumption says it is needless to pray for God's grace and to work for justice and peace. Both vices share an exaggerated estimate of myself and my world instead of a confidence in God's love.[34]

Charity is love as given by God's grace. This love must be ordered and its hierarchy is: (1) love for God, (2) for ourselves, (3) for our neighbor, (4) for our material possession including our bodily life.[35] In fact, we are meant to love life passionately, provided that we do not set it above our love for God, ourselves (meaning our moral self), and our neighbors.[36] Points (1) and (2) are strictly connected to each other: what is the meaning of loving God? For McCabe, the best answer is to ask what it is to love ourselves; and we can know the latter if we start asking what it is *not* to love ourselves (as we have seen in the chapter about ethics).[37]Whereas, points (3) and (4) easily conflict with each other in human lives and often we give up our love for the others because we are attracted by material lesser goods.[38]

Charity is a supreme value, or ultimate end: to stay in friendship is to treat it as more important than anything else, even life. It is to think that

---

32. McCabe, *God Matters*, 222; McCabe, *God Still Matters*, 71; McCabe, *God, Christ and Us*, 71, 6–7, 106.

33. McCabe, *God Matters*, 220–4; McCabe, *Teaching of the Catholic Church*, 56; McCabe, *God Still Matters*, 73.

34. McCabe, *Teaching of the Catholic Church*, 59–60.

35. McCabe, *Teaching of the Catholic Church*, 61.

36. McCabe, *God Christ and Us*, 65.

37. McCabe, *God Christ and Us*, 70.

38. McCabe, *Teaching of the Catholic Church*, 64.

sharing life is better than an individual life, it is better to die instead of living a long life alone.[39]

Personal friendship is the model for human society according to Aristotle, and also according to Jesus, who put his personal friendships as a model for reciprocal love within the church.[40]

In the New Testament the opposite of love is not hatred but *fear*, which, therefore, is the root of sin. What fear? Fear of not being loved, of thinking that one, in oneself, does not matter for the others (parents, for example), so that we must act a false role in disguise in order to be loved, but fearing that under the disguise there is nothing. Here McCabe diverges strongly from Aquinas, for whom pride is the root of all sins and is opposite to love. This disagreement comes from a misunderstanding: in fact, McCabe says that fear clashes with love because by the word "love" he means "to *be loved*." Whereas Aquinas says that pride clashes with love because by the word "love" he means "to love": pride is the only sin where aversion from loving God is not motivated by conversion to loving minor goods.[41]

Charity, like the other two theological virtues, is a gift from outside, we learn to love when we *are* loved, we cannot gain charity by introspection, because it is a sharing of life with God. Therefore, the root of love is faith, our faith that God loves us so that we can love ourselves and be grateful for the gift of ourselves. This is the meaning of "loving God."[42]

THE ONCE FUTURE THINGS

In Christian doctrine and also in popular religiosity there used to be four *novissima*, that is, "ultimate future things": death, judgement, heaven, and hell. But, after WWII, more and more quickly, this interpretative angle on human life has changed and almost vanished. "Hell" has almost disappeared from the preachers and conversations of Christians. We know this phenomenon from our personal experience, but there are also surveys,[43] and even Pope Francis has declared that the "souls" who refuse the saving love of God do not suffer the torments of hell but are "annihilated."[44]

When explicit Christian faith has so diminished and atheism so spread, to believe in God and in the life he provides his children is the important

39. McCabe, *God, Christ and Us*, 49.

40. McCabe, *God, Christ and Us*, 57.

41. McCabe, *God, Christ and Us*, 17, 70. Aquinas, *ST*, 2a-2ae, qu. 162, art.2.

42. McCabe, *God, Christ and Us*, 71; *The New Creation*, 72.

43. Parry, "Hell."

44. Scalfari, "Il Papa: 'È un onore essere chiamato rivoluzionario.'"

point, not the divide between hell and heaven. A reviewer of three recent monographs on the topic notices that they share a central idea: eschatology is concerned with "future hope" and, since it depends on God's initiative, not on human effort, it is impossible to figure out a "design" whereby to make predictions about the future, unlike Hegelian teleology.[45] This means that the harsh and long-lasting debates among the different Christian denominations about the means of understanding divine predestination to salvation or to damnation have become very rare outside of certain theological subgroups.

McCabe, on this point, does not provide any new interpretation. However, like almost everybody else, he does not mention hell either and adheres to what John E. Thiel and Katherine Sonderegger called the "non-competitive" eschatology that spread after the Second Vatican Council.[46] "Non-competitive" means that we do not visualize any "race" in which there are the losers (the damned) and the winners (the saved).

Summarizing McCabe's views on the four last things, we see a judgement that is not a weighing of evil and good;[47] a hell without a role, both theoretical and practical; a heaven that is embodied in the meaning of our life: and a death that is the center of human life because it offers us the opportunity to anticipate it, that is, to change an inevitable doom into a free choice, and reach the meaning of life: to give up our life for the sake of our friends.

To echo the title of T. H. White's tetralogy, we might rather call them the four "once-future-things" because once upon a time they were considered the last future things of human life, but much less in our time. McCabe does not address explicitly this historical point. As a theologian, he is content to be "apophatic," while speaking of the afterlife of the individual, and "radical," while speaking of the "revolutionary" ethical commitment in this life. As we have seen in the chapter about ethics, revolutions' outcomes are achieved in the future and are unpredictable, but revolutions themselves are undertaken now.

---

45. Horton, review, 94.

46. Sonderegger, "Towards a Doctrine of Resurrection," 116.

47 According to humanism, what is important in order in evaluating a human life is the algebraic sum of good deeds and bad deeds. According Christianity, this record does not matter. McCabe gives the example of Florence Nightingale's life, which would have been evaluated very good by humanists because of her good deeds in Crimea. But Christians know that, in the eyes of God, Florence's life was evaluated well because God could fill her with his powerful life in the moment of her death, regardless of Crimea.

Conclusions

18

A Recollection

SUMMARY

The recollection of Herbert McCabe's fragmented legacy—the main purpose of my toil—has been accomplished. On the one hand, from all McCabe's scattered (as for literary genre and editorial story) and fragmented (as for contents) works I could make visible a complex philosophical and theological system of thought, endowed with completeness and a logical structure. On the other, while treating each part, I continually explicated the conceptual connections with the others: of God's knowability with creation, of existence in general with the problem of evil, of anthropology with ethics and Incarnation, of ethics with redemption and grace, and so forth.

Both accomplishments are new in scholarship about Herbert McCabe, as is the thorough and scholarly study of most of its constituent parts. Another original achievement of my research—that of putting McCabe into historical context—was obtained in tracing A. D. Sertillanges, E. Gilson, and Victor White, the "existential" Thomists who influenced McCabe and provided him with that "apophatic" philosophical theology that allowed him to be comfortable with the development of natural sciences (Darwinian biology and Big Bang cosmology), social sciences (psychoanalysis, philology, and economics), and the radical questions coming from neo-Marxism.

263

In these conclusions I want to: (1) highlight some metaphysical features that pervade all the parts; (2) assess McCabe's communicative style; (3) underline some examples of concepts that can be usefully applied in our lives; and (4) select two methodological attitudes McCabe handed down to the theologians of today.

OVERALL METAPHYSICAL FEATURES

In every part of his system McCabe states a metaphysical realism, in between idealism and materialism: the world does not consist of facts but of things, concerning which there are facts—not just appearances but things with definite natures and which have appearances.[1] His realism is not materialistic, however. For instance:

> The perception is not itself a physical object; it is the relation of one physical object to others. It exists at a certain level of abstraction. Aquinas does not hesitate to say that the perceptions of brute animals are "spiritual," meaning that an animal acts in terms of such relations of relevance and not simply as, say, a billiard ball is pushed physically by another. "Spiritual," then, because belonging to the first move in transcending matter.[2]

Similarly ubiquitous is his stand in between immanence and transcendence. For instance:

> the point of human living cannot lie outside human living. I mean it cannot lie outside in the way that the point of being a machine lies outside itself. Machines exist to amuse and/or be useful to human animals. The point of human living cannot be either to amuse or be useful to other animals. I think it is true and very, very importantly true that the point of human living lies beyond itself, but not outside itself. This is because I think that in the end the point of human living lies in God, who is beyond us but not outside us. God, unlike the birds or any other creatures, cannot lie outside us because he creates us and sustains us all the time, making us to be and keeping us as ourselves. So to say that the point of our lives is in God is not to point to something outside us but to a greater depth within us.[3]

---

1. McCabe, *On Aquinas*, 17.
2. McCabe, *On Aquinas*, 35–36.
3. McCabe, *On Aquinas*, 53.

These two metaphysical features are the strongest landmarks of his insertion within the *perennis philosophia* coming from Aristotle and Aquinas.

STYLE

Among many others, Brian Davies notes that McCabe's talks (and writings, which most times were just the prepared text of his talks) presented difficult concepts "in a way that only the best communicators can manage," and "they were models of clarity and incisiveness."[4] Clarity is a characteristic that I have not found frequently in philosophical and theological texts, whereas I think it is a major intellectual virtue; and a moral one as well, as Turner says of Aquinas.

> One might say, likewise, that what humility is to the moral life, lucidity is to the intellectual, an openness to contestation, the refusal to hide behind the opacity of the obscure, a vulnerability to refutation to which one is open simply as a result of being clear enough to be seen, if wrong, to be wrong.[5]

McCabe sought precisely such clarity and depth. But he did not seek originality for its own sake. I completely agree with Davies when he says that "originality is very much context-dependent and can also consist in style and presentation."[6] McCabe himself, speaking of his own works, say that there are thoughts that "bear repetition because they are perennially forgotten."[7]

In accomplishing this task McCabe was unequalled. What he was doing was reviving and making intelligible major philosophical concepts from the tradition, which had become incomprehensible and blurry; ideas such as the transcendence of God, the non-substantiality of Trinitarian persons, and the many others that we have explored in the previous pages.

In this reviving of old concepts and in his admirable clarity we see his original style of communication on display. I call it "original" because it is so rare in academia, at least among metaphysicians of the last decades. Sadly, in the academic world clarity is often interpreted as shallowness, and the analysis of old concepts—regardless of its freshness and depth—is often perceived as non-originality. The penalty academia itself has to pay for this misperception is long-lasting and twofold: most academics are trapped

4. Davies, "Introduction," in McCabe, *McCabe Reader*, Kindle loc. 179.

5. Turner, "Foreword" to McCabe, *Faith within Reason*, viii.

6. Davies, "Introduction," in McCabe, *McCabe Reader*, Kindle loc. 487.

7. "Preface" to McCabe, *God Matters*.

either in a rigid and dumb literalism or in a talkative empty iconoclasm. Denys Turner, despite being an academic himself, admits:

> He [McCabe] didn't fit the fashions of the academic world either in style or theological method. So much the worse for that world, of course: he was simply a whole lot better than his theological peers, sharper, clearer, remorselessly more precise, and impossible to pin down to any fashion; and to this day the professional theologians find it difficult to know what to do with him.[8]

APPLICABILITY OF MCCABE'S IDEAS

As an intellectual, McCabe did not aim at being "up-to-date" with the intellectual fashions, let alone at flattering and being flattered by the allegedly "happy few" other intellectuals. For him philosophy and theology have their only worthiness in their helpful and, maybe, salvific applicability to the daily life of the human beings. Certainly, McCabe followed the example of his mentor Victor White, Jung's friend, who wrote:

> our present-day understanding of the psychological function of symbols and beliefs may help us to understand how eminently practical and inherently salutary such seemingly speculative treatises as those on the Trinity, the Incarnation, the Eucharist are.[9]

And McCabe introduces his most important volume finding "fascinating parallels with the anti-dualism and 'materialism' of St Thomas in the work of modern depth-psychology."[10] In fact, if there was not any practical applicability why on earth would these esoteric disciplines be worth caring for? But for McCabe, notes MacIntyre, the commitment and the enthusiasm was "to understand Aquinas both in his own terms and in ours and so to overcome the 'dry emptiness' that plagues many expositors of Aquinas."[11] Here I present some important examples.

One is the difference between creation and natural causality among creatures: the latter works within a world where every effect is potential: potentiality is there because other things already exist. Although not original,

---

8. Email to me on 22/5/2018.
9. White quoted in Nichols, *Dominican Gallery*, 69.
10. "Preface" to McCabe, *God Matters*.
11. MacIntyre, "Foreword" to McCabe, *God Still Matters*, vii.

this reflection revives a buried and forgotten doctrine and now we can use it against both the creationists (who claim to be able to build a cosmology and a biology from the allegedly understood nature of God) and the new atheists like Dawkins, who shape their counter-arguments relying on creationists' arguments.

Another example comes from the way whereby he presents God's transcendence, a way that is able to demythologize in depth the mainstream interpretation of the classical doctrine while sticking closely to it. In fact, he says that, given the radical difference between what is created and what is uncreated, God as Creator cannot be thought of as existing before creation—he cannot be something that existed before our universe and then made it. We cannot hold a proper concept of creation and are obliged to build an imaginary pattern representing the Creator God and the created universe alongside each other: "the model of God as another being over against us belongs (probably necessarily belongs), like the sacraments and all religious cult, to the era of man's alienation."[12]

The useful applicability of this point lies in debunking the widespread interpretation of a God who rivals human beings, a God who has to refrain from his omnipotence in order to guarantee freewill to humans, a zero-sum-game God who kindled the complaints of atheistic Feuerbach and Nietzsche.

From this same traditional doctrine of creation, and the entailed distinction between created and uncreated, McCabe draws a powerful demythologization of deification both in Incarnation and in redemption. In fact, to say that a man is God is not contradictory, whereas that a man is a sheep is contradictory. Just as we cannot infer anything about Fred from Fred being created, so we cannot infer anything about Jesus from Jesus' divine nature being uncreated; to be divine is not to be a kind of being, just as to be a creature is not to be a kind of being.[13]

Therefore, the "new creation" (our deification coming from redemption) is not an improvement of creatures, as it would happen to a man, for example, who became more virtuous and pious.[14] The useful applicability of this point is in debunking all the claims of the "born again" fundamentalists about their moral and even psychological superiority to all the not-yet-born-again others.

Still from the doctrine of creation and from the classical attribute of God's changelessness, McCabe produces a demythologization of both Jesus

12. McCabe, *God Matters*, 170.

13. McCabe, *God Matters*, 70–71.

14. McCabe, *The New Creation*, 3.

Christ and God. There is not any "moment at which the eternal Son was not Jesus of Nazareth," because in God's life there are *no* moments. The eternal life of the Son does not *precede* nor is it *simultaneous with* his human life: "there is not a story of God before the story of Jesus." There is not a "story" of God *at all* apart from the story of Jesus. McCabe observes that the claim that the triune God, as Creator, does not *pre*-exist the universe—for there is no temporality apart from the space-time of creation—is almost unintelligible to those who think of God as an individual actor within the universe.[15] But that is precisely the confusion that must be transcended if we are to think aright not only about God but also about God's world.

What is useful in this last idea that we could apply to our lives?

Perhaps the stress on what used to be called "Christocentrism" in the aftermath of the Second Vatican Council. The life and beliefs of a Christian are not the same as those of a generic theist. The profound and lively tie with history, a historical person, and a historical community provided by Christocentrism is the key to maintaining faith and standing up to contemporary atheism. McCabe himself witnessed this, keeping such a focus while slaloming among sciences, liberal capitalism, Marxist revolutions, medieval philosophy, church reform, secularization, and new atheism, and while remaining a loyal member of his church, though acknowledging that this church is morally corrupt and intellectually muddled.

The last example is my favorite one: following and reviving the Aristotelian tradition, McCabe wrote an entire catechism without employing the word "soul," not even once. As we have seen in the chapter about anthropology, he was acutely aware of the negative consequences for Christian faith coming from any philosophical dualism. Secular thinkers often ridicule Christian faith, especially for its alleged theory of an autonomous "soul," which is meant to be the "real" human person, like the body, only lighter and ethereal. McCabe's very paradoxical statement is that the brain is not the organ of thought because the human mind is fundamentally interpersonal, and the organ of thought is language. We are animals in which our sociality produced language, and we can translate the medieval word "spirit" and "intellect" with the word "language." Therefore, the collective mind (the "spirit") is *completely human* and is not God (unlike what Alexander of Aphrodisias maintained, and which worried Aquinas). The long-time incomprehensible "passive" and "active" intellects are explained by McCabe as the universal human capability to learn a language, and the actual language learned by a historical group. Once you realize that the lonely well-heated room of Descartes and the lonely sitting thinker of Rodin are deceptive

15. McCabe, *The New Creation*, 3.

icons of intellectual activity, you can find many-sided useful applications in education and politics.

APOPHATICISM AND TRAGEDY

There are two typical intellectual attitudes that McCabe brought to theology: apophaticism and a tragic view of human life. As far as I can tell, the former took root in the wider theological environment, but the latter did not.

Apophaticism has spread fairly widely throughout the theological scene. McCabe and David Burrell (and after them Denys Turner, Brian Davies, and several others) established in the theological environment that apophaticism is not at all a kind of fideism or mysticism, which was the mainstream interpretation beforehand, at least in the Catholic world. Today the many of the apologists who counter the arguments of the new atheists—people such as Denys Turner, Terry Eagleton, Rupert Shortt, and David Bentley Hart—rely directly on McCabe's non-mystical apophaticism.

Here, however, I want to suggest that several paths, opened up by McCabe, are still to be trodden. In Christology, for example, as Ian McFarland explained, we can "understand" Jesus' humanity, but his divinity is a mystery. Any improvement of our knowledge of Jesus' humanity does not involve a better knowledge of his divinity. According to many theologians, still nowadays, Jesus' humanity is mistakenly seen only in what is good and brave but still imitable, while the divinity allegedly abides in certain inimitable extraordinary qualities. But this temptation has to be resisted because we can only point to what is created, and those aspects are just human, not divine. However, most theologians have still to understand this crucial point of Christology.

Another theological path to be followed is in ethics and ecclesiology. In these fields kataphaticism rules, and the transient features of our preferred life-style as individuals and as community are presented as essential parts of Christian life. Whereas, McCabe tells us that self-denial is the watershed between failure and hope: when Jesus says "only the one who loses his self," he was talking about the meaning of human life as going always beyond a personal identity that has become a possession and a source of pride. In fact, "self-assertion is a failure to take the risks of living; it is settling for what we were, for the image in the mirror."[16] Whereas, every "structure," McCabe observes, be it the family, the church, or whatever other, is just to be "used"

16. McCabe, *God, Christ and Us*, 75–76.

by individuals throughout their path towards the ultimate end, because all structures are just "tents, shacks."[17]

Every structure, every collective institution, is unable on its own to account for the essence of human community. I think that an injection of apophaticism into ethics and ecclesiology will be something new, a refusal to confuse the "manuals" with the "rule-book" (to recall a powerful metaphor of McCabe).

Before concluding I want to mention another major intellectual aspect of McCabe's attitude: a tragic view of human life and history. To my knowledge, appearances to the contrary,[18] unlike apophaticism I conjecture that this tragic view has not taken roots yet. (I cannot provide this hypothesis with sound and detailed arguments here and this might be the subject of future research.) According to McCabe, human life is much more tragic than humanism holds. All of us should die in Christ, regardless of whether we do so publicly as the martyrs do, or privately; in fact, the same giving up of life is asked of all of us.[19]

Because of the evils of the world, all humans are asked to give up their lives: there is no casual death but only a choice between martyrdom and betrayal.[20] Our "hope" is different from mere optimism.[21]

I think that both on paper and verbally in the ethical debate this point of view is missing. Most philosophers and educators speak just of how we should seek a "flourishing" life,[22] so forgetting that even in the Aristotelian framework friendship was more important than success, justice more than wealth and health, and courage was praised as an active defiance of death for the sake of justice. (Actually, this is a powerful example of the degree to which a cultural bias that affects the mind of the current scholars can lead to a very misleading interpretation of an ancient author, in this case Aristotle.) Justice, yes; we know that McCabe saw himself as a revolutionary, not as a reformer. He took strong inspiration from the political revolutions

17. McCabe, *God, Christ and Us*, 4.

18. For example in Rowan William's *The Tragic Imagination*.

19. McCabe, *New Creation*, 75–76.

20. McCabe, *New Creation*, 125, 127.

21. McCabe, *God, Christ and Us*, 19. This idea from McCabe has been effectively developed by Terry Eagleton in his already mentioned *Hope without Optimism*.

22. Even though there is a new minoritarian tendency to studying virtue ethics in a less self-assuring way, i.e., the revisiting of Thomistic ethics from the point of view of "infused virtues." See Jean Porter's pioneering study "The Subversion of Virtue: Acquired and Infused Virtues in the 'Summa theologiae'," *The Annual of the Society of Christian Ethics*, Vol. 12 (1992), 32, 36; and Andrew Pinsent's book *The Second-Person Perspective in Aquinas's Ethics: Virtues and Gifts*, (Milton Park: Routledge, 2012).

of his times and from neo-Marxist movements. He was against hierarchies; he wanted equality.

Equality is not achieved by a creature through progressive improvements of its nature, it is not a sort of Lamarckian (that is, hierarchical) evolution, but, rather, it requires the end of any hierarchical structure. McCabe thinks that in us, linguistic animals, reason permits that natural hierarchies could be "slowly subverted by love."[23] However, we see that hierarchies and inequalities still spoil and dishearten the people of our time. For instance, in Western societies the neo-Marxist move towards "poverty" (decreasing food, weight, consumerism, waste, struggles for career and exploitation) produced a "therapy" for the few of us, for our "flourishing" and a progressive "improvement" of our human assets "according to nature." And so new, subtle, and hidden hierarchies are built and established because the people who do not "flourish" are secretively excluded and left behind.

Rather and instead, this move towards poverty could imply something different: a sort of "anticipation" of death. To every human being death is in any case inevitable, but this path of self-denial shows the possibility of dying before we are "naturally" meant to, to *choose* the risk of death instead of only to passively suffer it. McCabe reminds us that to believe in the cross, as distinguished from merely expecting it, "is to believe that this challenge to the world at the cost of destruction is not only right but the key to what human life is about, that in this act we have the revelation of the divine."[24]

23. McCabe, *God Still Matters*, 4–5.
24. McCabe, *God Still Matters*, 97.

Bibliography

Acta Apostolicae Sedis, Vl (1914), 38386; VII (1916), 15758.

Alfaro Jimenez, Juan. *Cristología y antropología*. Madrid: Ediciones Christianidad, 1973.

Anonymous. "Obituary: Dorothy Emmet." *The Guardian*, 25 September 2000.

Anononymus. "Father Herbert McCabe." *Irish Times*, 3 September 2001.

Aquinas, Thomas, *Summa Theologiae (ST), Summa Contra Gentes (SG), Commentary on the Metaphysics of Aristotle, Questiones Disputatae de Veritate, On Being and Essence, De Potentia*. In *St. Thomas Aquinas' Works in English*, edited by Joseph Kenny, 2013, online, https://dhspriory.org/thomas/, accessed on 28/3/2019.

Aristotle. *De Interpretatione*. In Works by Aristotle, online, http://classics.mit.edu/Browse/browse-Aristotle.html, accessed on 28/3/2019.

Augustine of Hippo. *On Correction and Grace; Sermones*. In Christian Classics Ethereal Library—Calvin College—Saint Augustine Works. Online, https://www.augustinus.it/links/inglese/opere.htm, accessed on 28/3/2019.

Aulén, Gustaf. *Christus Victor: An Historical Study of the Three Main Types of the Idea of Atonement*. Reprint, Eugene OR: Wipf & Stock, 2003.

Benedetto XVI. *Il Dio della fede e il Dio dei filosofi*. Rome: Marcianum, Kindle Edition, 2013.

Boer, Roland. "The Ethical Failure of Terry Eagleton." *Monthly Review*, 22 September 2010. Online, https://mronline.org/2010/09/22/the-ethical-failure-of-terry-eagleton/, accessed on 13 January 2020.

Bonansea, Bernardino M. "The Human Mind and the Knowledge of God: Reflections on a Scholastic Controversy." *Franciscan Studies* 40 (1980) 5–17.

Bonhoeffer, Dietrich. *Christology*. London: Collins, 1966.

Boyd, Gregory A. "What Is the Warfare Worldview?" *ReThink Everything You Thought You Knew*. Online, http://reknew.org/, 2 June 2014.

Bugyis, Eric, and David Newheiser, eds. *Desire, Faith, and the Darkness of God: Essays in Honour of Denys Turner*. Notre Dame, IN: University of Notre Dame Press, 2015.

Bugyis, Eric. "As We Were Saying." In *Desire, Faith, and the Darkness of God: Essays in Honour of Denys Turner*, edited by Eric Bugyis and David Newheiser, 328–62. Notre Dame, IN: University of Notre Dame Press, 2015.

Burrell, David. *Aquinas: God and Action*. 1979. Reprint, Eugene, OR: Wipf and Stock, 2016.

———. *Freedom and Creation in Three Traditions*. Notre Dame, IN: University of Notre Dame Press, 1993.

———. *Friendship and Ways to Truth*. Notre Dame, IN: University of Notre Dame Press, 2000.

———. *Knowing the Unknowable God: Ibn-Sina, Maimonides, Aquinas*. Notre Dame, IN: University of Notre Dame Press, 1986.

———, with Elena Malits, C.S.C. *Original Peace: Restoring God's Creations*. New York: Paulist, 1997.

Carol, Juniper B. "The Absolute Predestination of the Blessed Virgin Mary." *Marian Studies* 31 (1979) 180–87.

Clavier, Paul. "Sartre and Sertillanges on Creation." *The Review of Metaphysics* 69.1 (2015) 73–92.

Clayton, Philip. *"Creatio ex Nihilo* and Intensifying the Vulnerability of God." In *Theologies of Creation: Creatio ex Nihilo and its New Rivals*, edited by Thomas Jay Oord, ?–?. London: Routledge, 2014.

Clements, Simon. *The McCabe Affair. Evidence and comment*. London: Sheed and Ward, 1967.

Coackley, Sarah. "What Does Chalcedon Solve and What Does It Not? Some Reflections on the Status and Meaning of the Chalcedonian 'Definition.'" In *The Incarnation: An Interdisciplinary Symposium on the Incarnation of the Son of God*, edited by Stephen Davis, Daniel Kendall, Gerald O'Collins, 143–63. Oxford: Oxford University Press, 2002.

Cornwell, John. "MacIntyre on Money" (interview). *Prospect Magazine*, November 2010. Online, https://www.prospectmagazine.co.uk/magazine/alasdair-macintyre-on-money, accessed on 28/3/2019.

Corrin, Jay. *Catholic Progressives in England after Vatican II*. Notre Dame, IN: University of Notre Dame Press, 2013.

Cunningham, Adrian. "Herbert McCabe. Theologian, Philosopher and Radical Supporter of Christianity." *The Guardian*, Monday 16 July 2001.

Davies, Brian. "Foreword." In *The Good Life: Ethics and the Pursuit of Happiness*. London: Continuum, 2005.

———. "Introduction." In Herbert McCabe, *Faith Within Reason*, xi–xii. New York: Continuum, 2007.

———. "Introduction." In Herbert McCabe, *God and Evil*, xiii–xviii. London: Continuum, 2010.

———. "Introduction." In Herbert McCabe, *God Still Matters*, xi–xiv. London: Continuum, 1987.

———. "Introduction." In Herbert McCabe, *On Aquinas*, x–xii. London: Continuum, 2011.

———. "Introduction." In *The McCabe Reader*, edited by Brian Davies and Paul Kucharski, 1–29. London: Bloomsbury T. & T. Clark, 2016.

———. *The Reality of God and the Problem of Evil*. New York: Continuum, 2006.

———. "Thomas Aquinas on God and Evil." Lecture given at The Lumen Christi Institute on 11 April 2012. Online, https://www.youtube.com/watch?v=h1AZvn4tESs, accessed on 7 March 2019.

———. *Thomas Aquinas's Summa Theologiae: A Guide and a Commentary*. Oxford: Oxford University Press, 2014.

de La Peña, J. R. Ruiz. *Teologia della creazione.* Roma: Borla, 1986.

De Lubac, Henri. *The Mystery of the Supernatural.* Translated by Rosemary Sheed from *Le Mystere du surnaturel,* 1965. New York: Crossroad, 1998.

Doerge, Halden. "Herbert McCabe: The Underrated Theologian." *Inhabitatio Dei,* 7 August 2007. Online, http://inhabitatiodei.blogspot.com/, accessed in October 2015.

Duffy, Eamon. "Herbert McCabe." In *Oxford Dictionary of National Biography.* Oxford: Oxford University Press, 2004–16.

Eagleton, Terry. "Disappearing Acts." Review of *Thomas Aquinas: A Portrait* by Denys Turner. *The London Review of Books* 35.5 (2013). Online, [https://www.lrb.co.uk/the-paper/v35/n23/terry-eagleton/disappearing-acts, checked on 12 January 2020.

————. *The Gatekeeper: A Memoir.* London: Allen Lane, 2002.

————. *Hope without Optimism.* London: Yale University Press, 2015.

————. "Lunging, Flailing, Mispunching." Review of Richard Dawkins, *The God Delusion. The London Review of Books* 28.20 (2006). Online, https://www.lrb.co.uk/the-paper/v28/n20/terry-eagleton/lunging-flailing-mispunching, checked on 12 January 2020.

————. *Materialism.* New Haven: Yale University Press, 2016.

————. "Priesthood and Paradox." *New Blackfriars* 77 (1996) 316–19.

————. *Reason, Faith and Revolution: Reflections on the God Debate.* New Haven: Yale University Press, 2009.

Emmet, Dorothy. *Whitehead's Philosophy of Organism.* London: McMillan, 1938.

Encyclopaedia Britannica. Online, https://www.britannica.com/, accessed on 27 March 2019.

Erlenbush, Ryan. "The Beatitude of Poverty, the Gift of Fear, the Virtue of Hope." *The New Theological Movement,* 31 August 2013. Online, http://newtheologicalmovement.blogspot.com/2013/08/the-beatitude-of-poverty-gift-of-fear.html,   accessed 27/3/2019.

Fergusson, David A. S. *The Cosmos and the Creator: An Introduction to the Theology of Creation.* London: SPCK, 1998.

Figueiredo, Louis C. de. *C. G. Jung, Father Victor White and Privatio Boni.* Online, https://www.academia.edu/7344691/C._G._Jung_Father_Victor_White_and_privatio_boni, accessed on 27 March 2019.

Fletcher, Joseph F. *Situation Ethics: The New Morality.* Philadelphia: Westminster, 1966.

Flew, Anthony. "Divine Omnipotence and Human Freedom." In *New Essays in Philosophical Theology,* edited by Anthony Flew and Alasdair MacIntyre, 144–69. New York: Macmillan, 1955.

Friedman, Harvey. *A Divine Consistency Proof for Mathematics.* Athens, OH: Ohio University Press, 2012.

Garrigou-Lagrange, Reginald. *God, His Existence and Nature: A Thomistic Solution of Certain Agnostic Antinomies.* 1914. Reprint, Saint Louis, MO: B. Herder, 1949.

Gerber, William. *Anatomy of What We Value Most.* Amsterdam: Rodopi, 1997.

Gilson, Etienne. *The Christian Philosophy of St. Thomas Aquinas.* 1948. Reprint, London: Gollancz, 1957.

Gleeson, Andrew. "God and Evil: A View from Swansea." *Philosophical Investigations* 35.3–4 (2012) 331–49.

Gödel, Kurt. "Ontological Proof." 1941. In *Collected Works: Unpublished Essays & Lectures, Volume III*, 403–4. Oxford: Oxford University Press, 1995.

Gould, Stephen Jay. *A Wonderful Life*. London: Hutchinson Radius, 1990.

Green, Joel, and Mark Baker. *Recovering the Scandal of the Cross: Atonement in New Testament and Contemporary Contexts*. Downers Grove, IL: InterVarsity Press, 2000.

Gunton, Colin. *The Actuality of Atonement: A Study of Metaphor, Rationality and the Christian Tradition*. Edinburgh: T. & T. Clark, 1988.

Haldane, John. Review of *God and Evil*, by Herbert McCabe. *Notre Dame Philosophical Reviews, an Electronic Journal*, 29 November 2011. Online, http://ndpr.nd.edu/news/27487-god-and-evil-in-the-theology-of-st-thomas-aquinas/, accessed on 27 March 2019.

Hart, Trevor. "Redemption and Fall." In *The Cambridge Companion to Christian Doctrine*, edited by Colin Gunton, 189–206. 1977. Reprint, Cambridge: Cambridge University Press, 2001.

Hauerwas, Stanley. "Learning the Language of Peace: What It Means for the Church to Be Catholic." *ABC Religion and Ethics*, 13 June 2012. Online, https://www.abc.net.au/religion/learning-the-language-of-peace-what-it-means-for-the-church-to-b/10100474, accessed on 7/3/2019.

———. *Resident Aliens*. Nashville-TN: Abingdon, 1989.

———. "An Unpublished Foreword." *New Blackfriars* 86 (2005) 291–95.

Hegel, Georg Wilhelm. *Encyclopaedia of Philosophical Sciences*. 1830. Cambridge: Cambridge University Press, 2010.

Hobson, Theo. "Eagleton the Apologist." *The Guardian*, 9 January 2010.

Hodgson, Peter C., and R. Williams. "The Church." In *Christian Theology*, updated edition, edited by Peter C. Hodgson and Robert H. King, 249–71. Minneapolis: Fortress, 1994.

Horton, Michael. Review of *What Dare We Hope?* by Gerhard Sauter. *International Journal of Systematic Theology* 4.1 (2002) 100–104.

Houser, R. E. "Avicenna, *Aliqui* and the Thomistic Doctrine of Creation." Center for Thomistic Studies, University of Saint Thomas, Houston, TX, 2000. Online, http://t4.stthom.edu/users/houser/avicenna2000.pdf, accessed on 4 March 2019.

Irenaeus. *Against Heresies*. In *New Advent—Fathers of the Church*. Online, http://www.newadvent.org/fathers/0103.htm, accessed on 28 March 2019.

Jackson, Roy. Review of *An Introduction to the Philosophy of Religion*, by Brian Davies. *Ars Disputandi* 4 (2004) ?–?.

Jenson, Robert W. "The Church and the Sacraments." In *Cambridge Companion to Christian Doctrine*, edited by Colin Gunton, 207–23. Cambridge: Cambridge University Press, 1997.

Jung, Carl Gustav, and Victor White. *The Jung-White Letters*. Edited by Ann Conrad Lammers and Adrian Cunningham. London: Routledge, 2007.

Kant, Immanuel. "Transcendental Dialectic." In *Critique of Pure Reason*, in Online Library of Liberty, https://oll.libertyfund.org/titles/ller-critique-of-pure-reason, accessed on 28 March 2019.

Keating, James F. Review of *Aquinas and Radical Orthodoxy: A Critical Inquiry*, by Paul DeHart. *The Thomist* 79 (2015) 155–59.

Kenny, Anthony. *Brief Encounters: Notes from a Philosopher's Diary*. London: SPCK, 2018.

———. "Foreword." In Herbert McCabe, *On Aquinas*. London: Continuum, 2011.

———. *Medieval Philosophy*. Oxford: Oxford University Press, 2005.

Kerr, Fergus, *After Aquinas. Versions of Thomism*. Oxford: Blackwell, 2008.

———. *Theology after Wittgenstein*. London: SPCK, 1997.

Kilby, Karen. "Aquinas, the Trinity and the Limits of Understanding." *International Journal of Systematic Theology* 7.4 (2005) ?–?.

———. "Perichoresis and Projection: Problems with Social Doctrines of the Trinity." *New Blackfriars* 81.956 (2000) ?–?.

Kimel, Aidan. "Open Theism, Eternity and the Biblical God." *Eclectic Orthodoxy*, 14 November 2016. Online, https://afkimel.wordpress.com/2016/11/14/open-theism-eternity-and-the-biblical-god/, checked on 19 January 2020.

Lactantius. *De Ira Dei*. In New Advent—Fathers of the Church. Online, http://www.newadvent.org/fathers/0703.htm, accessed on 28 March 2019.

Ladaria, Luis. *Antropologia Teologica*. Casale Monferrato-Roma: Piemme-PUG, 1986.

Lammers, Ann Conrad, and Adrian Cunningham, eds. *The Jung-White Letters*. London: Routledge, 2007.

Lash, Nicholas. *Believing Three ways in One God: A Reading of the Apostles' Creed*. London: SCM, 1992.

———. "Considering the Trinity." *Modern Theology* 2.3 (1986) 183–96.

Lewis, C. S. *Mere Christianity*. London: Bles, 1952.

———. *The Problem of Pain*. London: Centenary, 1940.

Liccione, Mike. "On Evil and Omnipotence." In *Sacramentum Vitae*, 12 March 2008, Online, http://mliccione.blogspot.it/2008/03/on-evil-and-omnipotence.html, accessed on 28 March 2019.

Lindbeck, George. "The Church." In *Keeping the Faith: Essays to Mark the Centenary of Lux Mundi*, edited by G. Wainwright, 178–208. London: SPCK, 1989.

Lutheran World Federation and the Catholic Church. *Joint Declaration on the Doctrine of Justification*, Augsburg, 1999, #37. Online, http://www.vatican.va/roman_curia/pontifical_councils/chrstuni/documents/rc_pc_chrstuni_doc_31101999_cath-luth-joint-declaration_en.html, accessed on 7 March 2019.

Mackie, J. L. "Evil and Omnipotence." *Mind* 64 (1955) 200–212.

Marcuse, Herbert. *Eros and Civilization*. Boston: Beacon, 1955.

Maritain, Jacques. *Raison and Raisons*. Fribourg-Paris: Egloff, 1947.

Massa, Daniel. *PSI King-Maker: Thought and Adventures of Peter Serracino Inglott*. Valletta: Allied Newspapers, 2013.

McCabe, Herbert. "Analogy." Appendix 4 in Thomas Aquinas *ST, vol. 3, 1a, questiones 12 and 13—Knowing and Naming God*, edited by Herbert McCabe, 105–6. London: Blackfriars, 1964.

———. "Catholic Marxists." Letter to *The Spectator* 1 July 1966, 13.

———. "Coming to the Father" *New Blackfriars* 68.807 (1987) 320–23.

———. "Comment." *New Blackfriars* 46 (1964) 2–5.

———. "Comment." *New Blackfriars* 48.561 (1967) 228–29.

———. "Comment." *New Blackfriars* 60 (1979) 402–3.

———. "Dilemmas by Gilbert Ryle." *Blackfriars* 35 (1954) 548–55.

———. "Dr Robinson's Book." *CrossCurrents* 14 (1964) 25–34.

———. "Essays in Conceptual Analysis by Antony Flew." *Blackfriars* 37 (1956) 539–40.

———. "Evil." In *God Matters*, 25–36. London: Continuum, 2005.

———. *Faith within Reason*. New York: Continuum, 2007.

————. "Forgiveness." In *Faith within Reason*, 55–58. New York: Continuum, 2007.

————. "God and Creation." 1980. *New Blackfriars* 94 (2013) 385–95.

————. *God and Evil*. 1957. Reprint, New York: Continuum, 2010.

————. *God, Christ and Us*. New York: Continuum, 2005.

————. *God Matters*. 1987. Reprint, London: Continuum, 2005.

————. *God Still Matters*. Edited by Brian Davies. New York: Continuum, 2002.

————. *The Good Life*. New York: Continuum, 2005.

————. "Introduction." In *The Teaching of the Catholic Church*, ix–x. 1985. London: Darton, Longman & Todd, 2000.

————. "Knowledge." Appendix in Thomas Aquinas *ST, vol. 3, 1a, questiones 12 and 13—Knowing and Naming God*, edited by Herbert McCabe, 97–99. London: Blackfriars, 1964.

————. *Law, Love and language*. 1968. Reprint, New York: Continuum, 2004.

————. "Manuals and Rule Books." In *Considering the Veritatis Splendor*, edited by John Wilkins, 83–105. Cleveland, OH: Pilgrim, 1994.

————. *The New Creation*. 1964. Reprint, New York: Continuum, 2010.

————. *On Aquinas*. New York: Continuum, 2011.

————. "On Evil." In *Faith within Reason*, 67-92. New York: Continuum, 2007.

————. "Received Wisdom?" Review of *Received Wisdom*, by B. Hoose. *New Blackfriars* 75.888 (1994) 580.

————. "The Role of Tradition." In *God Still Matters*, 199–212. New York: Continuum, 2002.

————. "The Secularisation of Christianity." *New Blackfriars* 46 (1965) 696–98.

————. "Sense and Sensibility." *International Philosophical Quarterly* 41.4 (2001) 411–20.

————. "A Sermon for St Thomas." *New Blackfriars* 63.742 (1982) 193–95.

————. "Soul, Life." In *Faith within Reason*, 123–47. New York: Continuum, 2007.

————. "The Structure of the Judgement: A Reply to Fr Wall OP." *The Thomist* 19 (1956) 232–38.

————. *The Teaching of the Catholic Church*. 1985. London: Darton, Longman & Todd, 2000

————. "The Word in Liturgy." *Blackfriars* 38 (1957) 57–65.

McCarraher, Eugene, and C. Keller. "Meet the New Boss, Same as the Old Boss—Interview." *The Other Journal*, 27 January 2010, online, https://theotherjournal.com/2010/01/12/meet-the-new-boss-same-as-the-old-boss-an-interview-with-eugene-mccarraher-part-one-of-three/ , checked on 19 January 2020.

McCarraher, Eugene. "Radical, OP: Herbert McCabe's Revolutionary Faith." *Commonweal,* 4 October 2010. Online, https://www.commonwealmagazine.org/radical-op , checked on 19 January 2020.

McCarraher, Eugene. "Mammon: Notes toward a Theological History of Capitalism." *Modern Theology* 21.3 (2005) 429–61.

McFarland Ian A. "Spirit and Incarnation: Towards a Pneumatic Chalcedonianism." *International Journal of Systematic Theology* 16 (2014) 143–58.

MacIntyre, Alasdair. "Foreword." In Herbert McCabe, *God Still Matters*. New York: Continuum, 2002.

————. *God, Philosophy, Universities*. New York: Rowman & Littlefield, 2011.

McKinney, Stephen. "Aquinas and Philosophical Anthropology." *The Expository Times*, 120, July 2009, 514.

Mercier, Desiré-Félicien-François-Joseph. "The Nature of God—The Metaphysical Essence of God." In *A Manual of Modern Scholastic Philosophy,* vol. 2, edited by Cardinal Mercier, 60–64. London: Kegan,1917.

Meynell, Hugo A. "Faith, Objectivity and Historical Falsifiability." In *Language, Meaning, and God: Essays in Honour of Herbert McCabe,* edited by Brian Davies, 145–59. 1987. Reprint, Eugene-OR: Wipf & Stock, 2010.

Micheli, Jason. "Holy Week with Herbert: No Atonement Theories Necessary." *The Tamed Cynic,* 25 March 2016. Online, http://tamedcynic.org/, accessed on 28 March 2019.

Milbank, John. "Gay Marriage and the Future of Human Sexuality." *ABC Religion and Ethics,* 13 March 2010, online, https://www.abc.net.au/religion/gay-marriage-and-the-future-of-human-sexuality/10100726, checked on 19 January 2020.

Mondin, Battista. "Il problema della conoscenza dell'essere." In *Manuale di Filosofia Sistematica. Ontologia,* 93–109. Bologna: Edizioni Studio Domenicano, 2007.

———. *Il problema del linguaggio teologico dalle origini ad oggi.* Brescia: Queriniana, 1971.

Mulhall, Stephen. "Grammatical Thomism." In *The Great Riddle: Wittgenstein and Nonsense. Theology and Philosophy,* ?–?. Oxford: Oxford University Press, 2015.

———. "What Is 'Grammatical' about Grammatical Thomism? Or: Doing Theology in a Realistic Spirit." Paper presented at the Aquinas Colloquy at Blackfriars, Oxford, 3 March 2012.

Murphy, Francesca Aran. *Art and Intellect in the Philosophy of Etienne Gilson.* Columbia, MO: University of Missouri Press, 2004.

———. "The Why-Proof as a Contingency Cliff-Hanger." In *God Is Not a Story: Realism Revisited,* 89–93. Oxford: Oxford University Press, 2007.

Myers, Ben. "Why I Am (Finally) Going to Read Herbert McCabe." *Faith and Theology,* 12 March 2008. Online, http://www.faith-theology.com/2008/03/why-i-am-finally-going-to-read-herbert.html, accessed on 1 April 2019.

Nichols, Aidan. *Dominican Gallery: Portrait of a Culture.* Leominster: Gracewing Flower Wright, 1997.

O'Grady, Paul. "McCabe on Aquinas and Wittgenstein." *New Blackfriars* 93 (2012) 631–44.

Orme Mills, John. "Fr Herbert McCabe." *The Independent,* 25 July 2001.

Owens, L. Roger. "McCabe's Distinctive Wittgensteinian-Thomism. The Theological Ethics of Herbert McCabe, OP: A Review Essay." *The Journal of Religious Ethics* 33 (2005) 569–92.

———. *The Shape of Participation.* Eugene, OR: Cascade, 2010.

Parry, Robin. "Hell." In *What are we Waiting For? Christian Hope and Contemporary Culture,* edited by Stephen Holmes and Russ Rook, 98–111. Milton Keynes, UK: Paternoster, 2008.

Pasnau, Robert. *Thomas Aquinas on Human Nature: A Philosophical Study of Summa Theologiae 1a,* 75–89. Cambridge: Cambridge University Press, 2002.

Pérez de Laborda, Miguel. "La preesistenza delle perfezioni in Dio. Lo apofatismo di SanTommaso." *Annales Theologici* 21.2 (2007) 279–96.

———. *La ricerca di Dio. Trattato di teologia filosofica.* Roma: EDUSC, 2011.

Peters, Ted. "Six Ways of Salvation: How Does Jesus Save?" *Dialog* 45 (2006) 223–35.

PhilPapers Survey 2009. Online, https://philpapers.org/archive/BOUWDP, accessed on 28 March 2019.

Phillips, Richard Percival. *Modern Thomistic Philosophy, vol. 2, Metaphysics*. London: Burns, Oates & Washbourne, 1934.

Pinsent, Andrew. *The Second-Person Perspective in Aquinas's Ethics: Virtues and Gifts*. London: Routledge, 2012.

Popper, Karl Raymond, and John Eccles. *The Self and Its Brain*. London: Routledge, 1984.

Porter, Jean. "The Subversion of Virtue: Acquired and Infused Virtues in the 'Summa theologiae.'" *The Annual of the Society of Christian Ethics* 12 (1992) 19–41.

Powell, Samuel M. *The Trinity in German Thought*. Cambridge: Cambridge University Press, 2001.

Pseudo-Dionysus. *De Divinis Nominibus*. In *Early Church Fathers—Additional Texts*, edited by Roger Pearse. Online, http://www.tertullian.org/fathers/areopagite_03_divine_names.htm, accessed on 28 March 2019.

Ratzinger, Joseph. *Il Dio della fede e il Dio dei filosofi*. Roma: Marcianum, 2013, Kindle edition.

——— (Benedictus XVI). *Spe salvi*, 2007. Online, http://w2.vatican.va/content/benedict-xvi/en/encyclicals/documents/hf_ben-xvi_enc_20071130_spe-salvi.html, accessed on 1 April 2019.

Rist, John. Review of *The Great Riddle* by Stephen Mulhall. *Philosophical Investigations* 40 (2017) 188–92.

Rundle, Bede. *Why There Is Something Rather Than Nothing*. Oxford: Oxford University Press, 2004.

Ryan, Columba. "Homily at Herbert McCabe's Funeral." *New Blackfriars* 82 (2001) ?–?.

Sanders, Fred. "We Actually Do Not Need a Trinitarian Revival." *Christianity Today* 23 May 2017. Online, https://www.christianitytoday.com/ct/2017/may-web-only/we-dont-need-trinity-revival-fred-sanders.html, accessed on 11 March 2019.

Scalfari, Eugenio. "Il Papa: 'È un onore essere chiamato rivoluzionario.'" *La Repubblica*, 28 March 2018.

Schilleebeeckx, Edward. *Church—The Human Story of God*. 1970. Reprint, London: SCM, 1990.

Schindler, David L. "Introduction." In Henri de Lubac, *The Mystery of the Supernatural*, xi–xxxi. New York: Crossroad, 1998.

Serracino Inglott, Peter. *Peopled Silence*. Msida, Malta: Malta University Publishers, 1995.

Sertillanges, Antonin-Dalmace (Gilbert), O.P. "Dieu, II." *La Quinzaine* 64 (1905) 382–412.

———. *Somme théologique de S. Thomas d'Aquin*. Éditions de la Revue des Jeunes. Paris: Desclée, 1947.

Shortt, Rupert. *God Is No Thing: Coherent Christianity*. London: Hurst, 2016.

———. *Rowan Williams: An Introduction*. London: Darton, Longman, and Todd, 2003.

Smith, James. *Terry Eagleton*. Cambridge: Polity, 2008.

Smith, Ethan D. *The Praise of Glory: Apophatic Theology as Transformational Mysticism*. University of Dayton and Ohio, 2017. Online, https://udayton.academia.edu/EthanSmith, accessed on 28 March 2019.

Sonderegger, Kate. "Towards a Doctrine of Resurrection." In *Eternal God, Eternal Life: Theological Investigations into the Concept of Immortality*, edited by Philip G. Ziegler, 115–28. London: Bloomsbury, 2016.

Soskice, Janet Martin. "Creation and the Glory of Creatures." *Modern Theology* 29 (2013) 172–85.

Stump, Eleonore. Review of *An Introduction to the Philosophy of Religion* by Brian Davies. *The Thomist: A Speculative Quarterly Review* 49 (1985) 128–31.

Sumner, Darren. "What Is the Immanent Trinity?" *Out of Bounds*, 16 June 2016, Online, https://theologyoutofbounds.wordpress.com/2016/06/16/what-is-the-immanent-trinity-a-clarification-for-the-eternal-subordination-debate/, accessed on 1 March 2019.

Sykes, Stephen. "Foundations of an Anglican Ecclesiology." In *Living the Mystery: Affirming Catholicism and the Future of Anglicanism*, edited by Jeffery John, ?–?. London: Darton, Longman & Todd, 1994.

Ticciati, Susannah. "An Introduction to the Doctrine of the Person of Christ." Lectures from Kings College London. Syllabus online, https://www.kcl.ac.uk/artshums/depts/trs/modules/syllabi-2015-16/5aat2006-syllabus-2014-15.pdf, accessed on 28 March 2019.

———. *A New Apophaticism*. Leiden: Brill, 2013.

Titus, Craig Steven. "The Jung-White letters." *New Blackfriars* 91 (2010) 354–57.

Trelstad, Marit A. "The Fecundity of Nothing." In *Theologies of Creation: Creatio ex Nihilo and its New Rivals*, edited by Thomas Jay Oord, 41–52. London: Routledge, 2014.

Turner, Denys. *The Darkness of God*. Cambridge: Cambridge University Press, 1998.

———. *Faith, Reason and the Existence of God*. Cambridge: Cambridge University Press, 2004.

———. "Foreword." Herbert McCabe, *Faith within Reason*. New York: Continuum, 2001.

———. "The Price of Truth: Herbert McCabe on Love Politics and Death." *New Blackfriars* 98 (2017) 5–18.

———. *Thomas Aquinas, a Portrait*. New Haven: Yale University Press, 2014.

Vanni Rovighi, Sofia. *Elementi di Filosofia*. Brescia, Italy: La Scuola Editrice, 1941–50. Reprint, 2013.

———. *Il problema teologico in filosofia*. Lugano: Eupress-TFL, 2004.

Vatican Council II. *Gaudium et Spes*. Online, http://www.vatican.va/archive/hist_councils/ii_vatican_council/documents/vat-ii_cons_19651207_gaudium-et-spes_en.html, accessed on 28 March 2019.

———. *Lumen Gentium*. Online, http://www.vatican.va/archive/hist_councils/ii_vatican_council/documents/vat-ii_const_19641121_lumen-gentium_en.html, accessed on 28 March 2019.

Vella, Mario. *Reflections in a Canvas Bag*. Marsa, Malta: PEG, 1989.

Vos, Pieter. "Calvinists among the Virtues: Reformed Theological Contributions to Contemporary Virtue Ethics." *Studies in Christian Ethics* 28.2 (2015) 201–12.

Weaver, J. Denny, *The Nonviolent Atonement*. Grand Rapids: Eerdmans, 2001.

White, Victor. *God and the Unconscious*. London: Harvill, 1952.

———. *God the Unknown and Other Essays*. London: Harvill, 1957.

Wilder, Thorton. *The Bridge of Saint Luis Rey*. 1927. Reprint, London: Penguin Classics, 2000.

Williams, Rowan. "Foreword." In Herbert McCabe, *God, Christ and Us*. New York: Continuum, 2003.

———. "A Future for Natural Theology?" In *The Edge of Words: God and the Habits of Language*, 8–11. London: Bloomsbury Continuum, 2016.

———. "Interview" by Terence Handley MacMath. *Church Times*, 18 March 2016, 26.

————. "Interview" by Rupert Shortt. *Fulcrum*, 14 December 2010, online, https://www.fulcrum-anglican.org.uk/articles/rowan-williams-on-belief-and-theology-some-basic-questions/ , checked on 19 January 2020.

————. "On Making Moral Decisions." *Anglican Theological Review* 81.2 (1999) 295–308.

————. *The Tragic Imagination*. Oxford: Oxford University Press, 2016.

Wippel, John. "Thomas Aquinas on the Ultimate Why Question: Why Is There Anything at All Rather Than Nothing Whatsoever?" *The Review of Metaphysics* 60 (2007) 731–53.

————, ed. *The Ultimate Why Question: Why Is There Anything at All Rather than Nothing Whatsoever?* Washington, DC: Catholic University of America Press, 2011.

Yaure, Philip. "The Problem of Evil: The Privation Defence and Meaningful Belief." *Polymath: An Interdisciplinary Arts and Sciences Journal* 2 (2012) 103–8.

York, Tripp. "The McCabe Archives." *The Other Journal*, December 17 (2012). Online, https://theotherjournal.com/tag/herbert-mccabe/, checked on 19 January 2020.

INTERVIEWS

David Burrell, on 30 October 2017 via email.

Richard Conrad on 24 November 2015 at Blackfriars, Oxford.

Terry Eagleton on 27th January 2014 at King's Arms Hotel and on 23rd February 2016 at Lancaster University, Lancaster.

Simon Gaine on 24 November 2015 at Blackfriars, Oxford.

Stanley Hauerwas on 2 October 2017 via email.

Peter Hunter on 24 November 2015 at Blackfriars, Oxford.

Alasdair MacIntyre on 28 August 2016 via email.

Robert Ombres on 19 February 2016 at Blackfriars, Oxford.

Timothy Radcliffe on 26 February 2016 at Blackfriars, Oxford.

Denys Turner on 22 May 2018 via email.

Index